INTERNATIONAL LAW AS THE LAW OF COLLECTIVES

T0347386

The Ashgate International Law Series

Series Editor: Alex Conte, Consultant on Security and Human Rights

The Ashgate International Law Series brings together top-quality titles, principally in the area of public international law but also in private international law, under the label of a single international series. Each title represents work which is the result of high-level research, aimed at both the professorial and postgraduate academic market as well as the expert practitioner.

Also in the series

The Persistent Advocate and the Use of Force
The Impact of the United States upon the Jus ad Bellum
in the Post-Cold War Era
Christian Henderson
ISBN 978 1 4094 0173 5

Public Interest Rules of International Law
Towards Effective Implementation
Edited by Teruo Komori and Karel Wellens
ISBN 978 0 7546 7823 6

Terrorism, War and International Law
The Legality of the Use of Force Against Afghanistan in 2001
Myra Williamson
ISBN 978 0 7546 7403 0

A Dual Approach to Ocean Governance
The Cases of Zonal and Integrated Management
in International Law of the Sea
Yoshifumi Tanaka
ISBN 978 0 7546 7170 1

International Law as the Law of Collectives

Toward a Law of People

JOHN R. MORSS
Deakin University, Australia

Routledge
Taylor & Francis Group

LONDON AND NEW YORK

First published 2013 by Ashgate Publishing

2 Park Square, Milton Park, Abingdon, Oxon OX14 4RN
711 Third Avenue, New York, NY 10017, USA

Routledge is an imprint of the Taylor & Francis Group, an informa business

First issued in paperback 2016

British Library Cataloguing in Publication Data
A catalogue record for this book is available from the British Library

The Library of Congress has cataloged the printed edition as follows:
Morss, John R.
International law as the law of collectives : toward a law of people / By John R. Morss.
    pages cm. – (Ashgate International Law series)
  Includes bibliographical references and index.
  ISBN 978-1-4094-4647-7 (hardback)
  1. International law. I. Title.
  KZ3410.M685 2013
  341.01–dc23

                                                                    2013015214

ISBN 978-1-4094-4647-7 (hbk)
ISBN 978-1-138-25700-9 (pbk)

Contents

Preface

Grand Central Station, the concourse, viewed from above: just slightly above, the level where today's exciting new Apple products are on display. Any working day, rain or shine. Bunches of commuters flow and sway, blocks and fragments, concrete poetry in motion. Seems to me this is exactly what international law should be about: the people in movement. Not as solitary individuals, because patterns are plain to see even from here. Nor yet as a mathematical formula or as a bloc, a digitally generated crowd or alien army. Something in between all of those.

Some of the most problematic interventions in international law arise from assertions made in the name of 'the people', especially in the context of self-determination, or in the name of the state. Peoples and states would appear on their face to be collective entities of some kind. Yet international law opts to treat them as peculiar sorts of individual 'actor', replete with 'will' and a corresponding capability to give 'consent'. That is to say international law treats these collectives as kinds of sovereign. These terms – actor, will, consent, people, self-determination – are all problematic in their application to international law. It would be tedious to the reader for me to indicate their conceptual instability by means of scare-quotes on every occasion they are encountered. Let the scare-quotes in most cases be implied. One way of summing up many of the key problems is to say that these terms presuppose an individualistic or a homogeneous identity in the entities to which they refer. It is not novel to identify this frustrating difficulty within international law as we currently know it. Historian, theoretician and gadfly of international law Tony Carty has put it this way:

> [T]he whole contemporary edifice of international law, the trend towards so-called global constitutionalisation and the primacy of individual human rights, is based upon a demonisation of collective and community life in favour of an absolutisation of the autonomy of the individual person, whose sacral character lies precisely in the fact that it remains completely immune from scrutiny. This is how international law *misunderstands itself and thereby remains alienated from itself* at present. (Carty 2005: 551–2)

Meanwhile, legal philosopher Jeremy Waldron has been chipping away at this conceptual monolith from another direction. Among Waldron's many projects is the analysis of political society viewed as constitutional self-government, of which modern democratic versions are the most significant. Waldron has observed that on inspection societies break up into communities and communities into sub-communities, demonstrating what he aptly calls a 'fractal quality' (Waldron

2010: 400). There is rarely a feudal neatness to the nesting of social structures. But groupness is real. Rights and obligations, and other forms of jural interrelations by which human activity is structured, are not primarily characteristics of individual persons. In this context Waldron takes issue with the politics of identity, so often treated as the necessary concomitant of a respect for groups. Waldron has advocated 'group dignity without identity' and has commented that 'identity politics is a misbegotten evil in all its manifestations' (see Chapter 4 below). Waldron's concerns may be understood as a warning about the susceptibility of collective accounts to be reduced to accounts of uniformity. Waldron's warning on the dangers of identity politics connects up with, and helps to articulate, worries about the notion of 'will' in the context of collectives such as those that participate in international legal relationships. The purpose of this book is thus to look at international law in a different way.

As a first step in defining a law of collectives it will be argued that international law is currently conceptualised as a law of individuals. This claim has both an uncontroversial and a controversial, or at least a provocative, aspect. The uncontroversial aspect of this claim includes the familiar point that the international law of human rights, including much of humanitarian law (law in circumstances of armed conflict), is overwhelmingly a matter of the protection of individuals. The same applies to the international law of criminal prosecution. International criminal justice in some ways mirrors and also complements the law of international human rights, because the crimes that come to be dealt with by international tribunals are typically serious abuses of human rights perpetrated by individual persons whether in time of war or in time of state oppression. The more challenging aspect is the proposal that the law of state interaction is also a law of individuals. Moreover, the international law of self-determination – the law of 'peoples' – is also a law of individual entities, 'nations', 'tribes' or 'races' by another name.

It could be argued that international law has attempted to be a law of individuals at any expense, forcing its collective subject-matter into an individualistic explanatory framework. The effect of this is almost as if international law has been a law of sovereigns, of human Princes, Presidents and Popes, all along. The sovereign as the law-giving mobiliser of armies may be international law's nightmare from which it still struggles to awake. To mix the cultural referents, if there is any hope for the conceptualisation of international law it lies in the proles: in populations, not in potentates. All international law is law of collectives, and that, I suggest, is where the hopes and the fears of a global population meet.

At this point I am very happy to acknowledge the support and encouragement of mentors, colleagues and organisations. Research visits to the USA and Europe were supported by Deakin University including its School of Law and the Centre for Citizenship and Globalisation. It has been a privilege to accept Fellowship or visiting researcher status at the Lauterpacht Centre for International Law, and at Churchill College, University of Cambridge; at the Institute for International Law, Ludwig-Maximilians-Universität München; at the European University

Institute, Fiesole; at the University of La Verne College of Law, California; and at the Sheffield Centre for International and European Law, Sheffield University Law School, where final work on the manuscript was completed. Related papers were presented to colleagues at meetings of the Australian Society for Legal Philosophy and of the American Society for International Law, including the 2012 ASIL International Legal Theory Interest Group Symposium *Theoretical Foundations of Self-Determination*. In particular I wish to express my appreciation to the following: James Allan, Philip Allott, Christoph Antons, Tom Campbell, Tony Carty, Hilary Charlesworth, Richard Collins, Alex Conte, James Crawford, Marise Cremona, Jeff Goldsworthy, Joe Graffam, Douglas Guilfoyle, Matt Kramer, Brian Lepard, John Linarelli, Fethi Mansouri, Sundhya Pahuja, Dennis Patterson, Kim Phu, Thomas Pogge, Ottavio Quirico, Kim Rubenstein, Magnus Ryan, Tim Sellers, Gerry Simpson, Fernando Tesón, Mehmet Toral, Kevin Walton, Nathan Widder and Margaret Young. Helmut Aust has been an exemplary critical friend to this project, reviewing a number of chapters in draft and debating the issues with rigour and with comradeship. All errors and oversights remain my own. Karl Marx, years behind with a deadline, is said to have reassured an anxious publisher that all was now well, he had started writing. My beloved partner Maria Nichterlein understands exactly the joys and labours of writing, and this book is for her.

John R. Morss
Montmorency, Victoria, September 2013.

Chapter 1
Law, People, Peoples

Let My People Go

From time to time new states arise in ways that appear to represent the expression of some coherent population of people. 'The Palestinians' would be recognized by the long overdue recognition of the state of Palestine, 'the Kosovars' by the recognition of Kosovo. Sooner or later a seat with the name of the new state on it is (at least metaphorically speaking) created in the General Assembly of the United Nations. States that already exist may on occasion be held to correspond with, or to stand in the place of, a population coherent enough to be referred to as 'a people'. More commonly it is in the aspirational phase that the Palestinians, the Kosovars or the Kurds are identified in that way, in the context of a political argument for the legitimacy of future statehood. States, as usually understood, are kinds of individuals, legal persons (or 'subjects') at the international level. A state is an 'it', not a 'they' or a 'we'. Grammatically, 'a people' is like a state. It is also singular. And this is not just a matter of pedantry. In some accounts of geopolitics or modern history, emphasis is placed on the so-called 'nation state' as an entity in which statehood and nationality – peoplehood – are fused. It sounds as if, in this formula, the polity is co-terminous with the tribe.

There are a number of difficulties concerning the empirical and historical aspects of this usage. It is by no means clear how many, and which, modern states are accurately described as 'nation states'; when and where this phenomenon first emerged; whether it is on the decline and so on. The ease with which the term is used is in any case noteworthy. Peoplehood language switches to statehood language and back again. Versions of this permeability are familiar from nationalist rhetoric, from racist rhetoric and from anti-global rhetoric as well as from less loaded academic discourse. As we shall see in the next chapter, this trope is a major feature of political theorist John Rawls' influential book *The Law of Peoples* where nations are portrayed in a metaphorical, primal confabulation. Rawls' contribution to international law was very much from the outside, in a disciplinary sense. But there is a sense in which Rawls put his finger on the problematic in the ontology of international law. The kind of entity that it recognises is individualistic; and so is its methodology.

One could refer to the *singularist* sense of 'people' as in 'one people, two or more peoples'. It is the sense, if there is any, of the question that anyone may ask, 'what is my people?' The grammar of this term is not clear. Does 'the people' go with a 'who' (like an individual person) or with a 'which' (or a 'that') (like a state)? This sounds pedantic. But in this context it is important to be clear that the affective loading of the question and of the answer can be very great or it can be entirely absent. The phrase 'let my people go' still reverberates. This is, I think, because of its collective character. What it means is closely connected with the experiences of oppression suffered by African-American slaves and also by Jewish people in more ancient times, given that the narrative is derived from the Old Testament. At the same time for someone like myself who grew up in the majority population in cosmopolitan London, even as long ago as the 1950s, to refer to the English or the British as 'my people' would be to adhere to a reactionary ideology. Almost as bad it would be absurd. For others, a claimed identity with for example 'the Scots people' is still questionable in some respects – especially in its current manifestation among the Edinburgh elite – while being significantly less absurd than the corresponding claim to be 'English' would, I think, be.

In any event the extremes of affective loading are difficult to reconcile with the singularist concept of 'people'. Yet the discourse of international law persists in adopting the singular voice – 'the' people, 'the' state, 'the' international community. In some ways this seems at odds with observation. International law is patently concerned with people *en masse*, with populations distributed across geographical territories and between states, across affiliations and between affinities. International law is surely a law of collectives – complex collectives to be sure but collectives all the more. Notwithstanding their undoubted rhetorical impact, such unitary conceptual referents as 'the people' and 'the state' serve at best as proxies for different kinds of collective. At worst they obscure such collectives. The notion of 'people' is underdetermined and 'peoplehood' is defined with hindsight when an independent state has already been recognised (Oeter 2012: 116). 'Peoplehood' is after all only one way of reducing the complexity of global humankind to manageable conceptual proportions; 'statehood' but another. One way of expressing this state of explanatory affairs is to say that 'the people' and 'the state' are legal fictions (Oklopcic 2009: 701). The corresponding 'legal fact' so to speak would be collective in both cases. Looking at it this way makes the point that the singular form of expression has some function or effect. It is neither arbitrary nor trivial. It may even be a 'Good Thing'. But we will not know until we investigate.

Who Are We? Grammars of the Collective

How can one make sense of this confusing landscape of individualistic explanation in international law? One approach would be to embrace the individualism, and to endorse a natural-person variety of individualism in international law. Indeed person-centred positions in contemporary jurisprudence of international law are sufficiently influential as to present a serious challenge to the collectivist project which feels somewhat like swimming against the tide. As noted below, the contemporary person-centred approach to international law, with its focus on universal human rights, may be traced back at least to the writings of Hersch Lauterpacht in the decades around World War II (Lauterpacht 2010). In this tradition, Evan Criddle and Evan Fox-Decent (2009: 333) have urged that '[s]tates exercise sovereign authority as fiduciaries of the people subject to state power'. That is to say a relationship of trust must subsist between government and governed, where 'trust' is understood in the strong, legal sense as developed in the equity jurisdiction of English law over a number of centuries. Criddle and Fox-Decent have focused on the so-called 'peremptory norms' in international law, the *jus cogens* norms that are said to override all other kinds of international law including multilateral conventions. These peremptory norms 'express constitutive elements of sovereignty's normative dimension' (Criddle and Fox-Decent 2009: 332). For example, norms that many commentators include in the category of peremptory norm, such as the prohibition of slavery, seem to be straightforwardly understood as protections of individual persons as such. Criddle and Fox-Decent extend the category to include such norms or practices as due process of law even in situations of national emergency and the prohibition of public corruption.

In contrast the project of the articulation of the legal status of collectives on the international stage is a radically collectivist one. In brief it might be proposed that international law is concerned *only* with collectives. Looked at in this way, connections between law and people include the trivial, the profound, the ideological and the sacred. All law is about people in the plural and is in some sense made by people in the plural. It is probably a contradiction in terms for any law to be 'about' a single named individual. Of course there are examples of laws that have had the design and the effect of controlling the conduct or the freedom of a single person. But such laws have only made sense and achieved any effect through their context of legal frameworks governing groups or communities. So far so good. Much more challenging and complex is the connection between law and *a* people. Legal systems have often constituted themselves in the name of 'the' people, a local society or community with some notional boundaries, usually geographic but possibly ethnic. 'The law of a people' in many ways corresponds to what we generally understand by a legal system: by the legal system of Australia, of the USA, of India or of Japan. In Charles Taylor's words, this is what is often thought of in terms of 'the Law of a people, which has governed this people since time out of mind, and which in a sense defines it as a people' (Taylor 2007: 163).

Expressed in this way, the law of nations is straightforwardly *the law of peoples*: the law of the plurality of these tribal jurisdictions. Much of international law as it has developed over many centuries fits into this familiar conceptual framework. The book of this name, *The Law of Peoples*, by political philosopher John Rawls, published first in 1999, is but one version of this vision of international law as a framework of regulation of discrete national entities. Rawls' status as theorist of justice and fairness, probably the foremost philosopher of political liberalism of the twentieth century, guaranteed that attention would be given to his intervention in the theory of international law. It will be argued in the next chapter that the attention was not really justified by the content of the contribution. To put it bluntly, *The Law of Peoples* is a distraction at best from the project of articulating a politically and philosophically sophisticated account of international law. But offering a critique of Rawls' later work is not the main purpose of the present book. It is the larger and older senses of that phrase that need to be scrutinised – the many 'non-Rawlsian' understandings of 'law of peoples' that have dominated scholarly thinking and geopolitics. While the phrase 'law of people' risks bathos, this risk seems worth taking. Bathos is understood as a style of the commonplace approaching absurdity in comparison with the gravity of the subject matter with which it deals. As Burke put it, '[t]he most wonderful things are brought about in many instances by means the most absurd and ridiculous; in the most ridiculous modes; and, apparently, by the most contemptible instruments' (Burke 1997: 667). International law is in many ways an absurd practice and an absurd discipline; it continues to make the attempt to curtail the foolishness of our leaders, both elected and non-elected, who refuse to learn from each experience of fudge and of failure. 'History consists, for the greater part, of the miseries brought upon the world by pride, ambition, avarice, revenge, lust, sedition, hypocrisy, ungoverned zeal, and all the train of disorderly appetites' (Burke 1997: 680).

International law should then not be thought of as law of 'peoples', nor law of nations, nor law of states. And to be clear at this opening point, neither should it be thought of as law of individuals. 'Law of people' is intended to connote law of *people in collectives* or international law as the law of collectives. States are collectives; nations are collectives; empires are collectives; 'peoples' are collectives. 'Non-state actors' are collective entities; so are non-governmental organizations, including those designated 'international' (INGOs). International institutions are collectives (Klabbers 2012).

In many ways it is the term 'peoples' that presents the most complex challenge to this bathetic project. What is a people? And why does there seem to be such an intimate relationship between 'peoples' and law, so that 'law of peoples' appears to make sense? A later chapter will look in detail at the concept and the practice of 'self-determination' which in many ways is international law's operationalization of this notion of a people. Here, some more general comments may be made on what might be called 'peoplehood' (Smith 2003). One reason for focusing on this at the start, rather than on the state, the nation or indeed the individual person, is the emotional dimension. Sometimes rivalled by attachments to nations or to religious faiths, but rarely exceeded, identification with a people generates intense passions. International law prefers to avoid affective displays, except for the orchestrated and temperate enthusiasms of the preambulatory statement. But the terminology of 'peoples' is, so to speak, inherently emotive: it reminds us that the subject-matter of international law includes people's most cherished projects, projects for which as individuals and as groups the preparedness to risk or even to embrace death may be all too present. And the dead play a role also:

POBLACHT NA hÉIREANN/ THE PROVISIONAL GOVERNMENT OF THE IRISH REPUBLIC TO THE PEOPLE OF IRELAND/ Irishmen and Irishwomen. In the name of God and of the dead generations, from which she receives her old tradition of nationhood, Ireland, through us, summons her children to the flag and strikes for her freedom. (Davies 2011: 649)

The Easter Rising of April 1916 saw the first declaration of an Irish Republic. Up to that point Ireland had been ruled by feudal chiefs, or ruled directly from England as purportedly conquered territory or administered as some kind of colony or assimilated province by London (Carty 1996). The appeal was made to, and on behalf of, 'The People of Ireland'. Unilateral declarations of independence before and since have similarly been made in the name of 'the people'. The Constitution of the United States of America begins, 'We the people of the United States ...' A much more recent example is the declaration made on behalf of the people of Kosovo: 'We, the democratically-elected leaders of our people, hereby declare Kosovo to be an independent and sovereign state'. And in what might be called a 'multilateral declaration of interdependence', the United Nations Charter of 1945 begins 'We the peoples of the United Nations ...'

The 'self' to which reference is made in the term self-determination, or which may be constructed in retrospect, can therefore be said to be 'a people'. Within many disciplines it has become commonplace for somewhat imprecise reference to be made to ethnic, national or religious populations as constituting 'peoples'. Historians, for example, are happy to do so. Timothy Parsons writes in his Conclusion to *The Rule of Empires* that 'Basques, Northern Irish, Kurds, Tamils, East Timorese, Tibetans, and many other peoples seeking national homelands continue to endure a form of subjecthood. However, their struggles are with nations, not self-described empires' (Parsons 2010: 428). To describe '[the] Northern Irish' as a 'people' suggests a significant lack of precision in Parsons' analysis. The concept of 'a people', at least in terms that are not informed by international law, seems to invite loose thinking of a kind that Parsons exhibits. Of course, such usage around the humanities and social sciences derives more from the larger political traditions of the Declaration of Independence (of the USA) and of the Charter of the United Nations than from the technicalities or prescriptions of international law as such. The more salient question must therefore be posed, as to whether writings in international law eschew such imprecision. The question whether international law has successfully solved that conceptual problem, by showing how the term can be precisely defined and applied, will be examined in more detail in Chapter 6 below.

In the declaration of Irish independence, referred to above, among the appeals to patriotism and to idealism was an appeal to Ireland as 'she': as some kind of person. Of course it is commonplace to personalise countries, one's 'own' or others, by describing them as a 'him' or a 'her', rather than as an 'it'. This may be done with patriotic pride, with patronising affection, or of course with the laziness of journalistic habit. Many such usages are on the same clichéd level as treating cities as gendered, as in historian Alistair Horne's question 'has any sensible person ever doubted that Paris is fundamentally a woman?' (Horne 2002: xvii). Horne's gendered approach to the historiography of great cities may seem outdated for 2002

('London … has always betrayed clearly male orientations, and New York has a certain ambivalence'). Yet the general practice is more than arch, stylistic flourish. The gender dimension is a reminder that linguistic habits may interconnect with more weighty matters: the personal is the political.

What is My Country?

The trope of country as person is sometimes employed in a deliberate manner as an analogy. Norman Davies' invaluable *Vanished Kingdoms: The History of Half-Forgotten Europe* provides a series of studies of kingdoms, republics and other state entities that have existed in past centuries across Europe, their boundaries cross-cutting or engulfing the state borders which in many respects seem natural to the contemporary eye. While border disputes are not unfamiliar to the international lawyer, there seems to be a common habit of thought by which a geographical heartland is locked in place for a political entity, 'France' for example. For non-historians like myself there is probably a confused sense that 'this is the region where people speak such-and-such a language'. Such inchoate assumptions are of a kind with the more populist understandings of 'self-determination': 'of course the people of Poland should determine their own governance'.

Davies' book sets in question such uninformed certainties, reminding us of the instability and the fluidity of political arrangements and divisions across the territory of Europe. Both the specific examples and the general patterns that Davies presents are pertinent to the aims of this book. But Davies' feet also are made of clay. In a concluding overview he suggests that

> [i]n order to survive, newborn states need to possess a set of viable internal organs … [If not], they lack the means to sustain an autonomous existence, and they perish before they can breathe and flourish. The 'Republic of One Day' in Carpatho-Ukraine illustrates this point nicely. Since its executive body did nothing other than to declare its independence, it may be said to have been stillborn … No state is as vulnerable as in the very early days of its existence, and the vultures begin to hover as soon as the infant takes its first breath. (Davies 2011: 737)

The state-as-person analogy connects up with the larger trope of the *developmental* conceptualization of change in the human and in the natural world. The application of a developmental form of description and explanation to the career of the individual human person from infancy through adolescence to adulthood is extremely familiar from its enthusiastic adoption within the discipline of psychology. It might seem that the context of the human individual lifespan and its changes is the authentic or natural home base for the developmental approach, the source of the metaphor so to speak in Davies' discussion. As it happens even this familiar usage is theoretically loaded and has been subjected to criticism (Morss 1990; 1996). But the application to geopolitics and history, and to international politics and international law, is especially troublesome.

Most of the time Davies' employment of the analogy is restrained in an exemplary manner, and serves to aid explication or at least illumination of the historical processes, without taking over the sense to a deleterious extent. To describe Georgia as 'again gasping for air ... in the hostile environment of Russia's "near abroad"' (Davies 2011: 738) would seem perhaps to be crossing the line into partisan rhetoric or at least into journalese. Elsewhere the effect is harder to pin down. Thus in the concluding section 'How States Die', '[t]he strange death of the Soviet Union ... suggests that a typology of "vanished kingdoms" is worth attempting. Bodies politic clearly expire for a variety of reasons ...' (Davies 2011: 729). 'Bodies politic' is a term that seems unhelpfully pluralised. 'The body politic' is a familiar phrase but like 'the nation state' its employment is rarely interrogated. In combination with the birth and death motif, Davies' rhetoric suggests that states can usefully be described as if they are like individual human persons.

The point of this observation about Davies is not to carp at historians for being successfully approachable in style. Rather it is that the grammatical or stylistic trope of treating countries (states, nations, 'peoples') as forms of individual is fraught with risk. It is one of the tasks of the theorist of any of the disciplines affected by this practice, to enquire into the implications and consequences of the practice. It is, to put it grandiosely, a matter of the *ontology* of the discipline: what kind of entity is it about? What is the ontology of international law? Because, of course, countries are not 'he's' or 'she's'. More importantly, and harder to avoid or to address, they are only in carefully defined senses, 'its'. Countries, states, nations are not things. They are conglomerates, institutions, systems or structures.

A Plague on Both Your Houses

Some of international law as we currently know it is said to be about individual natural persons, as in human rights law. Much of international law is said to be about states. International law has discussed legal relations between states for centuries, indeed in a recognizably 'modern' manner since the sixteenth century if not before. It has discussed the international legal status of individual human persons also for a surprisingly long time even if focused attention on this task has been a recent phenomenon in the discipline. Pirates and monarchs have been with us, with their demands and their depredations, for millennia, and a law of nations has had to take them on board so to speak. The same may be said about diplomats, at least insofar as they are treated as state agents. States and individuals have thus been, with rare exceptions, thought of as the two available options for the role of 'subject' of international law. The differences between theorists of international law and between schools or generations of international lawyers have often taken the form of disagreement over the relative weight to be placed on state-centred versus individual-person-centred forms or levels of explanation. Even a theorist as innovative and rigorous as Hans Kelsen, for whom international law was above all a matter of norms rather than of 'subjects', may be said to have contributed to the 'statist' orientation in the discipline as against a person-centred alternative.

But states and individual persons do not exhaust the ontology of international law. There are other ways of imagining and of describing the processes that demand our attention on the world stage and that seem to call for legal expression if not regulation. The approach taken in this book is 'a plague on both your houses!' For however distinct states and individual persons might be, as objects of theoretical scrutiny, they share singularity. To put it inelegantly, a state is an 'it' and so is a person. My argument is that international law is about pluralities. It is about 'we', 'they', 'them', and our grammatically plural vocabulary needs to be matched by pluralistic concepts. My code word for this attention to the pluralistic is 'collective'. It seems to me that attention to the collective dimension of international law is needed if the discipline is to make the contribution that it should to larger debates over cosmopolitanism and global justice, for example, as well as to immediate problems arising in conflict zones or in regions threatened by environmental hazard. What I will suggest is that when international law talks about states it is actually talking about kinds of collective.

Further, when it talks about individual human persons and their needs, international law is also, as it turns out, talking about collectives. All human rights, I suggest, are collective rights. That view would generate new perspectives on what may have seemed familiar about the conceptual structure of universal human rights instruments, as well as challenging orthodox viewpoints on the role of states in international law, for example. In order to make this case, it is important to say a little more about the deficiencies of the two orthodox approaches.

International Law as State-centred

While criticisms of orthodox international law as state-centred are very familiar, and themselves comprise an orthodoxy, some aspects of this issue need to be re-examined. For international law, states have been traditionally seen as kinds of individual – indeed, for the discipline of international law, 'our' kind of individual. The state as an individual is part of the self-serving self-image of geopolitics. As James Crawford remarks, 'in practice States hunt in packs but like to be seen as hunting alone' (Aust 2011: 2). Despite Crawford's characteristically pithy observation, international law is conventionally thought of as a series of agreed obligations between a plurality of fundamentally independent polities scattered around our globe. This model of a plurality of sovereignties is often referred to as the 'Westphalian' system, in reference to the provisions of the peace treaties that ended the Thirty Years War.

While individual natural persons may be the ultimate beneficiaries of protections thus established, and while individuals in positions of power are increasingly at risk of being prosecuted as criminals if they transgress, states treated as independent geopolitical actors still dominate the conceptual landscape. When whales are hunted for 'scientific' purposes in the South Pacific, conservationists' concerns lead not to any criminal or civil processes but to a dispute between two states, in this case Japan and Australia, as currently (2013) before the International Court of Justice.

It is of course in relation to a state-centred perspective that the claim of a general individualism in the theory of international law requires particular attention. What will be proposed is that states are dealt with in international law as if they are kinds of individual. Much of international law is routinely treated as constituted by the interactions between such individuals. States are the predominant variety of 'subject of international law'. The most senior international tribunal, the International Court of Justice, is concerned almost entirely with disputes between states. International law is frequently said to be the creation of states, especially by means of express agreement between them or by means of state conduct generating customary international law. There are many ways in which the role of states in modern international law is closely analogous to the role that emperors and 'princes' used to have in earlier centuries. The political and military context is comparable. The style of advice that Niccolo Machiavelli offered to one specific Prince – Lorenzo de' Medici – in the early sixteenth century, is in many ways echoed in the advice offered to the head of a state such as the USA by a Henry Kissinger in more recent times (Hitchens 2002). What is understood as the collective dimension in international law is thus for many commentators the collective dimension of states acting together. To the extent this perspective on an international community of states emphasises collaboration and complicity between states, it is helpful. But to the extent the analysis is based on a notion of atomic entities in interaction, it is not only partial but deeply erroneous.

International Law as Person-centred

The international protection of the human rights of individuals, and the international prosecution of former heads of state or other high officials as individual criminals, seem emblematic of a historical trend away from abstract constructs such as the state and toward the solid ground of individual needs and individual liabilities. There is a sense in which international law has been removed from the palsied hands of the diplomats – that detached and over-professionalised cadre of *Yes Minister*'s Sir Humphrey Applebys – and entrusted to the passions and energies of a new generation.

There is no denying the immense growth of a global human rights consciousness over the last seven decades. I will argue later in this book that collective rights play an important part in this story, but the major objective of this movement has undoubtedly been to define and to celebrate rights possessed by individuals as individuals. The thinking behind this is derived from what might be broadly termed liberal theories of politics, which emphasise liberty and autonomy at the expense of more collective or communitarian parameters. Early statements of universal rights at the time of the American War of Independence, and the French

Revolution, laid stress on inalienable rights of individuals as such. Consistent with this tradition, it is thus sometimes claimed that the overriding purpose and justification of international law is in the regulation, protection or empowerment of natural persons. This claim has often been expressed in terms of universal human rights, as in the monist tradition represented by Hersch Lauterpacht. It is sometimes expressed as a story about a significantly escalating trend, or even a revelation of the true purpose of international law. A contemporary version is the claim that peremptory international norms (*jus cogens* norms) are to be understood in terms of fiduciary responsibilities of states toward their nationals, with such responsibilities largely couched in terms of the needs and rights of natural persons (Criddle and Fox-Decent 2009; Gaeta 2010).

It should also be noted that a line of argument drawing inspiration from philosophical traditions, especially from Kant, converges on the claim that international law should be thought of as focused on the needs and rights of natural persons, and evaluated in those terms (Perreau-Saussine 2010). In this approach, 'deontological' presuppositions such as the dignity of the individual person play a central role. Pat Capps has recently explored this approach in the context of contemporary international law (Capps 2009). It should be emphasised that the sophistication and richness of such traditions will have to be matched by any competing analysis. Evan Fox-Decent (2011: 48) has proposed that a fiduciary view of authority should be thought of as applicable to all levels of societal control from states and entities with 'state-like administrative powers' all the way down to the parent-child relationship. The fiduciary obligation is 'fractal'. The project which the present book seeks to further is to treat the collective as fractal: to argue that political life is collective all the way down.

A Critique of Individualism?

As may be apparent, there are several ways in which the argument of this book might be described as a critique of 'individualism' in the theory of international law. This is correct up to a point, although there are problems with such a project which should be indicated upfront. The most serious limitation is the imprecision of such a campaign. 'Individualism' is an elastic and in many ways ambiguous term as Martha Nussbaum has pointed out (Nussbaum 2007: 441). An extreme, methodological individualism has indeed been international law's ideology of choice in some epochs, such as the late nineteenth century, but not at other times (Koskenniemi 2011: 111). In any event a project thus conceived would hardly be innovatory. Critiques of individualism may be said to have already been made within international law. International law is not entirely immune from trends and movements within the social sciences and humanities, although that may sometimes seem to be the case, and the latter disciplines have been subjecting individualism to critique for quite a while. This is the case even if 'individualism' is scarcely better defined in those disciplines than it is in relation to international law. The social constructionist movement in psychology and other social sciences is cognate with the constructionist school within international relations theory. It is in many ways a critique of individualism.

Various critical writings in international law over recent decades have taken on board the widespread intellectual suspicion of the autonomous individual as centre of political life. Feminist theory in international law provides some of the more closely argued examples (Charlesworth and Chinkin 2000: 38). The autonomous individual has often turned out to bear the insignia of an adult, white, heterosexual and able-bodied male, further adding to the disquiet. Stepping further back, large philosophical traditions such as Marxism, as well as much of the work of Rousseau and Hegel for example, might be said to comprise alternatives to individualism especially as represented by liberal theory. The writings of Derrida and Deleuze, among more recent thinkers, recast our understanding of individuality and of the social in a variety of ways (Kellogg 2010; Patton 2010).

What is the Collective Approach?

There are many political theories and ideologies that de-emphasise the interests and the value of the individual as individual, by placing weight on some larger group or society. Totalitarianism in politics offers a range of alternatives including communist and fascist forms of collectivist ideology and practice. In philosophy, Hegel explored community and the nature of a collective ethical life as formative of the subjectivity of individuals. In the decades following Hegel, around the middle of the nineteenth century, other German-speaking philosophers were emphasising the racial and linguistic basis of culture. Nationalism, in its many varieties, represents a way of foregrounding collectives or populations, and laying stress on their common identity. To explore collective dimensions of international law requires a willingness to deal with such forces and their conceptual derivatives, for example in the context of self-determination. It would certainly be naïve to suggest that shifting from an individual to a collective register is a merely technical matter.

It should also be observed that a sharp distinction between individualistic and collective orientations within political theory can itself be misleading. For example classical liberal theory lays stress on the autonomy of individuals as they make choices and act on them. However there is a strong implication, and occasionally express argument, that society as a whole benefits from such an arrangement. The United States Constitution explicitly sets up a society on these lines. There are thus communitarian (or societal) arguments intimately connected with liberal individualism. Correspondingly, more sophisticated communitarian arguments in political thought, such as that of Hegel, involve detailed and complex claims about the rights, obligations and available subjectivities of the individual citizen. A related argument is that made by Arendt, that 'one needs to be part of a political community in order to make claims'. (Schwöbel 2010: 537)

In any event it may be asked whether there is anything new about looking for the collective in international law. Even those who know little of international law, but especially those who do, may already be wondering if the collective wheel is being at best reinvented, at worst overlooked or misrepresented. For it is clear that in some senses, much of international law is already about collectives. Minorities, children, people with disability, women, are all collectives of some kind. All are the subjects (or possibly the objects) of international agreements and instruments. Whatever can be said about 'peoples' in international law, for example in the context of self-determination, is surely about collectives. But it may well be that in the orthodox account of international law, these are thought of as marginal or anomalous instances of regulation and that the rest of the discipline is not about collectives at all. More significantly, even when collectives such as a particular indigenous people are the subject of discussion, the discourse is often framed in ways that obscure that collective dimension. The indigenous people becomes 'a subject of international law', alongside states. It (the 'people' as a singularity) becomes as it were an atom, or to use another analogy it becomes a pawn on the Westphalian chessboard. In international law, collectives are turned into kinds of individuals.

Overview of the Book

The next chapter overviews the contributions of major traditions in legal and political philosophy to the collective project in international jurisprudence. It discusses some aspects of legal and political theory from the time of Hobbes up to the later twentieth century, with a view to sketching the background to a collectivist enquiry into international law. The range of writers whose contributions are discussed here is large and diverse. In the earlier part of the chapter the focus is on the social contract tradition within liberal theory as this developed in the last four centuries or so in Western Europe. This tradition is taken in a pragmatic spirit to encompass Locke, Rousseau and Kant as well as Hobbes himself, and comment is also made on such important critics of social contract theory as Hume. Other than by reference to Rousseau, no attempt is made in the chapter to deal with communitarian traditions even to the modest degree of coverage of the social contract tradition.

The latter part of Chapter 2 discusses the work of legal theorists of the twentieth century, from Hohfeld up to Hart and Rawls, with particular attention to the relevance of their work for international jurisprudence. Hohfeld himself did not in any way sanction such a project. But rights and duties can be attributed to groups, not only to individual persons – or at least such is argued by a significant cadre of contemporary legal philosophers. The attempt should at least be made to see if Hohfeld can assist on the world stage as well as in his own preferred domain of property disputes between neighbours. Rawls' book *The Law of Peoples*, originally published in 1999, presents an account against which some crucial components of the present approach will be defined and defended. Without turning Rawls into some kind of intellectual nemesis for the present author – in a struggle for which he is ill-prepared – it needs to be admitted that Rawls' *The Law of Peoples* is for him something of a *bête noire*. Rawls' status as one of the most important legal and political philosophers of the twentieth century is unassailable, a circumstance which seems to make his late writings on international relations and global justice doubly unfortunate. With its use of the word 'peoples' as the plural of 'a people', *The Law of Peoples* seems to promise an examination of self-determination and of international law, perhaps about their conditions of possibility or their consequences. It will be suggested that the book does not represent such a contribution, but is at best a distraction from that task.

Chapter 3 examines both the history of international law, and the role of history within international law, with a view to the role played by individualistic and by collectivist approaches to its subject matter. It is concerned with historiography more than with history: that is to say with questions about how the history of international law is understood and constructed. This chapter thus contributes to the overall project by overviewing selected aspects of the history of international law with an eye to the distinction between the individual and the collective styles of analysis. The selection of topics is deliberately restricted. It is intended to highlight the ways in which the history and the historiography of international law have, on the one hand, recognised or, on the other hand, overlooked the role of collectives. For example the supposed milestones in the development of international law as represented in orthodox accounts may need to be re-examined in the light of the collective viewpoint. Relatedly, the common assertion that 'old' international law was all about the relationships between states but that contemporary international law is increasingly about individual persons is an historiographic frame that must be subjected to scrutiny.

While the emphasis is more heavily weighted on recent contributions and analysis, the overall chronology is broadly parallel to the times covered in the review of the legal and political philosophers. The discussion thus begins with the seventeenth century, the era when Hobbes was writing *Leviathan*. The iconic date of 1648 looms large in the historiography of international law. Lake comments that '[i]t is the myth of Westphalia, rather than Westphalia itself, on which today's understanding of the principle of sovereignty rests' (Lake 2009: 48). Important conceptual matters within international legal thinking, including matters of vocabulary and of methodology, can be usefully discussed in the context of what has been aptly referred to as 'Westphalia and all that' (Wright 2006: 262). Indeed it could be argued that any attempt to identify collective possibilities in international law, or to advocate for a collective analysis, needs to get to grips with the presuppositions that are in many ways enshrined in the idea of 'Westphalia'. For if the commonly received understanding of what happened in international relations at the conclusion of the Thirty Years War is correct, the collectivist project might appear to be doomed. As David Kennedy remarked in a related context, the approach of most historians of international law is one 'which both presupposes and proves the continuity of the discipline of international law

– reaffirming in the process that the project for international law scholars is and always was to construct a social order among autonomous sovereigns' (Anghie 1996: 334).

Many aspects of the more popular account of Westphalia are questionable, even if attempts to entirely debunk its claimed significance may be an overreaction. The points of concern here arise from the almost mythological status of Westphalia as a point of supposed origin for a modern geopolitical world – the world of the United Nations for example. Some contributions to a collective focus within international law are then reviewed. Particular attention is paid to the contribution of post-colonial scholars in international law, for whom international law is historically conditioned as a consequence of European expansion and global domination over the past several centuries. With their sensitivity to the collective experience of those who were the colonised, post-colonial accounts of international law might be expected to demonstrate sensitivity to the collective more analytically as well.

The next two chapters address contemporary debates relating to international jurisprudence. In Chapter 4 a major focus is on the conceptual analysis of the rights of groups, a topic of central importance for a collectivist agenda. If rights and other legal attributes are only valid when attributed to individual human persons as such, then the collectivist project is in difficulties. Fortunately substantial arguments are available that support the view that rights and other jural relations may properly be attributed to groups. On this basis the scheme of Hohfeld, for example, can with caution be called upon in the context of collectives. In this chapter attention is focused almost entirely on the contributions and the debates of later generations of legal theorists, our contemporaries. In common with Rawls and Hart, the works of these contemporary scholars cover a range of topics and aspects are selected for discussion on the basis of direct relevance to the current project.

Particular attention is paid to the writings of Jeremy Waldron, a political theorist as well as a legal theorist and one of the foremost legal philosophers currently writing on international law. Waldron has written extensively on rights, the democratic process and the rule of law. Waldron's writings have for some years included topics that bear rather directly on the jurisprudence of international law. Self-determination (of 'peoples'), sovereignty, the privileges of heads of state and the concept of an international rule of law are among these topics. Waldron's contributions are discussed towards the end of the chapter.

As noted this chapter includes an attempt to demonstrate the significance of the scheme of jural relationships developed by Hohfeld. Contemporary applications of Hohfeld include applications in the context of group rights and collective rights. The notion of group rights, and the articulation of the consequences of recognising rights and obligations in groups, are examined. Matthew Kramer's analysis of rights, as well as his related exegesis of Hohfeld, are important resources for the current project. It is at this point that the important matter of the 'interest' versus 'will' debate in the legal theory of rights is explored (Kramer, Simmonds and Steiner 1998). It is argued that the will (or choice) theory of rights is peculiarly inappropriate to the group or otherwise collective context. For the will versus interest debate within the jurisprudence of rights, a debate in which Hart plays an important role, can be connected up with international law's difficulties over 'will' and 'consent' as pertaining to entities like states or 'peoples'. On the other hand, the interest approach seems promising in this regard.

In Chapter 5 the focus is on statehood, especially formal and systemic aspects of statehood, including the concept of 'consent' in relation to states. Statehood is a concept central to much of international law's theoretical framework. Topics include the question of state complicity. Complicity between states is becoming a key area for theoretical debate within the discipline of international law (Aust 2011). While circumstances such as 'rendition' of suspected terrorists present contemporary examples of such complicity, the practice is not new. British, German and Italian naval forces collaborated in 1902 in seizing the fleet of Venezuela and enforcing a blockade, as well as bombarding coastal cities, in order to enforce the settlement of foreign debt (Rajagopal 2003: 33). The vocabulary of state complicity, as it develops, will make it possible to describe the collective conduct of states without recourse to imprecise terms such as 'the international community'. Precision is after all one of the chief merits of international law as a discipline. In turn it will become possible for political concepts such as 'solidarity' to be articulated with international law. Extending the notion of complicity among states, attention to the ways that multi-state 'assemblages' function is a contribution to the 'withering away of the state' within international law. Rather than the solid ground of the discipline, the high ground surrounded by compromise and uncertainty, statehood seems more reminiscent of the shifting sandbanks and treacherous channels described by Erskine Childers in his *The Riddle of the Sands* (Morss, forthcoming). States seem to be effects rather than causes. The demarcation of states one from another, as well as their interactions one with another, are consequent to larger processes. This is an approach advocated from outside the discipline of international law in recent times, as well as from inside it, but in many ways it is an approach that can be attributed to Hans Kelsen (von Bernstorff 2010).

Chapter 6 discusses self-determination. Self-determination by definition concerns collectives, often in this context referred to as 'peoples', so that it is important to investigate the ways in which international law has conceptualised and addressed this issue. It may turn out to be the case that international law's understanding of self-determination provides a template or other form of guidance for the larger collective project. On the other hand it may be that international law's understanding of self-determination is compromised by the same individualistic thinking as identified elsewhere, or by other conceptual deficiencies. That this may be so is suggested by the insistence of international law on using the term 'the people' without, it may appear, much in the way of precision or clarity. It is certainly the case that international law's instruments (such as international agreements on civil rights and so on) purport to confer or to affirm rights to self-determination 'of peoples' on a wide scale. Article 1 of the Charter of the United Nations is an important example. Indeed the Charter as a whole is announced in the name of 'We the peoples of the United Nations'. In what seem to be thought of as easy cases – stable and familiar states, or the peaceful emergence of new, post-colonial nations – 'peoples' and the fulfilment of their self-determination are treated as straightforward descriptions. But the recognition of some population as constituting 'a people' is in such easy cases circular or at best, retrospective. The package of legal prescriptions, proscriptions and formulae that we label 'self-determination' illustrates the centrality of the collective question to the discipline of international law but does not go very far toward answering it.

As with self-determination, cultural rights and the rights of minorities are topics where a collective orientation seems both unavoidable and, more to the point, familiar. In other words the stated aim of this book might seem to call for a celebration of the vocabulary and the methodology of international law in these areas, and their expansion into much wider aspects of the discipline. If all rights are collective rights then it could be argued that all rights are cultural rights as already understood. If states are special kinds of collectives, then it may be that states can be treated as cultural entities. If international law's understanding of cultural and minority rights is already satisfactory, if only in its broad strokes, then so to speak the wheel of the collective in international law should not be reinvented. The twin targets of state-centred and individual-centred international law might turn out to be twin straw men, artificial enemies that have already been challenged by a third way. Certainly there are contributions to the theorization of cultural rights and of minority rights that give rise to substantive challenges to both 'straw men'. But what will be argued in Chapter 7 is that theorization in these areas has been held back by the hegemony of the predominant, individualised approach of the discipline. Just like other aspects of the field of international law, our discipline's understanding of cultural rights and of the rights of minorities needs to be 'collectivised'.

In Chapter 8, insights and articulations from the discipline of international relations are discussed. International relations is a discipline sharing many common concerns as well as much common history with international law. Its two main camps are usually referred to as a 'realist' and a more recent 'constructivist' perspective. As to the former, Hans Morgenthau stated bluntly that '[i]nternational politics ... is a struggle for power' (Morgenthau 2005: 32). The most important communality from a conceptual point of view is the state. In both disciplines, the state plays a key role yet is increasingly recognised as problematic from a theoretical point of view as well as giving rise to practical difficulties. The response to this challenge has been different in international relations as compared to international law. There are therefore instructive ways in which the search for alternative theoretical frameworks has unfolded in the sister discipline. International relations is in some respects closer to the social sciences than is international law and has been more extensively affected by recent trends within the social sciences. Over the last three or four decades a reaction to the more quantitative and positivist forms of methodology in the social sciences has manifested itself as a turn to hermeneutic, phenomenological and other interpretive traditions. Social constructionism, for some decades now an important theoretical approach within psychology and social anthropology for example, now constitutes an important 'school' of international relations. This approach has had much less impact on international law except for its contribution to critical work in legal theory more generally. Examining the social constructionist approach to international relations, then, opens up enquiry into an important and relevant approach in the social sciences and humanities more generally. As the discussion in the chapter demonstrates however, social constructionism at least as understood by international relations theory fails to constitute an adequate framework within which to reimagine international law. Other aspects of international relations theory are also discussed. The chapter concludes with a discussion of sovereignty.

In Chapter 9 an attempt is made to bring the strands of argument together if only in an indicative and occasionally an aphoristic manner. This chapter attempts to articulate the challenge to international law that the focus on collectives represents. In these final two chapters, the opportunity is taken to make brief reference to a wider range of critical, scholarly traditions. Some support can be found for the view, espoused in this book, that both state-centred and individual-person-centred forms of analysis of our political life are inadequate. Some of these traditions may offer helpful alternative formulations, including suggestions concerning cosmopolitan, communitarian or otherwise collectivist orientations. At the same time the sharpening of the theoretical task for international law may generate some questions and even some challenges for those wider projects. As indicated in the chapter that follows, the phenomena with which international law grapples have been with us for a while. It is time for some name-dropping.

Chapter 2
From Hobbes to Rawls:
Covenants, Social Contracts and the
Law of Peoples

States of Nature and Original Positions

This chapter begins the task of setting out the major contributions from legal and political philosophy that inform the current project. The emphasis in this book is on contemporary debate: jurisprudence and related philosophical resources of the twentieth and twenty-first centuries. However some remarks must first be made on relevant contributions of political philosophers of earlier centuries. Some of the arguments of Hobbes and Locke in the seventeenth century, and of Rousseau, Hume and Kant in the eighteenth, are of sufficient significance for the current project that overviews of their arguments should be included. These earlier contributions are the work of social and political philosophers rather than of international lawyers, or of scholars of international law, as such, although such distinctions are not always applicable.

The material here is broadly chronological although some thematic discussions interrupt that sequence. After tracing some lines of thought up to Hegel and Marx, the chapter continues with a brief discussion of the legal philosophy of the twentieth century. This contains many strands, most of which have more in common with political and social philosophy than with particular content areas of law or professional practices within law. Initial remarks are made here about the contribution of Hohfeld although a more extended discussion of his contemporary relevance is postponed until Chapter 4. Some contributions like that of Hart, who was of the next generation after Hohfeld, are central to contemporary legal theory and need to be taken account of in any essay into international jurisprudence. Hart offered some preliminary comments on international law and his work continues to inspire theoretical debate on a number of related topics.

The chapter concludes with a discussion of John Rawls' contributions to understanding the law of nations. Rawls' theory is in many ways a sophisticated version of social contract theory. Rawls' work is thus the culmination of a long tradition of liberal political theory applied, in the case of *The Law of Peoples*, to international law. In any event social contract theories make assumptions about the global domain. As Martha Nussbaum has commented, '[s]ocial contract theories take the nation-state as their basic unit. For reasons internal to the structure of such theories, they are bound to do so' (Nussbaum 2007: 92). If Rawls' book on the law of nations is something of a dead end, as will be proposed, it is a cautionary one.

Earlier Contributions

Without attempting to be comprehensive, some comments should be made on the contribution of longer traditions in legal and political philosophy to a collectivist program in international jurisprudence. In many ways Western philosophy has focused most of its attention on individual human beings and their place in a world of objects, concepts and values. Ethics in Western traditions is predominantly a matter of obligations for the individual person. It is a commonplace to contrast such individualistic preoccupations with a more collective, holistic or mystical set of traditions emanating from the lands to Europe's east. To the extent this contrast is valid, it no doubt reflects among other things the varied influence of the larger spiritual movements. For example significant versions of Christianity since the time of Luther have focused on the knowledge and the faith of the individual person. There is no doubt that John Locke's account of governance and of the relationship between ruler and citizen was strongly influenced by Protestant forms of Christianity with their emphasis on the individual believer's 'covenant' with God. Kant and Hegel were in a significant sense Protestant Christian philosophers. But even within Western philosophical thinking, including the work of Locke himself, many traditions of thought have addressed questions of community and of plurality (Locke 1997: 290). Those traditions strongly influenced by religious commitments also provide examples of a more collective style. Roman Catholic theology has been a major contributor to the development of natural law as a body of thought, and relatedly to notions of political life that emphasize the community of the faithful as a living whole rather than the individual believer.

Turning to more directly political concerns, the limits of legitimate political domination of the many by the one, as in monarchy, and the point beyond which such domination becomes tyranny, were explored by the ancient writers as well as by scholars of the Renaissance. Also, in the sixteenth century, religious turmoil stoked by the Reformation gave rise to renewed debate on the relationship between monarchy and the divine. When a sovereign of England, Henry VIII, came for quite different reasons to sever his ties of spiritual deference to the Pope, it became urgently necessary to delineate the role of divine guidance and of delegated divine authority in the person of the monarch. By the time James I of England (already James VI of Scotland) came to the throne, he found it necessary to strongly assert a divine status: it was not taken for granted.

Hobbes and Locke

Against this background, modern political theory in the West from Hobbes onwards attempted to define the nature of governance and thus the relationships between the ruled and the ruler. Thomas Hobbes was born in Elizabeth's reign (in the year of the Great Armada), and his long life spanned an extraordinary period in English history. It included the reign of James VI and I, the English Civil War, the trial and execution of the son of Elizabeth's successor King James and the restoration of the monarchy following the republican experiment. Hobbes' *Leviathan*, published in 1651, examined the varieties of sovereignty, including monarchy and rule by an assembly (Covell 2004: 32; Runciman 1997). Hobbes examined the ways in which interests of large communities could be served or at least accommodated by such arrangements. The notion of the covenant was therefore of key interest to Hobbes (Covell 2004, 23). In many ways Hobbes stood back from the specifics of constitutional arrangements, taking the institution of sovereignty rather than its particular manifestations as his subject matter. Hobbes also discussed political relationships among nations. While the conventional view is that Hobbes' approach to international law was a version of what came to be called the realist orientation, with its jaundiced view of human conduct whether individual or collective, it has been argued that a somewhat more benevolent, natural law perspective is a more accurate categorization (Covell 2004: 147).

Covell argues that Hobbes stands in a line of natural law theorists of international law that includes Grotius some decades earlier, and Vattel a century after Hobbes. According to Covell each of these thinkers held, although in different ways, that relationships between sovereigns are constituted by law which is not entirely of their making (Covell 2004: 7). As Koskenniemi argues, for Grotius 'the sovereign is merely an agent of the normative order' (2005a: 99). Towards the end of the seventeenth century, philosopher and international jurist Pufendorf (Wright 2006: 273) proposed that nations are in a state of nature and hence are governed by natural law. Pufendorf's contemporary, John Locke, was also much concerned with this idea.

The liberal tradition, to which Locke contributed, investigated relationships between individuals, for example in relation to ownership of property, both prior to and after a state of civilized society had emerged. The 'state of nature' represented for Locke a methodological device for delineating the effects of law-based governance. The latter was characterized above all by the necessity of consent of the governed, as manifested at least by a constitutional framework with legislative and executive powers laid out.

The status of competing independent nations was sometimes to be seen by later commentators as anarchic, and in that respect characterized by the 'state of nature'. But Locke's 'state of nature' was a more nuanced one. Indeed for Locke, as described in his *Second Treatise of Government*, it is unregulated monarchy that more nearly converges on anarchy (Locke 1997: 276). An example of this would be where a 'prince' arrogates to himself the nomination of a successor without the legal framework to legitimate such a momentous decision. In Locke's own times, the nomination by Charles II of his brother James to succeed him gave rise to a constitutional crisis. For a monarch to claim a 'divine right' based on genealogy – tracing his status back through the generations, perhaps back to William the Conqueror if not Adam – was for Locke entirely without foundation. The state of nature bears only the minimal characteristics of civilization, but it does accord to natural law and to divine law. In particular, the state of nature brings with it inherent rights to certain kinds of property. It is, so to speak, not so much a jungle as a (very primitive) village. '[T]he whole community is one body in the state of nature, in respect of all other states or persons out of its community' (Locke 1997: 261). The 'or persons' clause is itself of some interest.

Thus when Locke stated that 'all commonwealths are in the state of nature one with another' (Locke 1997: 272) he was not describing a universe bare of rights and obligations. The state of nature can include the making of promises, for trade or on a personal basis, even though it falls far short of the effects achieved by combining into a commonwealth. The state of society is among other things an administrative improvement, an improvement in efficiency and what we might now call 'good governance'. Humans can get along without it. Indeed the state of society brings with it many burdens such as agreeing to majority rule, as discussed in Chapter VIII of the *Second Treatise*. Absolute monarchy – a form of the state of nature – is much less demanding in that sense. In the state of nature man has liberty over self-preservation much more widely than in the state of society. In the state of society self-preservation is regulated and curtailed. Similarly, the punishment of wrongdoers is, in the state of society, given over to an executive which the citizen agrees to assist.

Locke's understanding of the state of nature thus involved not only rights to property but on many occasions also the honouring of those rights, for example by informal and reciprocal arrangements or perhaps by custom or by the sovereign's command. All of these kinds of processes are for Locke not truly 'social' in the full sense of the state of politic society. Locke sets the bar high for politic society. The arrangements he envisaged and advocated for in Britain would reach that bar. This was a constitutional monarchy, with exclusion of Catholic princes. Presumably the republican arrangement under Cromwell may at times have met this standard. But the Stuart monarchs (James I and Charles I) clearly had not met Locke's stringent criteria, nor the Tudors before them. To reiterate, for Locke the state of nature is capable of great sophistication and efficacy: it is just so much a second best to the heights of the social. Emphasis must be laid on this in view of Rousseau's radically different and equally influential take on the state of nature in the century following.

Turning to intercourse between nations, for example in time of war, even in a state of nature the rights of the conqueror are for Locke severely delimited (Locke 1997: 273). There may be rights and obligations at work in the international sphere, despite the absence of an integrated legal infrastructure as in a true (bounded) 'commonwealth', *because* that sphere represents the state of nature. It will be an empirical matter, a matter of history and contingency, whether rights are honoured and obligations recognized. In part because Locke set the bar so high for properly constituted commonwealths, he in effect recognized considerable scope for regulation and order at the international level too. In some respects Locke thus anticipated the views of Hart on this question. Locke's account of international law is, one might say, a 'glass half full' picture. And although Locke discusses, as was commonplace, the relationships between princes as constituting international law to some extent, his focus on commonwealths as the unit of independent polity itself contributes to a collective analysis. Locke's constitutional investigations were entirely opposed to the identification of the populace with a single leader, especially a monarch. Indeed one of the important outcomes of Locke's analysis was to provide a vocabulary with which revolution might be articulated (Taylor 2007: 160). There are continuities between the analysis carried out by Grotius at the start of the seventeenth century and that of Locke towards its end. In some ways they shared the experience of a new world order, which had emerged in the sixteenth century, founded on the pillage of the lands beyond Europe (Sassen 2006: 83). Despite his methodological adherence to a 'top-down' framework for international normativity, Grotius was something of an apologist by vocation, especially in relation to the 'aggressive trading policy' of the Dutch East India Company (Koskenniemi 2011: 110). His application of a natural law theory to international relations was thus a quietist one (Taylor 2007: 159). Locke in contrast was a radical. Among the consequences of Locke's writings was their influence, three-quarters of a century after his death, on those who drafted the US Declaration of Independence and the US Constitution. By then further political ideas were in the air.

Rousseau and Hume

Developing a tradition of thinking from essayists Montaigne and Montesquieu, Jean-Jacques Rousseau's accounts of a general will in the population flirted with the irrational yet were sufficiently down to earth to inspire political activists across the world (Nussbaum 2007: 36). For Rousseau the individual 'puts in common his person and his whole power under the supreme direction of the general will; and in return we receive in a body every member as an indivisible part of the whole' (Rousseau 1997: 425). Rousseau's picture of the contracted society is at the same time a contribution to communitarianism and to liberal theory. As to the former it anticipates Hegel and Marx in apparently defining the individual person entirely in terms of the group. This organic whole, a cross between a beehive and a human village, is a kind of collective but a radically communitarian one. For Rousseau, this whole is 'a moral and collective body, which … receives from this same act [of association under the social contract] its unity, its common *self*, its life, and its will' (1997: 425). Rousseau continues: 'This public person, which is thus formed by the union of all the individual members' may be called 'Republic', 'body politic', 'State' or 'Sovereign'. When it is 'compared to similar bodies', that is to say internationally, it is called *Power* (1997: 425–6). Thus the whole entity (what Locke would have called a Commonwealth) exhibits the characteristics of a kind of macro-individual. The state is a kind of a person so that interaction between states may be thought of as interaction between these sovereign persons. Without having invented this usage, Rousseau undoubtedly established a highly influential version of it.

Like Locke, Rousseau's scheme had a central place for the state of nature and the consequences of human society transcending that state. Rousseau's state of nature is a much more primitive state than Locke's. It is also expressly an anthropologically prehistorical state, and an early stage in the evolution of civilization. Rousseau is by no means dismissive of the up-side of the state of nature; the sense of natural liberty is celebrated. But this is a somewhat nostalgic kind of appreciation. Rousseau's account is characterized by an anthropological admiration of the exotic. Thus to the extent Rousseau sees international law as exhibiting the state of nature, he will have a darker, glass-half-empty attitude compared to Locke.

As Nussbaum emphasizes, Rousseau was no liberal and his account of the social contract does not involve a contract between independent individuals (Nussbaum 2007: 25). He was however a kind of 'positive libertarian', one who conceived of freedom as 'an "exercise" concept rather than as an "opportunity" concept' (Shapiro 2012: 317). This is an important indication about Rousseau's understanding of a collective 'will'. For Rousseau the transition from the state of nature to the civil state is from appetite to right, from physical 'impulsion' to duty. It is a transition from the mere possession of objects, by force or at best on the basis of such bare customs as 'finders keepers' to ownership under legal title. Rousseau's leap from the state of nature to the social contract is a quantum leap (that is to say a qualitative jump) much more dramatic than the change envisaged by Locke. From might to right – from physical inequality to legal equality.

Like Locke however, Rousseau presented the state of civil society (in Rousseau's vocabulary, the 'social contract') as the solution to a problem. Some aspects of Rousseau's account are indeed similar here to Locke's: the social contract gives rise to an holistic infrastructure by which individual rights such as to life, as well as property rights, can be guaranteed. In its absence there is just too much uncertainty. Also consistent with this aspect of the liberal tradition of Locke was Rousseau's insistence that the individual retain his freedom in this law-ruled polity. This liberty is 'conventional' because it is based on a contract, yet it is a radical, even an absolute liberty.

David Hume was at one time a significant supporter of Rousseau in the latter's peregrinations. More resistant to romanticism, Hume was something of a sceptic in relation to political theory. Hume dismissed the social contract as a serious account of the legitimacy of societal arrangements. He pointed out that the notion of popular, individual-based consent to prevailing political order – for example the reign of a monarch – is entirely implausible. Hume made the comparison with the position of a man carried on board a ship when asleep: can he be said to have consented to the captaincy of that ship, to which he finds himself subject when awake? Indeed the inhabitants of any state are in much the same position. They 'wake' at birth under a certain regime. Generally speaking they have no practical possibility of relocating elsewhere, undermining any claim as to their express consent to the prevailing power relationships. Even if a 'company of men' manage to leave their native country and its prince, and settle elsewhere, their prince may well seek to maintain his authority over them and this effort would likely be treated as legitimate on an international basis. The attitude of governed citizens to their rulers may include views on legitimacy of that rule, for example a belief that King X is their rightful monarch even if he has been displaced by a usurper. But this does not amount to a belief, still less an actuality, that the sovereign's legitimacy is constituted by the population's 'consent'. There is no place here for promises and the reliance on promises. Instead, for Hume, all is a matter of convention, of social arrangement.

From Kant to Marx

David Hume died in the year in which independence was declared by Britain's former colony, the United States of America, and Rousseau two years later. This event was epochal however for the younger contemporaries of Hume and Rousseau across Europe. The first European state to recognize the USA as a fellow, independent state, by signing an agreement with it, was Prussia, home state to Immanuel Kant (Hoeffe 2006: 11). Kant adhered to an extensively modified version of the social contract, declining to follow Hume's extreme scepticism on this point while avoiding the more simplistic accounts of a state of nature. As is well known, Kant's philosophic task focused on the individual, knowing subject, the rational animal confronting a universe of spatiotemporal reality and of ethical challenges and striving for principled cognition in relation to both. In much of his writings Kant set the contingencies of human social and political life at a distance, and emphasized that the social consequences of ethical principles are irrelevant to the validity of those principles.

Kant's thinking on right and on the state was firmly in the liberal tradition. 'Right is ... the sum of the conditions under which the choice of one can be united with the choice of another in accordance with a universal law of freedom' (Hoeffe 2002: 92). A universal law of freedom could not for Kant depend on or be evaluated against mere contingencies or consequences. He was no utilitarian. Yet at the same time Kant recognized some social contingencies as inescapable, and relatedly he valued certain social outcomes. The 'sheer fact' of human coexistence (Hoeffe 2002: 93) means that one universe is shared by many moral actors, giving rise to conflicts and challenges. Similarly, limited space on the globe gives rise to challenges for the peaceful coexistence of the large, delimited communities of people called states or nations.

Where some philosophers might have been seen as apologists for international conflict, seen as inevitable, Kant was unapologetic in his vision for world peace. The state of peace is for Kant 'a direct duty' (Hoeffe 2002: 183). Hoeffe is surely correct to observe that 'Kant is the first thinker and to date the only great thinker to have elevated the concept of peace to the status of a foundational concept of philosophy' (Hoeffe 2006: xv). Kant's writings include 'a scathing criticism of colonialism' consistent with his support for the American revolution against British rule, and '[a]bove all, it overcomes the prevailing tendency to restrict legal and political philosophy to the "national" level, [responding] to its concentration on single communities with a global and cosmopolitan perspective' (Hoeffe 2006: 2). Kant was also a supporter of the French revolutionary republic, despite the Terror and the execution of the former monarch. Good outcomes may be associated with unworthy means, without thereby compromising those outcomes (Hoeffe 2002: 177). Kant's cosmopolitanism should also be seen as a significant departure in the legal theory of the West. Kant took the juridical relationships between states seriously in the context of a philosophical analysis of rights. Indeed his contribution stands out from subsequent writers almost as much as from earlier scholars. Hoeffe comments as follows:

> From Hobbes, Locke, and Rousseau to Hegel, and to some degree also to Marx, and in the twentieth century from Kelsen and Hart to John Rawls, up through Dworkin and Habermas, the prominent texts deal almost exclusively with the juridical order of a single state. (Hoeffe 2006: 13)

This is an exaggeration, particularly with respect to Kelsen, but the point is well made. The inclusion of the name of John Rawls on this list might seem even more surprising. It is justified, I think, on the basis that Rawls' substantial contribution to legal and political theory is indeed a contribution to our understanding of justice within a polity. As we will see when discussing Rawls, *The Law of Peoples* fails to engage with international dimensions. Importantly, Rawls' attempt to do so is itself a development of Kant. Kant's approach is, before Rawls, the 'clearest example of [the] two-stage approach' to global justice (Nussbaum 2007: 231). A 'two-stage approach' is one in which some kind of social contract between nations is postulated as an adjunct to the various social contracts by which those nations are themselves brought into being. Two-stage versions of social contract theory treat the social contract between nations (what might be called an external social contract) as secondary to the internal (constitutional) social contracts.

　　Kant's version is framed in terms of personhood. A state 'is like a household situated alongside others' and in Kant's words is 'a moral Person living with and in opposition to another state in a condition of natural freedom' (Nussbaum 2007: 231). Treating states (or nations) as so many persons is inherent to this scheme. As Nussbaum observes, Kant 'does not press the analogy between persons and states' as far in his later work as in his earlier work. Certainly Kant's account of statehood as a kind of personhood is a sophisticated one. In *Perpetual Peace* Kant puts it as follows:

> [A] state is not a property ... as may be the ground on which its people are settled. It is a society of human beings over whom no one but itself has the right to dispose. Like the trunk of a tree, it has its own roots, and to graft it on to another state is to do away with its existence as a moral person, and to make of it a thing. Hence it is in contradiction to the idea of the original contract without which no right over a people is thinkable ... The custom of marriage between

states, as if they were individuals, has survived even up to the most recent times ... (Kant 1997: 571–2)

A 'state of nation states' or *Weltrepublik* was for Kant the only way for states to transcend 'the lawless state of constant war' and like 'individual persons, give up their savage (lawless) freedom' for a '*civitas gentium*' (Byrd and Hruschka 2010: 199). Kant argued that a league of nations, which he thought of as a minimal arrangement for non-aggressive cohabitation but with no overarching legal framework, would constitute a rather poor second best (Nussbaum 2007: 49).

Post-Kantian philosophy in the early decades of the nineteenth century explored ways of articulating relationships between an individual thinker and a complex universe of both natural and social phenomena. It treated questions of ethics as matters of particular human societies, rooted in particular time and place. The study of human languages and their supposed connections, including connections of derivation and ancestry, supported the view that populations with shared cultural identities were the natural components of an international settlement. Hegel's writings on an evolution of spirit towards communal as well as towards individual expression was in many ways the culmination of this development, although Marx was to take the approach in further directions still. Hegel himself should be considered, like Rousseau, as one of the 'positive libertarians' for whom individual freedom is linked 'to participation in social and political institutions – participation in ways that will lead people to realize their potential' (Shapiro 2012: 317). Hegel's focus on the ethics of a community was more subtle than that of Marx was to be, and considerably more ironic, but it was of course not designed to inspire revolutionary activism. It was Marx and his followers who harnessed the philosophical resources supplied by Hegel, suitably diluted, to a political program. The Marxist and the subsequent Leninist theoretical accounts of society and of its constituent parts were designed to inform and to fuel the activities of a leadership cadre which would express the interests of the whole class and thereby would drive historical change. People and the relationships between people would be transformed for ever. A dictatorship of the proletariat would turn on its head the ancient fear of tyranny.

In the twentieth century alongside Marxism there developed various traditions that also focused on communitarian questions. In recent decades Charles Taylor has been perhaps the most well-known advocate of a communitarian approach. Theories of democracy and of republicanism are in active development within political philosophy, as are accounts of political obligation and collective action (Gilbert 2006; Kutz 2000; List and Pettit 2011; Pettit 2010). The republican traditions are intertwined with the history of law and continue to provide essential resources for articulating a law of nations (Sellers 1998; 2006). The point of this whistle-stop tour is to suggest a number of things. While the role of the individual retains pride of place broadly speaking, political philosophy from ancient times has also been concerned with collectivities of various kinds. Communities, societies, tribes and classes have been analysed in the course of the articulation of theories on government, sovereignty, democracy and institutions of state. While it will be argued that legal philosophy in general, and the jurisprudence of international law in particular, has failed to adequately address collective questions, there is no lack of ideas relevant to those questions within philosophical literature. If the jurisprudence of international law is to pay more attention to the centrality of collectives to its task, it cannot ignore this rich and diverse resource. It should also be noted that important traditions in legal philosophy have derived from (for example) Hegel or Marx, bringing with them certain traces of a communitarian tendency in one of its many variants. Marxism continues to inspire international lawyers (Marks 2008). But attention should now be turned to the legal philosophy of the twentieth century and beyond.

The Twentieth Century: Hohfeld, Kelsen and Hart

Wesley Hohfeld's work has a unique place in legal philosophy. The various writings of authors such as Hart, Raz, Dworkin and Rawls were composed over the course of extended careers and were influenced by ongoing scholarly interactions and debates, they are extensively cited and discussed and their internal consistencies and inconsistencies continue to be debated. In contrast Hohfeld's highly circumscribed contribution has acquired canonical status as a kind of founding formula for an analytical tradition in jurisprudence. In a paper originally published in 1913, subsequently expanded and republished, Hohfeld outlined a scheme by which legal relationships between private individuals can be categorized and the logical implications drawn out. Hohfeld was inspired by earlier writers on rights and duties, who had pointed to the troublesome consequences of what might be called a unilateralist understanding of rights. If a right is viewed as a kind of property, or of 'dominium', it seems that too much is being taken for granted and too many questions begged. Rights held by persons in respect of other persons (such as legal rights) are not like the powers with which persons may freely deal with inanimate objects or with beasts. In contrast, they involve reciprocal relationships.

This argument about rights as correlative with obligations goes back to the seventeenth century if not earlier. One of the founders of this sceptical or parsimonious tradition was Samuel Pufendorf, who among other things was an important contributor to international law. For Pufendorf, writing in the middle seventeenth century, inherent rights are conceptually troublesome,

> For 'tis ridiculous Trifling to call that Power a *Right*, which, should we attempt to exercise, all other Men have an *equal right* to obstruct or prevent us. (Tuck 1979: 158)

To identify what Hohfeld called 'claim-rights' (as held by one party), without identifying corresponding duties or obligations (owed by another party), is thus an empty gesture (Tuck 1979: 158). This argument about rights as correlative with obligations was enthusiastically taken up by Jeremy Bentham in his positivist campaign for the reconceptualization of law. It is connected with the utilitarian methodology of weighing up costs and benefits of legal regulations, as contrasted with a 'deontological' or ethics-based orientation such as that of Kant (Tuck 1979: 160). Hohfeld did not follow Bentham's prose style, with its diatribes against over-extended claims concerning inherent universal rights as 'nonsense upon stilts'. In a broadly positivist style, Hohfeld however followed Bentham in seeking to unpack legal relationships and to work out the necessary implications that follow from particular jural connections. Any legal relation excludes all others to the extent that the content of and relevant parties to the relation are the same. In other words the linked pairs are like atoms. Molecules can only be formed by combinations of those atoms. Hohfeld's career was cut short by his early death. Contemporary explorations of Hohfeld are discussed in Chapter 4.

Hans Kelsen was born only a few years after Hohfeld, towards the end of the nineteenth century, but had by contrast a long and productive career, albeit a career severely disrupted by the political events of the times. Kelsen explored the nature of legal norms both in the municipal and in the international context. It was his insistence on the formal and abstract characteristics of law's normativity that set Kelsen apart from other legal theorists. Traditional legal positivism had emphasized the social facts of the constitution of law by sovereign command, by parliamentary edict or (grudgingly) by the ineffable processes of Common Law. Normativity is considered to be of the essence of law from a natural law perspective, but that approach focuses on the content of such proper laws. Up to Kelsen's time, at least, the natural law perspective defined legitimate law as law with good content. In contrast, and expressly rejecting the values-based natural law orientation, Kelsen incorporated the norm-centred position into a positivist framework. With some success Kelsen attempted to remain grounded in the practical realities of law, including international law, without losing sight of its more abstract qualities.

One important area explored by Kelsen was the conceptual status of individuals within the context of legal systems. Much of Kelsen's work emphasizes the ways in which the legal person (the individual citizen as a person under law) is constructed by a web of legal relationships including state-derived constitutions (Kelsen 1967: 172). Without suggesting that he thought humans nothing more than such constructed entities, it is certainly the case that Kelsen de-emphasized the role of individual persons as such (as voluntary and autonomous agents) in respect of the operation of legal norms. Thus 'even the so-called physical person is an artificial construction of jurisprudence ... even the so-called physical person is actually only a "juristic" person' (1967: 172). Thus, 'a legal person is the unity of a complex of legal obligations and legal rights'. Here it might be noted that Kelsen was of one mind with Hohfeld on the question of reciprocity of jural relationships ('the right of the one presupposes the obligation of the other': 1967: 170). For Kelsen (1967: 129) it is a vestige of 'natural-law doctrine' to assert that rights, such as a right to property, can pre-exist a legal order in which reciprocal obligations are set out. Legal orders do not emerge in response to such inherent, 'subjective' rights. In a somewhat analogous manner

Kelsen's account of international law proposed that states, as they operate on the international stage, are more accurately thought of as the creatures of international legal norms rather than those norms being the creatures of the conduct of those states. Kelsen's view of the relationships between national and international legal orders is admittedly subtle (1967: 332). It is certain that Kelsen did not treat 'sovereign' states as quasi-individuals, competing and bargaining with each other and giving rise by their willed conduct, their decisions and their agreements to international law as we know it. Even in the sphere of private law, Kelsen emphasizes, there is no 'self-determination' by individual persons if by that is meant the autonomous creation of legal rights and obligations by assertion or even by negotiation. Such processes rely for any lawfulness on law-creating functions conferred by the prevailing legal order itself (Kelsen 1967: 170). Kelsen's norm-focused alternative to that traditional view of sovereign individuals at the international level is not of course the alternative to be focused on in this book, yet Kelsen may be said to have been labouring in the same vineyard.

Certainly Kelsen would have found it difficult to accept the suggestion that international law can be reduced to a series of universally applicable, uniform protections of individual human persons. As previously noted, that view was carefully explored and advocated by Kelsen's contemporary Hersch Lauterpacht. From Kelsen's perspective a focus on uniform protections would obscure the ways in which international norms are structured, and on the ways in which municipal and international norms interrelate. It would be to put the cart of the implementation of law before the horse of lawfulness. Consistently with this approach, Kelsen rejected any role for affect in the relationship between individual persons and the law; whether a person is bound by the laws of State A or State B is an objective matter independent of the person's feelings, positive or negative. 'The question whether an individual belongs to a state is not a psychological but a legal question' (Kelsen 1967: 288). Kelsen was just as sceptical about consent or the social contract as explanatory frameworks in international law (von Bernstorff 2010: 159).

Herbert Hart's writings on legal theory have shaped English-speaking jurisprudence for the last half-century or more. Especially with *The Concept of Law* (first published in 1961) Hart established an approach to legal philosophy that brought together an analytic style derived from Bentham with an attention to social and institutional contexts, and to language use, that responded to twentieth-century developments in philosophy. With Bentham, Hart insisted that laws are human products, imbued with moral worth only in partial and contingent ways. Legal systems, and individual laws, do not express higher values. While the exact shape and strength of Hart's brand of legal positivism is still debated, and may not have been stable across his writing career, Hart's position was quite definitely opposed to natural law traditions. Hart emphasized that legal systems are made up of people making decisions in systematic ways, in effect following rules, where important institutional roles are played by officials as well as by the general citizen. While officials have the function of interpreting and implementing some of the rules, not just obeying them, their conduct is just as much rule-bound as that of the citizens.

Above all, officials operate in the institutional context of rules about rules, higher-level rules that govern what lower-level rules are legitimate. The 'rule of recognition' which plays a central role in Hart's account is the prototype of such a higher-level rule. In his brief discussion of international law, Hart observes that many of the features of legal systems in the municipal realm (the realm of nations) do not seem to exist in the international domain. This commonplace observation is accompanied by a number of remarks on ways in which international law does still manifest lawfulness.

One of several areas of legal theory to which Hart contributed was the theory of rights. Where Hohfeld had focused on the puzzle of the interrelationships of right, duty and so on, Hart was more concerned with the exercise of rights and with the source of the legitimacy of their implementation. Two broad schools have been identified in this area: the 'will theory' and the 'interest theory' of rights. Hart's name is usually associated with the former. The will theory of rights emphasizes the voluntary nature of legitimate implementation of rights, exemplified just as much by the waiving of one's rights as by insisting on one's enjoyment of them. Rights are subjective in that sense and seem to presuppose significant mental capacity in their bearer. Hart observed that there are limitations on the applicability of this approach. As well as the general point that the will theory has difficulty with the rights of anyone lacking the capacity of a competent adult (for example, children or animals, the sleeper or the drunkard), Hart accepted that the existence of legal officials restricts the voluntary aspect of the deployment of rights. For example if the officials are governed by a national constitution, and even if it is only partly adhered to, voluntary decisions by individual rights-holders must on occasion come into conflict with higher demands. Hart remained on the 'will' side of the will/interest divide, but his writings make it clear that the deployment of rights in a society governed by law is itself an institutional matter. There are important connections between these points made by Hart and the claims of the interest theorists, for whom rights are objective social facts that can legitimately be defended by others. As will be shown in Chapter 4, such matters are important at the collective level as in international law. Hart's direct contribution to the conceptualizing of international law is generally held to have been a modest one, constituted almost entirely by the final chapter of *The Concept of Law*, a chapter whose status is in the manner of a 'postscript' or a Tolstoyan Epilogue to the preceding chapters. Hart's indirect contributions are more numerous (Morss 2005).

John Rawls and 'The Law of Peoples'

From the point of view of the current project, one particular contribution must sooner or later be scrutinised: John Rawls' *The Law of Peoples*. John Rawls' status as one of the twentieth century's most influential political philosophers was secured by *A Theory of Justice* which originally appeared in 1971. Rawls developed a modern account of social contract theory. Rawls as a thinker in the liberal tradition focused on 'the basic rights and liberties of citizens as free and equal persons, a requirement of absolutely first importance for an account of democratic institutions' (Rawls 1999b: xii). Consistently with this, Rawls valued tolerance and diversity, acknowledging that rational persons of goodwill may disagree over many of the most important judgements that we have to make in social life. Diversity and disagreement, in the form of competition, are of course central to capitalism, a system with which some forms of liberal theory are therefore comfortable. But his acceptance of plurality did not for Rawls constitute an argument for the legitimacy of competitive capitalism, under which inequalities are exploited and amplified. Market forces do not of themselves generate justice. Command economies are no better. How then may a just society be achieved?

Centralized decision-making by a monarch or by an elite, claiming special knowledge as to the proper allocation of goods and of burdens, was for Rawls no better an option than the free market. Nor was a calculus based on the costs and benefits, the pains and pleasures of various alternative arrangements. Rawls described his project as 'a reasonably systematic alternative to utilitarianism, which in one form or another has long dominated the Anglo-Saxon tradition of political thought' (Rawls 1999b: xi). For this reason and others, Rawls can be thought of as reinvigorating a Kantian tradition in political thought. As Hoeffe observes, 'Rawls' categorical imperative ... turns out to be that imperative of *rights* in which lies the fundamental task of a Kantian theory of law and the state' (Hoeffe 2002: 217). For Rawls, like Kant, thought of justice as a political matter just as much as a personal matter.

How to establish some kind of conceptual 'level playing field'? Employing a version of the 'state of nature' paradigm as earlier used by Locke and Rousseau among others, Rawls set out to establish a kind of benchmark or template, a default condition for the optimal distribution of life's advantages. For every real person who reflects on the unequal distribution of goods and opportunities, either in their own society or internationally, will be both influenced and limited in their thinking by their own particular circumstances. They might focus too much on their own personal circumstances or those of their immediate family or neighbourhood. Or they might try to take account of others' circumstances but they would generally fail to do so successfully, if only as a result of trying too hard.

Rawls' strategy for facilitating a more detached view was the conceit of the 'original position', a circumstance in which one's own place in the pecking order (gender, nationality, class and so on) is as yet concealed from one's view. As Rawls noted, Kant's own 'categorical imperative' has some similar aspects to the veil of ignorance in its bracketing of the contingent in order that general principles may be revealed (Rawls 1999b: 118).

A certain kind of self-interest could then be allowed to drive the argument, for an intelligent and cautious kind of self-interest in one thus blinkered would have to take a larger view of the best approach to the distribution of goods. In particular, mechanisms which would guarantee sufficient for the worst off, or provide for improvements for the worst off, would be favoured under the modestly enlightened self-interest posited by Rawls. Clearly, then, the rationality of the parties is assumed in the original position (Rawls 1999b: 123). These are economic actors. But it is also important to note that while the actors are very much liberal individuals, 'they are choosing principles for a public conception of justice'. Rawls points out that this aspect of his account might be said to be Kantian, as expressed by the latter in *Perpetual Peace* (Rawls 1999b: 115). In other words the universe for which principles are being defined by this individualistic process is itself a collective one. Moreover the process requires some kind of consensus to be reached so that it is a 'prior collective agreement' that comes to determine the society's future planning (Rawls 1999b: 495).

In a much more sophisticated and nuanced way than I have suggested here, Rawls thus set out the claim that fairness is the most firm and most valid foundation for justice. Rawls was a kind of liberal Machiavelli, designing and advocating for a system that accepts human frailty (in the form of self-interest if not selfishness) while harnessing it to a vision of a society that operates for the welfare of all. True to the liberal tradition, and despite the considerations just noted, Rawls' account is based on the cognition and the decisions of an individual subject. In the words of Nathan Widder, the Rawlsian subject is a 'hypothetical ... subject that stands apart from its values, talents and identity in order to choose principles of justice'. This is one reason for the limitations of Rawls' account, connected with the appeals to 'moral or political principles deemed universally applicable or rational' (Widder 2012: 135–6, 125). Rawls' project has been described by Paul Patton as utopian (Patton 2010: 186) and in this connection a comment by Connolly that Rawls is centred on stasis should also be noted. As Connolly suggests (Patton 2010: 225), Rawls' approach has trouble dealing with change.

Rawls' 'methodological individualism' has been criticized by proponents of a communitarian approach to social and political life such as Michael Sandel (Campbell 2001: 43, 111; Widder 2012: 4). Communitarian philosophies, which offer perspectives on collectives of humans, have benefitted from the particular challenges presented by Rawls. For whereas other influential liberal theories such as those of Nozick are unapologetic in their defence of a 'libertarian' capitalism, Rawls attempted to synthesize liberal individualism with the aspiration to a welfare economy. It should also be emphasized that scholars such as Thomas Pogge and Martha Nussbaum continue to find value in Rawls' earlier work, as discussed below.

Rawls' overall approach as expressed in *A Theory of Justice* is of relevance for the present project in various ways. But it is his later *The Law of Peoples* that is of more direct significance. Published first in lecture form in 1993, and then in 1999 (Martin and Reidy 2006: 7), *The Law of Peoples* attempts to extend to the international sphere a version of the 'original position' methodology from *A Theory of Justice*. The earlier book set up the paradigm of individual people within some notional society stepping back from their knowledge of that society and of their place in it, to something like a (cognitive) state of nature with the slate wiped clean or turned over. *The Law of Peoples* treats nations or states in an analogous way, imagining them as kinds of individuals existing in relationship with each other but able (for the purposes of the exercise) to step back from the actuality of the global society and think 'outside the square' so to say. Cogitating behind a 'veil of ignorance', just as Rawls' individual human subjects had done in the earlier book, these nations are able to give consideration to alternative schemes for their social arrangements insulated from an awareness of contingent differences between them. For example they are not aware of which is a world power, which is struggling to emerge from poverty, and so on. For Nussbaum, Rawls is working in a Kantian tradition here:

> Both Kant and Rawls ... recognize the importance of confronting issues of justice between nations. But the logic of their theories leads them to pose this question at a second stage, and derivatively. They imagine that after states are established, relations among them still resemble a state of nature; so further principles must be chosen to regulate their dealings with one another.
>
> Thus, in this two-stage approach, states are treated as isomorphic with 'free, equal, and independent' persons in the first stage of the argument. (Nussbaum 2007: 18–19)

Nussbaum is sympathetic to Rawls' methodology and to many of his claims, and shares the tradition of liberalism. But Nussbaum is unequivocal in her judgement on the book. While Rawls' *The Law of Peoples* 'represents his attempt to make good on [his] claim' that the problem of international justice can be dealt with by an extension of his general conception of justice, it fails to deliver. 'It does not in fact ... give a satisfactory account of those issues' (Nussbaum 2007: 23). Rawls' theory of justice 'offers no principles whatsoever' (Nussbaum 2007: 24). Thus,

> [A]dequate criticism of the hierarchy among nations requires a kind of radical re-thinking of national boundaries and basic economic arrangements that cannot be achieved if we simply imagine the contract doctrine applied a second time over, as nations already constituted, *and imagined as virtual persons* who are rough equals, contract for the best cooperative deal among them. (Nussbaum 2007: 32; emphasis added)

Onora O'Neill's evaluation of Rawls has been summed up as follows: 'Rawls's conception of a people, on whom [sic] he builds his account of justice beyond borders, is in fact remarkably state-like ... there is little to distinguish liberal peoples from liberal states'. The same commentators continue: 'Rawls is anchoring his account of justice in agents who are not well exemplified in the real world, but if they were so exemplified, they would need the (realist state-like) capacities from which he seeks to detach his agents' (Booth, Dunne and Cox 2001: 10).

In *The Law of Peoples* Rawls' approach is consistent in his continuing employment of the methodological individualism implemented in *A Theory of Justice*. Rawls' focus in *The Law of Peoples* is, in his own words, on 'the particular political principles for regulating the mutual political relations between peoples'. Thus 'the Law of Peoples is developed within political liberalism. [It is] an extension of a liberal conception of justice for a *domestic* regime to a *Society of Peoples*' (Rawls 1999a: 3, 55). Rawls observes that 'The Law of Peoples regulates the most inclusive political subject, the political Society of Peoples'. He seems to be saying that the Law of Peoples argument is a way of completing the whole picture, initiated in *A Theory of Justice*, by presenting an account that covers all levels of political life ('all politically relevant subjects'): 'for free and equal citizens and their governments, and for free and equal peoples' (Rawls 1999a: 86).

The Law of Peoples thus represents a development of Rawls' larger concerns with liberal politics viewed as a philosophically rigorous enterprise. It can be thought of as an attempted synthesis of two traditions, the social contract tradition of the formation of civil society and the Kantian tradition of practical cosmopolitanism as explored in *Perpetual Peace*. Other features of a Kantian style of philosophy, more closely aligned with liberal theory, may also be discerned. Kant's notion of the categorical imperative involves the notion of a single thinker's rational willing of universal principles, irrespective of consequences. The validity of universal principles does not depend on consequences, whether viewed objectively or subjectively. In the Kantian tradition that validity is a deontological not a utilitarian matter. Similarly, for Rawls, the decision on principles to be made by the people under the 'veil of ignorance' is one that it must treat as simultaneously universal, that is, applying to all peoples. As for Kant, the argument is centred on an epistemic subject: an individual who thinks and knows. Rawls' understanding of 'a people' is based on such an analogy. As Tasioulas remarks, 'peoples' are the 'Rawlsian counterparts' of sovereign states (Tasioulas 2010: 114).

Under the second original position, that is to say where it is peoples that are taking part in the mythic scene of arbitration, 'peoples are modelled as rational' (Rawls 1999a: 32–3). '[P]eoples' rights and duties in regard to their so-called sovereignty derive from the Law of Peoples itself, to which they would agree along with other peoples in suitable circumstances' (Rawls 1999a: 27). In a manner that corresponds closely to the argument for the first original position, 'peoples' are portrayed as kinds of individuals, reflecting on the general principles under which their flourishing might best be guaranteed. Some of the attitudes of such peoples are announced by Rawls. Even though they are not aware of the detailed circumstances of their own society, nor the circumstances of others' societies, they already possess values according to Rawls. Thus '[n]o people will be willing to count the losses to itself as outweighed by gains to other peoples' (Rawls 1999a: 60). These claims about the naturalness of a parochial preference for its own citizens by a people are very much of a piece with the claims about 'laws' of moral development as sketched in *A Theory of Justice* in which family attachments are treated as natural (Rawls 1999b: 429). In *The Law of Peoples*, Rawls refers to a people's self-respect in Rousseauian terms. In *Emile* Rousseau had defined two kinds of self-esteem in the growing individual, and Rawls discusses 'a people's proper self-respect of themselves as a people, resting on their common awareness of their trials during their history and of their culture with its accomplishments' (Rawls 1999a: 34). While this form of self-respect is manifested in the expectation of mutual recognition (by other peoples), and is thus not merely inward-looking, this orientation is consistent with Rawls' commitment to what Thomas Pogge calls 'explanatory nationalism'. This is 'the idea that the causes of severe poverty and of other human deprivations are domestic to the societies in which they occur' (Pogge 2006: 217).

Many criticisms have been levelled at *The Law of Peoples*. While there are numerous legal and political theorists who find at least some of it persuasive or stimulating, it is probably not inaccurate to say that it is generally considered unsuccessful. In the words of Leif Wenar, '[e]ven Rawls's most sensitive and sympathetic interpreters have registered unusually deep misgivings about the book' (Wenar 2006: 95). David Miller comments that reviewers of the book tended to concur that Rawls had 'lost his bearings' (Miller 2006: 191). Many of the perceived inadequacies are outside the scope of the present project. Here, some specific aspects are of concern. At this point it is important to note that much of Rawls' book is no more objectionable than many other works on international law or politics. Rawls shares some habits (or choices) of analysis with large and venerable traditions. Treating nations, states or 'countries' – seemingly the least loaded of terms for the members of the global polity – as kinds of individual is a target for general criticism in this book. It is treated here as a significant conceptual commitment, not a mere form of words. Rawls may be said to have reinforced this usage, and added some authority to its persistence, although Rawls can hardly be taken to task for such a widely shared practice. What is of concern in particular is Rawls' use of the term 'people' in this context. 'Peoples' are the quasi-individuals who (or which) give hypothetical consideration to their interrelationships. It sometimes seems that the term 'people' may be little more than a synonym for 'state' or 'nation'. But there is more to Rawls' choice of terms than this. One motivation seems to be that statehood is a conceptual formula with too much baggage in political theory. 'Peoplehood' seems to involve less assumptions about constitutional matters, about sovereignty and so on. It does not connote the power to make war in the way that is conveyed by 'states as traditionally conceived' (Nussbaum 2007: 246). But by using the term 'people' in this way, as a personification of that kind of collective, it can be argued that Rawls has contributed in substantial ways to the obscuring of the role of collectives at the international level.

What Rawls does in effect, in some instances of this usage, is to treat international states as co-terminous with coherent ethnic populations. It is surely done with a pragmatic purpose, in order to develop the 'originary position' argument on the world stage. It would be idle to castigate Rawls for not understanding the technical details of the international law of self-determination. He did not pretend to expertise in international law. But the problems caused by Rawls' easy sliding from states to peoples and back again are substantial. If taken seriously the model of homogenous nationality and citizenship offered would verge on the nationalist.

As Nussbaum comments, '[w]e do not need an extra concept to talk about [the] bond between citizens and the basic structure within which they live'. Thus 'the concept of "people", with its vague suggestion of social homogeneity, offers no useful clarification' (Nussbaum 2007: 245–6).

As suggested above, *The Law of Peoples* has never enjoyed the same reputation as Rawls' earlier work on justice. One reason for this may well be that *The Law of Peoples* is a somewhat brief account of a large and complex topic, inevitably leaving gaps in argumentation. It is a tentative, exploratory investigation of a Rawlsian approach to international justice, an 'essay' in the earlier sense of that word. One aspect of the book that has aroused criticism is the role played by a definition of decency in states, a categorization of states as either acceptable or outlaw. As in *A Theory of Justice*, liberal democracies are not the only kinds of state thought of as valid. Yet Rawls' theory runs into some of its most serious difficulties when illiberal nations are considered. As Nussbaum comments, it is extremely idealistic to hold that some representative of an imperfectly democratic state could nevertheless represent its people's most fundamental interests (Nussbaum 2007: 233). Similarly, Nussbaum's concerns with the inadequacy of a self-sufficiency model of states (as required by Rawls' version of the two-stage social contract theory) are empirical concerns (Nussbaum 2007: 234). But independence or self-sufficiency of states is, for international law scholars, much more than a mere contingency. It has sometimes been doctrine, for example in the form often referred to with the tag of the *Lotus* decision by the Permanent Court of International Justice in the 1920s.

Some other comments should be made on Rawls' reception by scholars of international law and of international relations. In an examination of self-determination, Cara Nine adopts a 'Rawlsian inspired' orientation, suggesting that '[a] people must ... demonstrate the capacity to meet minimal standards of justice' in order 'to qualify as a candidate for self-determination rights over territory' (Nine 2012: 52, 3). Allen Buchanan has both positive and negative comments to make. He finds Rawls to be supportive of the view that a moral account of international law does not depend on a preference for one particular institutional form such as the liberal democracy (Buchanan 2004: 45); in other respects he is critical of Rawls (2004: 16, 209).

Certainly the questions raised directly about *The Law of Peoples* are substantial. From the standpoint of international law, it seems at best naïve. Elements of the larger theory of justice which themselves seem speculative, but which seem to be legitimated as steps in an argument by their context in that earlier work, seem crude in the context of *The Law of Peoples*. Thus the notion of a primal debate (the original position), a first-principles conference from which various details are veiled, plays a useful role in the general theory of justice. It allows principles of distribution to be clarified, and enables one to see the wood in spite of all the trees, so to speak. Even so its value is limited. Rawls' approach, as exemplified by this image, is after all a direct descendent of the social contract tradition of Hobbes and Rousseau (Sen 2012: 12).

Thomas Pogge is a significant commentator on Rawls and a significant contributor to the debate on global justice. Pogge is supportive of much of Rawls' earlier work. But in the context of examining global poverty and the causes of its persistence, Pogge has argued that *A Theory of Justice* over-emphasizes characteristics internal to states, such as 'political culture'. '[T]he design of the global institutional order' is ignored (Pogge 2010: 417, 418; 2006: 206). Pogge puts his finger on a key difficulty with Rawls, one also observed by Sen (Sen 2012: 11). As Nussbaum describes (Nussbaum 2007: 264), Pogge has also put forward the speculative proposal that the original position formula might be applied globally but in one stage rather than two. The notion here is of national origin (into what nation, state or people one is born) being thought of as one more of the contingent factors which is concealed behind the 'veil of ignorance' along with gender, class and so on. Every individual person in the world may be thought of as having participated in the delineation of the principles by which goods should be allocated. This 'one-hit' original position formula has the virtue of eliminating some of the problems with Rawls' two-stage account, although it scarcely deals with the larger difficulties of Rawls' social contractarian model in the international law context (Buchanan 2004: 18).

As a consequence of focusing on the philosophical developments, both legal and political, the topics discussed in this chapter have provided limited insight into the role played by international law and its theorization, within the chronological span examined. Attention therefore needs to be paid to some selected historical matters from a somewhat narrower, disciplinary perspective, as a component of the same overall project. Along with related questions of historiography in international law, this is the task of Chapter 3.

Chapter 3

Historiography of the Present: Collectives, Colonies and the Chronicle of International Law

Do We Progress?

Chapter 2 focused on important contributions from legal and political philosophy of past centuries to the project of describing international law as the law of collectives. As described there, the diverse traditions in legal and political philosophy that emerged from the time of Hobbes onwards present us with a range of tools and conceptual frameworks for describing legal relationships at the international level. These include examinations of sovereignty, of the legitimacy of various forms of government and of the ways in which the citizenry are to be described and their powers and obligations articulated. Such enquiries had been made since ancient times, and sovereignty had been a lively issue for the medieval scholars such as Bartolus and Baldus. Seventeenth-century analysis of tyranny, for example, built on classical foundations, for Rome had regulated tyranny – at times of emergency, dictatorial leadership was legitimate. However the writings of Hobbes, Locke and Rousseau and of their various contemporaries on these continuing topics are recognizably modern in terms of geopolitics. They were composed in the era of contesting kingdoms and emerging republics within Europe and of the accelerating settlement and exploitation by European nations of the 'New World' as well as of territories to the East. Relationships between Princes in the sixteenth century were already driven by demands of trade as much as by aspirations of status or the greed for conquest. The profession of diplomacy already had many of its familiar, contemporary characteristics (Kissinger 1994; Wright 2006). Hobbes, Locke, Hume, Rousseau: all had experience of working in the diplomatic service, broadly defined (Damrosch 2007: 168, 424). That said, the previous chapter discussed relevant lines of thinking in legal and political philosophers for most of whom international law was a secondary or indirect concern. In the present chapter a focus on international law is adopted, still in a historical context. This will assist in clarifying the lineaments of the collective project, both within and outwith international law as a discipline, before going on in the chapters that follow to consider some topics in greater depth and with a more contemporary focus.

The argument of this book is that two powerful ideas have dominated thinking in international law over decades and over centuries. The first is that countries, nations or states are to be thought of as kinds of individual, in relationships with each other. The second is that international law is fundamentally about individual natural persons: about protecting them or prosecuting them. In current orthodoxy these two ideas are sometimes amalgamated or yoked together. In some formulations this seems to work: after all the main agents for protecting individual human rights are states. It is states that sign up to the international conventions. Responsibilities of states can be thought of as fiduciary duties to their nationals, that is to say matters of trust. The international institutions that are increasingly being set up in order to deal with the most serious criminal acts committed by individuals are set up precisely by multilateral treaties drawn up between states. The *historical* trend may therefore be defined as characterized by the convergence and synergy of these two components, states and individual persons, as subjects of international law.

But the yoking is often less comfortable. Indeed in some ways these two tendencies pull in different directions. When this is recognized, so that they are presented as alternatives, the usual formula is for the first (state-centred) approach to be portrayed as old-fashioned or traditional, and the second (human individual-centred) to be portrayed as progressive. In other words, they are presented in terms of the old way and the new way. Thus the orthodox dichotomy referred to above between a state-based and human-individual-based approach has sometimes been taken to correspond to a historical development from the former to the latter, a matter of progress in thinking. In effect, the dichotomy generates a framework for the history of international law, with an enlightened universalism of human rights struggling to liberate itself from the repressive, dead weight of a state-centred orthodoxy.

The dualistic picture of states and individual persons is therefore connected with the history of international law in several senses, such that attention to the history of international law is called for. Alternative versions of the dualism correspond to different views of international law's past and of its future. There is much to commend both narratives. The convergence or synergy account, which focuses on complementarity between these two components, has the virtue of pragmatism. The progressivist account, with statehood as archaic and universal human dignity as the program, is a powerful formula, especially when deployed against representatives of oppressive regimes. But it does have its limitations. The connections to political liberalism, with the focus on the freedom of individuals *contra* state, are an indication of some of these limitations. What is important to note at this point is the affinity between the dualistic picture itself – the model of two kinds of focus in international law – and accounts of international law's history. It could be said that the duality model is a historiographical model – a proposal for ways of reading history. Historical aspects, assumptions or frameworks are therefore important to bear in mind when an alternative to the duality – a third way so to speak – is being examined. Several questions arise. Does the introduction of a collectivist orientation enable an escape from these historiographic trappings? It might be that the collective paradigm opens up new approaches to the history of international law. On the other hand, perhaps the history of international law shows us that the question of collectivity has been addressed in the past and even, perhaps, transcended.

One way of thinking about this point is to observe that like so many other dualities in international law, the distinction between state-based and human-individual-based orientations to international law can be reduced to Martti Koskenniemi's archetypal dichotomy of 'apology' versus 'utopia' (Koskenniemi 2005a). According to Koskenniemi, international law in its practices, theories and institutions can be portrayed in terms of the tensions between these poles. International law 'ascends' to idealistic aspirations, and 'descends' to the grubby level of the mere retrospective rationalization of state conduct. In some respects, international law has thus swung like a pendulum between uncritical description (apology) and evaluative advocacy (utopia). The historical version of the orthodox duality fits nicely with this formula. A focus on statehood is gradually displaced, across the centuries, by respect for individual personhood. Indeed, state-centred international law is in many ways 'apologetic' of the conduct of nations and of their leaders, seeking to describe and to find patterns in their behaviour rather than criticizing or advocating for change. In past centuries this approach has been thought of as defining a 'scientific' methodology of international law. In contrast, human rights law and its cognate areas such as humanitarian law and international criminal law have a strong utopian streak.

While the historical understanding of this dichotomy is seductive, the dichotomy itself may be a false one. For both of these powerful ideas may of course be reduced to the one thought: that individuals, of some kind or another, are the units of international law. A new dichotomy might need to be defined. Looked at this way, it is the collective analysis of international law that represents the alternative paradigm. A warning note should therefore be sounded at once. A dichotomy between individualistic and collective approaches to international law could itself be neatly glossed as 'apology versus utopia' respectively. The collectivist project might be tempted to claim the ideological high ground. If individualism in the theory of international law is the old way (of apology), then collectivism in international law is the new way or, better still, the way of the future. Further, we could excavate the history of international law to seek early 'insights' into the collective approach. One might say that not only does the Koskenniemian formula re-emerge in a synchronic sense, that is to say with a disregard of history, but its historical (diachronic) manifestation also looms large. Clearly there are dangers of circularity and of prejudice in such a triumphalist project. As Thomas Skouteris has shown, historical ruminations in international law are over-supplied with tendentious examples of 'progress' (Skouteris 2010).

These caveats are important and a sensitivity to forms of explanation and of reasoning (to philosophy of science, in effect) as well as to forms of historical understanding is going to be required. Everything said in this chapter should be seen in light of these qualifications and circumscriptions. But historical enquiry, while speculative and tentative, should not be proscribed. There may be some lessons to be learned and the notion of a collectivist orientation to international law may be illuminated by this exercise, perhaps in unexpected ways.

Attention to the historiography of international law is important in other ways. The ways in which the history of international law has been written and the contours of the stories that are most generally told about the past of the discipline themselves reveal important aspects of the questions addressed in this book. Comments are made on the historiography of international law throughout the chapter, in the course of the examination of some selected chronological questions. Historiography is in general a weak point of the scholarship of international law. Historical accounts have been narrowly focused and narrowly conceived. Thus the history of international legal theory as such is generally thought of as conceptual work internal to international law as it has developed over the centuries, as a profession and as an academic discipline, largely independently of legal and political philosophy. No doubt common frameworks and shared assumptions, as well as a variety of reciprocal influences, could be shown. Mainstream 'internal' histories of international law tend to neglect such contexts, partly for this reason falling into the traps of simplistic progressivist thinking as discussed by Skouteris. As suggested above, the understanding of individualism and collectivism in international law is bound up with progressivist assumptions. Nothing illustrates this progressivism better than the legend that has been constructed around the Westphalia agreements of 1648. This is the next topic of this chapter.

1600–1815: Footnotes to Westphalia

It is a commonplace in the literature of international law and of international relations for the peace treaties that were established at the end of the Thirty Years War in continental Europe to be treated as marking a 'watershed' (Klabbers 2002: 17), or paradigm shift in geopolitics and international relations. A system of multiple, independent states, none presuming any right of intervention in the 'internal' affairs of another, is frequently referred to as the 'Westphalian' system. A popular view is that in order to establish some prospect of peace in central Europe, following decades of war between empires and other conglomerates, a system of independent 'sovereign' states was conjured into being or at least that a strong 'nudge' was given towards this modern-looking arrangement. The term 'nation state' is often rather loosely associated with the components of the post-Westphalian dispensation. Thus for Morgan, sovereignty is 'a concept with a long lineage that can be traced to the Peace of Westphalia (1648) and the consolidation of a system of sovereign states in Europe' (Morgan 2011: 104). According to international relations theorist John Ruggie:

> The very concept of the modern state was made possible only when a new rule for differentiating the constituent units within medieval Christendom replaced the constitutive rule of heteronomy (interwoven and overlapping jurisdictions, moral and political). And the modern system of states became conceivable only when the constitutive rule of reciprocal sovereignty took hold. (Ruggie 2005: 125)

The Westphalian model is sometimes treated as anarchic, or as a 'state of nature'. With a more positive spin it is sometimes understood as a tacitly consensual or even a quasi-democratic system for global cohabitation, adumbrating the General

Assembly of the United Nations. Dystopic interpretations are also available, which however concur on the significance of the Westphalia settlement. For Nussbaum, 'the Peace of Westphalia established religious pluralism *among* nations, allowing repression within each nation' (Nussbaum 2007: 303).

'Westphalia' can be taken to represent this discourse or narrative with its sense of an evolutionary step from a 'medieval aspiration to universality' (Kissinger 1994: 56) based on Pope, Emperor and Church to an increasingly secularized, state-based and participatory polity. Several aspects of the Westphalia agreements and of their context therefore deserve closer attention in the context of the current project. Adopting a strong reading of what might be termed 'the Westphalia discourse', international law is inevitably a matter of individuals – and not individual natural persons but individual, sovereign states. Individual states are independent, not interdependent: they are 'atoms' in the ancient Greek sense of indivisibles, or 'monads' as Leibniz was to discuss in the eighteenth century, entities with no 'insides'. The rhetoric of Westphalia is powerful and part of its power is in its claim to objectivity. For international law, with its limited sensitivity to the scholarship of history, the authoritative reference to historical fact plays a significant role (Lake 2009). Crucially the world thus described is treated as a fact – a non-negotiable circumstance within which international law must find its explanatory place. So far as international law is concerned the argument tends to the circular: the geopolitical landscape is divided up thus and so; international law is by definition concerned with the interrelation of just those kinds of entity into which the landscape is divided. This is in many ways an example of Koskenniemi's notion of the 'apologist' stance.

Debate continues among historians as to the significance of the Westphalia agreements. Like other iconic events such as the French Revolution or World War I, there are differing accounts of the scale of any posited differences between the 'before' and the 'after', and differing views on postulated long-term effects of the event. Something should therefore be said on the 'before'. To sketch the understandings of international law that preceded the era of Westphalia, it is important to indicate some of the ways in which thinkers of the sixteenth and the early seventeenth centuries – the 'early scholars' of Koskenniemi (2005a: 95) – had discussed the law of nations and similar concepts. Thus, writing in the mid-sixteenth century, when Spanish colonization of the New World was in full swing, Salamanca theologian Vitoria sought to base international law 'on an objective foundation irrespective of the will of the states' and thus 'to conceive international law as a law above states' (Gross 1948: 34). In Vitoria's follower Suarez, who was writing in the early years of the seventeenth century, 'the objective foundation is at least overshadowed if not replaced by a subjective foundation in the will of the states' (Gross 1948: 34). Thus Suarez emphasized the voluntaristic aspect of nations' conduct. This trend can also be seen in the writings of Suarez' contemporary Gentili for whom 'the sovereign's assumed subjective authority' needs to be taken into account when reference to a normative order is found to be inadequate (Koskenniemi 2005a: 106).

The Dutch jurist and political adviser de Groot, usually known in Latinized form as Hugo Grotius, was of the next generation after Suarez and died during the last years of the Thirty Years War, in 1645. It has been suggested that the fundamentals of international relations have changed little since Grotius. Thus '[i]n our day, as in Grotius' time, the fundamental unit through which people exercise this fundamental aspect of human freedom [forming law through association with others] is the nation-state ...' (Nussbaum 2006: 257). On this interpretation the Westphalia settlement represented a crystallization, or institutionalization, of processes that were correctly identified by Grotius a few decades ahead.

Progress in secularization is itself frequently attributed to the Westphalia process. '[T]he victors gathered at Westphalia are widely understood to have elevated secular rulers to positions of ultimate authority in their realms and secured the dominance of political authority over other possible authorities, especially that of the universal church' (Lake 2009: 46). Religious difference was a major source of conflict in the Thirty Years War, which took place 100 years after the Reformation, at least in its earlier phases. The Holy Roman Empire under the Habsburg dynasty had initiated the conflict, partly in an attempt to cement in place the Catholic Counter-Reformation. In 1648, a kind of structural religious toleration was installed by virtue of the disaggregation of the Holy Roman Empire into multiple entities, many of which were ruled by a Prince (or equivalent) and entitled in effect to select a religious affiliation out of three options: Lutheran, Calvinist or Catholic. As well as the Holy Roman Empire itself, and not always treated distinctively, one of the supra-national political agencies thus dethroned is supposed to have been the Papacy in the sense of a pan-European Catholic hegemony headquartered in Rome. It is certainly the case that much of the 'imperial governmental machinery' was dismantled under the Peace of Westphalia (Wright 2006: 266). After 1648 the Holy Roman Empire was 'a federative state' – a loose union somewhat comparable to the European Union or the British Commonwealth (Hughes 1992: 97, 117). But the form of sovereignty after Westphalia in some cases amounted to no more than a transfer of title, with cities retaining their rights *ante bellum* even while a new Prince added the title deed to his collection (Neff 2005: 114): not at all the image of a plurality of new entities awaiting, as if behind a veil of ignorance, the contingencies of faith and so on that would derive from the edicts of a Prince.

By the time of the Westphalia agreements the Empire was divided 'among more than 300 sovereigns, each free to conduct an independent foreign policy' (Kissinger 1994: 65). It had formerly comprised some 900 identifiable territorial units (Gross 1948: 27). Princes of German units attained sole authority to enter into agreements with other states; no longer could cities do so as before. The polities, even if very small, were becoming more centralized in governance (Hughes 1992: 94). But miniature polities were not the norm across Europe. By contrast with what was becoming a kind of fragmented, federated Austria-Germany, a victorious and centralized France emerged as the dominant country in Europe. This was thanks in particular to the brilliance of Richelieu and his concept of *raison d'état*. The French regime's foreign policy aimed at the long-term weakening of any German entity, and a 'divided and impotent Germany' as resulted at Westphalia, was consistent with that objective even if the Westphalia agreements in themselves did not bring this about (Gross 1948: 21; Hughes 1992: 97). In the words of Bertrand Russell, what emerged was 'a number of petty principalities which were at the mercy of France' (Russell 1961: 691). The plurality of entities within the Empire/Germany was thus but one component of the bigger picture which was dominated by large powers such as France and Sweden. Thus even within Europe, nothing like a 'level playing field' plurality of equal sovereignties emerged from Westphalia and of course beyond Europe the situation was at least as diverse. It is a distortion to read into the Westphalia settlement a pluralistic system of states as kinds of individual legal entity, operating under the same set of rules.

Nor was non-intervention a uniform commitment. Under the Treaty of Munster, France was empowered to intervene internationally 'when necessary in order to vindicate the principle of the sanctity of treaties' (Gross 1948: 21). France and Sweden became guarantors of the Imperial Constitution (of the post-War Holy Roman Empire) and thereby enjoyed the right of intervention in its affairs (Fulbrook 2004: 60). Even under the terms of Westphalia, some states were more equal than others. 'A major result of the treaties was to make foreign interference in German affairs a permanent and important factor' (Hughes 1992: 97). Small states now in post-'48 Germany were even more dependent on the Emperor for protection than before (Gross 1948: 27).

Some safeguards for religious minorities were indeed provided by Westphalia. This was not entirely a new development. The Peace of Augsburg just under 100 years before (Lake 2009: 46) had already set out the principle that religious affiliation, which at that time meant either Catholic or Lutheran, was at the disposal of each Prince. Under the Westphalia agreements, some protection was given for private worship. Such 'confessional' protections were in many ways overshadowed by the increasingly state-centred and bureaucratic character of religious observance (Fulbrook 2004: 62). Also some territories were now defined as adhering to Catholicism by fiat as in the case of the traditional lands of the Habsburgs themselves, centred on Austria and Bohemia. Significant population movements resulted (Hughes 1992: 109). Consistent with the comments of Nussbaum noted above, if anything, secularism and religious tolerance took a backward step in that sense. Most generally, 'members of any of the three legal faiths established in a state in 1624 could stay there' (Hughes 1992: 95). Those not covered by this provision were allowed to relocate with their property or to remain in place without molestation.

According to Gross, one consequence of Westphalia was to consolidate a subjective or voluntaristic approach to international legal thinking. For example this orientation is seen by Gross to dominate the influential writings of Emer de Vattel, in the mid-eighteenth century. By the time of Vattel, 'the will of states seems to explain both the contents and the binding force of international law' (Gross 1948: 37). According to Gross, the Vitorian concept of the Family of Nations 'recedes in the background'. Gross thus links the agreements at Westphalia and their consequences to the historical process of 'liquidating' the Middle Ages idea of an objective order of things personified by an Emperor. Historian Wright takes a similar position. Thus Vattel is said to have described the state as 'an autonomous individual' (Wright 2006: 289). '[S]he deliberates and takes resolutions in common; thus becoming a moral person, who possesses an understanding and a will peculiar to herself, and is susceptible of obligations and rights' (Wright 2006: 289). Wright comments that 'the state as a moral actor was a conceit that would endure'.

There is no doubt that evidence can be found for such a libertarian, state-centred analysis in Vattel. It is probably correct to highlight this ideology as Vattel's major influence over the international law of the next (nineteenth) century. But this was as much due to the triumph of liberalism more broadly as it was due to Vattel's influence *per se*. Vattel was more nuanced and the argument of Covell (2004) that Vattel needs to be seen in the context of the natural law tradition is well made. Following his teacher Christian Wolff, Vattel explored the consequences of separating out the top-down, normative aspects of the law of nations (governed by natural law) from the bottom-up realities consequent on the autonomy of sovereign states (Koskenniemi 2005a:108). Wolff had suggested that both states and nations should be regarded 'as individual free persons living in a state of nature' (Domingo 2011: 635). For Vattel (2008: 170) the independence of states is to be directly contrasted with the conceit of Popes or Caliphs for whom state boundaries are as nothing, for example all Catholic countries being thought of by the former as together comprising one true state. Religious tolerance within states, a virtue of such countries as Holland in Vattel's view, itself logically requires independence of states. But the independence is not absolute. 'The natural law of nations ... produces between nations ... an *external* obligation wholly independent of their will' (2008: 8). Natural obligations include some duties to strangers, deployed by states on behalf of their constituent citizens, including assistance in time of famine (2008: 263); and relatedly, some rights of intervention in the affairs of other nations 'who openly violate the laws of the society which nature has established between them' (2008: 73, 77). Vattel's admittedly rather 'thin' version of normativity in the international sphere is a gesture toward the collective, just as it is in the writings of Vitoria. This sensitivity is not absent although it is marginal. It might also be remarked that Vattel's contribution to the laws of warfare reflect an increasing focus on the role of populations in times of conflict. Reflecting more than anything else the increasing professionalization of warfare (Neff 2005: 114) Vattel's discussion paid attention to the entitlements to non-molestation of disarmed enemy soldiers, women, children and the sick. Necessarily, an attempt to describe or to prescribe legal regulation of conduct towards foreigners, or towards merchants in time of war, as well as early forms of international humanitarian conduct, is a contribution to international law of collectives. At least it helps to put in perspective the components of Vattel's writing that seem to be conceptualizing international law as the interaction of independent sovereigns ensconced in their independent sovereign states.

Moving forward again from Vattel, into the early decades of the nineteenth century, the Congress of Vienna provides a footnote to Westphalia. The Congress comprised an extended series of meetings in Vienna as Napoleon's Empire reached its final days. Beginning long before Napoleon's breakout from Elba and the 100 days leading up to Waterloo, the Congress of Vienna was dominated by the major European powers. But it received representation from a diverse range of constituencies and sovereigns. The list is of interest as an indication of what may be called the ontological pluralism of international law – the pluralism of the entities with which it deals and by which it is formed. Representation at Vienna included:

> [R]epresentatives of the four Hanseatic cities (Hamburg, Lübeck, Bremen and Frankfurt); of the city of Mainz; of the Chamber of Commerce of the city of Mainz; of the Teutonic Order; of the firms of Bonte & Co., Kayser & Co. and Wittersheim & Bock, creditors of the government of Westphalia, which had been abolished; of the Bishop of Liège; of the subjects of Count Solms-Braunfels. One delegation of Catholic clergy demanded full restitution under Papal authority; another, consisting of four delegates led by the Bishop of Constance, called for the institution of a new German national Catholic Church. The Pope's delegate, Cardinal Consalvi, was there to oppose this. There was also a delegation … representing eighty-one German publishers and demanding a copyright law as well as freedom of the press. And there were J.J. Gumprecht and Jakob Baruch of Frankfurt and Carl August Buchholz of Lübeck, representing the interests of the Jews. They were one of the few groups eager to preserve changes made by Napoleon, who had granted them full equality, of which the authorities in many German states were now attempting to strip them once more.
> (Zamoyski 2007: 257–8)

The multitudinous representation at Vienna, with all the various and overlapping constituencies involved, if nothing else indicates the limits of the Westphalian narrative. It also provides a glimpse of the realities of the interests at play and of the diversity of forms of collective at a key moment in geopolitical history.

Contributions to a more collective view of international law in the nineteenth century included the continuing traditions of normative or transcendental approaches. Romanticism and a new concern for history played a part. For example, as an alternative to the influential state-centric formulations of Vattel, and seeking to reconnect more closely with Roman models, Heffter argued that a more inclusive understanding of the law of nations was required in which states did not have the central and dominating role. Thus:

> Even though the law of nations did not recognize any human authority superior to independent and sovereign states (having history as its ultimate or highest court), it tended by nature to unify the human family, bringing it closer together in one grand and harmonious community. (Domingo 2011: 637)

The grand and harmonious community is one vision of international law as the law of collectives, but the court of history has seen others.

The Post-colonial and the Collective

As noted above, the history of international law has often presented itself in isolation from wider social and intellectual currents. Much of the work of contemporary critical scholars within international law precisely consists of exploring the broader intellectual influences on the writings in the canon of international law. In a complementary fashion, the socio-political contexts of international law's history are scrutinized. Post-colonial scholarship in international law is an important genre of this critical movement within the discipline. Consistent with the greater sensitivity to social and political factors, increased attention to collective dimensions charaterizes much of this work. For an example that introduces and illustrates a number of key points, the contribution of Antony Anghie is discussed first. A number of limitations in Anghie's work will be suggested, but these limitations should be thought of as the limitations of a pioneer whose work has both stimulated and inspired the contributions of others. Critical remarks will also be offered on the contributions of other scholars in this field.

Anghie's project is to prepare the ground for counter-histories of international law, such as 'history from the vantage point of the peoples who were, in many ways, the victims of international law' (Anghie 2007: 12). In support of this provocative formulation, Anghie argues that the histories of a legal positivist approach to international law, and of colonialism, are closely intertwined. Looked at in this light, the understanding of international sovereignty that had emerged by the early twentieth century in Europe and North America was in many ways a reflection of colonial rhetoric. According to Anghie's analysis, a 'naturalist' understanding of international law had prevailed in European thinking in the centuries prior to the colonial era and retained influence during that era. 'Naturalism' in relation to international law here refers to an approach derived from natural law traditions and focused on a law of nations that transcends state boundaries. An important, early version of this approach was, in Anghie's analysis, provided by the writings of Vitoria (Anghie 2007: 54). This approach asserted that 'a universal international law deriving from human reason applied to all peoples, whether European or non-European' (Anghie 2007: 35). Naturalistic international law had, according to Anghie, exhibited an inclusive and relatively tolerant approach to the discovery of the New World and of its inhabitants.

In contrast, the positivist international law of the late colonial era was designed to serve and to explicate the divisions between the civilized and the uncivilized (Anghie 2007: 35). 'The late nineteenth century was … the period in which positivism decisively replaced naturalism as the principal jurisprudential technique of the discipline of international law'. Positivist jurisprudence 'is based on the notion of the primacy of the state' (Anghie 2007: 33). The consequence has been, according to Anghie, that colonized peoples have only with difficulty entered 'the realm of sovereignty' (2007: 31). They have attempted 'to pursue their interests and aspirations through a "universal" language of international law which, arguably, was devised specifically to ensure their disempowerment and disenfranchisement' (Anghie 2007: 31).

As can be seen from this brief summary, Anghie's revisions to international legal theory, via historiography, involve a reorientation that is in some ways towards the collective. Attention is focused on 'colonized peoples', on 'the victims of international law'. Anghie distances himself from a view of international law as being defined by the conduct or will of states as individual actors. But there is rather little analysis of this collective dimension. As discussed further below, the theoretical framework is if anything weighted toward the psychological and subjective; that is to say to the individualistic as traditionally conceived in the social sciences. Purported motivations of the theorists and publicists of international law are discussed as in the quotations above. In places, Anghie's argument is expressed in a somewhat simplistic manner, as here in the language of victimhood and even of conspiracy. This polemical style is characteristic of much writing in a self-consciously post-colonial vein within international law scholarship. In any event the history of positivism in international law is somewhat more complex. For example as Kelsen points out, the emergence of legal positivism in the nineteenth century was strongly conditioned by the presupposition of inherent rights grounded in history:

> The function of a positive legal order (i.e, of the state), which terminates the state of nature, is – according to this doctrine – to guarantee the natural rights by stipulating corresponding obligations. (Kelsen 1967: 129)

Anghie claims that 'there appears to be an inherent reflex within international law which conceals the colonial past on which its entire structure is based' (Anghie 2007: 112). This begs several important questions. For it points to a perceived absence and interprets that perceived absence as indicating a conspiratorial cover-up. The same can be said of the claim that 'positivists themselves [of the late nineteenth century in particular] vehemently set out to detach themselves from their naturalist past' (Anghie 2007: 112). Of course, while over-simplification can be deleterious to the argument, polemic can be an effective technique by which to prepare the ground for more nuanced ideas and to set out a framework within which complexities may be scrutinized. For example, Anghie himself notes the diversity of the colonial experience and of the resistance to colonialism, across the globe (Anghie 2007: 12, 72). But this important observation would seem to cast doubt on the unitary concept of 'the colonial past' as the hidden secret of international law. The complexities discussed by Liliana Obregón seem pertinent (Obregón 2006).

Anghie's account of the role of positivist jurisprudence in the international law of the late nineteenth century, as it grappled with the practicalities of colonial expansion, leads him into accusations of deviousness that may not be warranted and, more to the point, may foreclose the analysis. By the late nineteenth century many international agreements had been reached between colonial powers and presumed representatives of indigenous communities. New Zealand's Treaty of Waitangi of 1840 would be a good early example of such agreements. John Westlake's attempts to delimit the obligations of 'uncivilized tribes' in treaties with European states were, as Anghie relates, wholly inadequate. But rather than illustrating a dogmatic positivist exclusion of 'natives' from international law they seem rather an awkward, paternalistic and pragmatic attempt to assimilate them (Anghie 2007: 79). As Anghie notes, the status of non-European 'entities' (such as chief-led tribal parties to international treaties) in the European international law of the period was 'ambivalent', 'lacking in international personality and yet necessarily possessing it if any sense was to be made' of such treaties (Anghie 2007: 81; 79). 'Ambivalence' seems a more apt description than the ideological and formalistic rigidity that Anghie elsewhere seems to discern.

Again, over-simplification can interfere with the larger argument. In Anghie's account, the agreements reached at the Peace of Westphalia are treated as more of a watershed in the development of sovereignty than they probably deserve (Anghie 2007: 311). While indicating that colonialism is an alternative candidate (to Westphalia) for the role of founding moment in international law, Anghie retains a view that Westphalia represents 'the emergence of the modern state system' in Europe (2007: 311). Anghie is not alone in this position, but the claimed complementarity of his imperial or colonialist model of sovereignty with the Westphalian account (2007: 315) threatens to weaken his argument. Over-emphasizing the effects of Westphalia leaves less scope for the more interesting argument that international law's concepts of sovereignty emerged in tandem with the extended colonial era. More seriously perhaps, Anghie's reduction of all questions of sovereignty in international law to 'the construction of the "other"' (2007: 318) seems to flatten out the complexities and diversities that Anghie has elsewhere insisted on. If both the Peace of Westphalia and the colonial expansion of the European powers are covered by this description, it seems that a personal or even quasi-psychological level of analysis is replacing a cultural, historical or geopolitical one. Thus the contemporary denial by the USA of imperial ambitions, while undertaking imperialist adventures, is explained by the fact that (Anghie 2007: 319) 'an important aspect of its history, its identity as a nation that emerged through a war of independence against colonialism, provides a powerful resource of self-criticism and questioning' so that 'the "other" is not external to the self, but within'. The 'self' being discussed here, with its internal structures, is the 'self' of the USA. Such language while familiar, and often innocuous, seems inadequate to the context of postcolonial analysis.

Anghie is rightly critical of the pseudo-anthropology called on by Westlake in his attempts to rationalize the limitations on sovereignty for native entities, by 'divining [the] consciousness' of Makololo chiefs (Anghie 2007: 80). But the jargon of 'self and other' by itself achieves no greater depth or precision, it might be suggested, than Westlake's efforts over 100 years earlier. Needless to say, self and other as conceptual formulae have been explored with great subtlety within many disciplines in the twentieth century, including phenomenological strands of philosophy. But consciousness has also been explored with more sophistication since Westlake's day, again within those phenomenological traditions in particular if not by psychology. Dismissing and even ridiculing Westlake's efforts and those of his contemporaries achieves very little. In any event, Anghie's analysis of the nineteenth-century international jurists' writings on sovereignty and the colonial would seem to illustrate the role played by their reductive sense of the state as legal person (Anghie 2007: 43). If tribal or nomadic people encountered under the expansion of empire gave rise to theoretical problems for international law, some at least of these problems were symptomatic of the limitations of the theory of state sovereignty and of the 'will' of the state.

As argued by other post-colonial writers on international law, 'naturalist' alternatives with their appeal to ethical universals fare no better than the approaches normally labelled 'positivist'. Indeed Anghie agrees that 'the basic structures of colonialism … are reproduced in all the major schools of international jurisprudence', including naturalism (Anghie 2007: 195). Coming to grips with the collective nature of international law's intellectual subject-matter requires more of a paradigm shift. Anghie casts doubts on the emancipatory potential of such a project, to the extent that '[t]he colonial origins of the discipline are re-enacted whenever the discipline attempts to renew itself, reform itself' (Anghie 2007: 313). David Kennedy is appealed to on this general point of the repetition of old patterns in the discipline (Anghie 2007: 292). This point is surely over-sold and the pessimism a little too formulaic. If the discipline's contamination is so deep and so ubiquitous, its foundational (Anghie 2007: 316) concepts so hollow, then it is difficult to understand how the contribution of any contemporary scholar from within the discipline can use that disciplinary vocabulary even to describe that situation let alone alter it. Above all, the orthodox formulations and formations of international law are conserved.

Sundhya Pahuja's *Decolonising International Law* (2011) significantly extends the debate beyond Anghie's contribution both in theoretical depth and breadth. Even so, some limitations may be suggested, from the standpoint of the current project. Pahuja is concerned with 'development, economic growth and the politics of universality' in the context of Third World experience of First and Second World policies. (The Second, Communist World in effect disappeared with the end of the Cold War). The development narrative that underpins much Western policy-making is subjected to critique on several grounds (Pahuja 2011: 185). Pahuja self-effacingly understates (2011: 138) her differences with Anghie, which include methodological differences as well as differences in focus. One example of the difference is over Westphalia: for Pahuja, endorsing a comment of Strawson, the Peace of Westphalia 'granted a monopoly of legal personality to the European powers' (Pahuja 2011: 57).

Pahuja incorporates a range of conceptual vocabulary from across the social sciences and humanities. Pahuja articulates a sophisticated view of the universalism claimed by international law, one that recognizes the paradoxes involved (Pahuja 2011:256). As she notes, 'the claim to represent universal values is a familiar mode of power', but 'the universality of international law is also heir to the progressive values of the Enlightenment'. Thus '[l]aw's anti-imperial dimension arises from the inclusivity that universalism invites'. Pahuja subverts Anghie's analysis according to which inclusivity is, almost with a hint of nostalgia, associated with a 'naturalist' international law of earlier centuries, an approach to international law grounded in an appeal to rational values. The deontological form of universalism (universal values based on ethics or morality) is thus rejected. '[T]he solution is not to succumb to the siren song of the neo-Kantians, searching for "genuine" universals by which to recalibrate our normative compass' (Pahuja 2011: 259). Pahuja is not of course referring to Anghie in this quotation. Elsewhere Pahuja says that a neo-Kantian approach would 'offer a normative reconceptualisation of justice (re)founded in a "genuine" universality'. But 'such a move would be to succumb to a gesture that would precisely foreclose the instabilities of international law that [Pahuja is] seeking here to reveal, and the political possibilities those instabilities may offer' (Pahuja 2011: 42). Thus Pahuja's argument is that the contingent character of such categories as 'the nation' and 'the international' must never be lost sight of even while their claims to universality are addressed with what might be called respect (Pahuja 2011: 40). In this way political multiplicity and diversity are recognized. The pluralist methodology of economist and political theorist Amartya Sen is called upon (2011: 24).

Pahuja's analysis of the post-colonial context for international law endorses and places greater weight on the kind of ambivalence noted by Anghie. International law's role in decolonization has been ambivalent, with 'its capacity to be both regulatory and emancipatory, both imperial and anti-imperial' (Pahuja 2011: 45). Of course this recognition of ambivalence can easily be transmuted into the language of 'contradiction'. Pahuja cites Partha Chatterjee (Pahuja 2011: 55) on the contradictions of nationalism: nationalist thinking 'reasons within a framework of knowledge whose representational structure corresponds to the very structure of power nationalist thought seems to repudiate'. The identification of 'inherent contradictions' in reactionary political or institutional frameworks has a long history in political philosophy of the Left dating from the time of Marx and Engels, for whom the methodology was a strategic application of the Hegelian apparatus. In its stronger forms, the identification of contradictions was a kind of deconstructive technique in the sense that these contradictions were understood to constitute instabilities in the repressive socio-economic systems themselves, lines of weakness that would sooner or later bring the entire edifice crashing down. The more apocalyptic variants of this approach are long discredited, but more tempered versions are still of significance in the many approaches to international law influenced by Marxism and by post-Marxist thought (Marks 2008). Some of this style is apparent in Pahuja's reference to 'critical instability' in 'the heart of international law' (Pahuja 2011: 42, 255). As noted above, for Pahuja the instability represents an opening to political possibilities; however it still has a Hegelian ring.

Has progress been made in relation to collectives? Like Anghie, Pahuja is in some respects concerned with collectives throughout her account (Pahuja 2011: 57). Detailed analytic attention is given to questions of individuals as against states. Pahuja cites the observations of Anne-Marie Slaughter, liberal theorist in international law, for whom international law theory of the twentieth century has converged on a state-centred analysis (Pahuja 2011: 82). According to Slaughter, a 'realist' tradition in international law treats states as opaque units in competition, and a 'legalist' international law tradition treats state autonomy as a 'normative precondition' for a global rule of law. Neither tradition properly recognizes individual persons in their relationships with states, according to Slaughter. Pahuja does not endorse this liberal argument for individualism of the person within international law, but nor does she take this opportunity to explore collective alternatives. Thus in discussing the important role played by the progress narrative and nineteenth-century evolutionism '[a]t this moment of transition ... peoples who were not nations were not *yet* nations ... Admittedly the *possibility* existed within this form of reason for everyone to be a (modern) nation one day' (2011: 56). The 'everyone' is deliberately bathetic, yet the side-effect is to smudge the sense of 'a people' as having any precision. To be even more pedantic, the use of 'peoples who' (instead of the impersonal 'peoples which' or 'peoples that') also contributes to this vagueness of tone. However Pahuja avoids the more florid or aphoristic styles in which theoretical analysis of international law and of its history is sometimes couched. Pahuja cites Fitzpatrick, apparently with approval, when he writes that 'if modern occidental law is the child of imperialism, [it is] a child with oedipal inclinations, one whose ultimately uncontainable being opposes ... its imperious parent' (Pahuja 2011: 37). Yet the intellectual sophistication of Pahuja's analysis would seem to move well beyond the social sophistication of such *bons mots*, for example with her exploration of the pluralism of 'a universalism which is not one' (Pahuja 2011: 9).

This chapter has focused on two broad issues within a historically sensitized understanding of international law: the legend of the Westphalian settlement, and the question of the relationship between international law and colonization. The former encapsulates the notion of the independent sovereign state as the centrepiece of international law. It glorifies a particular form of political collective. The latter attempts to deal with marginalized collectives of people, people defined to some extent as individual persons but even more so in terms of their social and cultural forms of organization, namely as 'tribal' or otherwise uncivilized. The history and the historiography of international law provide evidence that the task of coming to conceptual grips with collectives remains on the table. What is important to consider next are contributions to this task from the philosophy of international law and from legal and political philosophy as we find these disciplines in the twenty-first century. To this we next turn.

Chapter 4
Grouphood, Rights and Waldron's Warning: Respecting the Collective

A Crisis of Identity

This chapter returns to the task, commenced in Chapter 2, of exploring the major contributions from legal and political philosophy that inform the current project. The emphasis is now on contemporary debates and resources, that is to say jurisprudence and related literature of the late twentieth, and of the present centuries. The only exception to this is the more detailed examination here of the contribution of Wesley Hohfeld, which originally dates from a century ago (Morss 2009). Hohfeld's contribution is particularly relevant in the context of contemporary jurisprudence of rights, including the question of group rights, especially as examined by Jeremy Waldron and by Matthew Kramer. The writings and interests of these contemporary philosophers of law and of politics are extensive and diverse. Both Waldron and Kramer have written extensively on rights, from a broadly analytic perspective. Both have written on the legitimacy of group rights. Kramer has focused more detailed attention on Hohfeld and on developing a version of legal positivism that as he sees it avoids the pitfalls of the more extreme, 'exclusive' versions of that tradition (Kramer 1999).

Waldron's writings have for some years included topics that bear rather directly on the jurisprudence of international law. Waldron has written extensively on individual rights and collective rights, on the democratic process and on sovereignty. Self-determination (of 'peoples'), the privileges of heads of state and the concept of an international rule of law are among the topics that are directly connected with the jurisprudence of international law. Both Waldron and Kramer adopt the interest approach to rights rather than the will approach, albeit in differing ways. Both find that approach consistent with Hohfeld's contribution.

The notion of group rights is a major focus of the present chapter. Does it make sense to describe a collective as, like an individual person, bearing rights or liberties, or as bound by obligations? If states and peoples are to be thought of as collectives then these questions need to be addressed. In this connection international law's understanding of the term 'will' needs to be examined. Closely related to the notions of sovereignty and of independence in the context of nations, 'will' seems to connote an individualistic and autonomous subject. In many ways that one word, when thought of as a term of art of international law, encapsulates the problematic that this book sets out to interrogate. One of the ways in which legal philosophy can be called upon to assist in this project derives from its own examination of 'will' in the context of the theory of rights, where a contrast is made between a 'will theory' and an 'interest theory'.

The present chapter will thus contribute to this collectivist project by focusing on one aspect of the vocabulary of international law, specifically the term 'will', a term which it could be argued presupposes an individualistic and, so to speak, 'subjective' analysis. Clearly the term 'will' either refers to, or expresses an analogy (or perhaps a 'legal fiction') with respect to, a subjective state of mind as more commonly thought of as pertaining to a natural person. Now it must be stressed that the nominal identity of this component of the lexicon of both disciplines – the word 'will' as such – is not in itself evidence for any significant overlap of meaning, still less for congruence. Arguments from legal philosophy to international law, or vice versa, need to be made with caution. But it will be argued below that the deficiencies of the 'will' position in rights theory, as demonstrated by advocates of the 'interest' theory of rights, are deficiencies that are informative for the scholar of international law. Correspondingly the 'interest' theory of rights is illuminating when alternatives to 'will' in international law are being sought. Some arguments will be presented in support of the latter, constructive point. The proposal therefore is to reconceptualize 'will' as 'interest'. A telegraphic story can be made in which the will theory of rights is connected up with an individual-centred international law (including an orthodox state-centred international law that is to say), in which case the interest theory is a candidate in the development of a (collective-centred) alternative for international law. In the case of Kramer it is therefore the analysis of rights, in the 'interest' tradition, as well as the exegesis of Hohfeld, that is of focal concern here.

Further, the question of identity is raised by these debates. If groups are acknowledged as valid entities, acknowledged ontologically so to say, then it might appear that a strong notion of identity follows. If so the relationships between groups would manifest a kind of identity politics. There are dangers with this prospect, to which Jeremy Waldron has alluded. Discussions of the political and philosophical status of groups or of communities, for example in the context of self-determination, often focus on the question of group identity. It is sometimes argued that identity is the essence of any collectivity that is more than an ephemeral happenstance of time and place.

In the context of international jurisprudence, any discussion of rights runs up against the notion of the 'will' of a state or of a people. Such references abound in international law. In both contexts, state and people, the term has a long and respectable pedigree stretching back at least to the Romans (the notion is captured in the venerable phrase *vox populi, vox Dei*) and through Rousseau among many contributors to Western legal and political thought. Too much weight should not be placed on terminology. The word 'will' has undoubtedly become a term of art within international law and has thus acquired specialized meanings within the discipline, meanings removed to some extent from its ancestral ones. But exploring its effects and seeking alternative terminology may be worthwhile. One reason for thinking that this might be the case is that there are close conceptual linkages between 'will' and 'consent' within international law and the theoretical significance of the latter term cannot be doubted. In relation to states, for example, will is associated not only with the so-called 'consent' of states but also with states' quasi-subjective 'beliefs' concerning the legal status of international customary norms.

Meanwhile, within the jurisprudence of rights, there continues a major debate between the 'will' (or 'choice') and the 'interest' theories of rights (Kramer, Simmonds and Steiner 1998). The voluntarist and subjectivist tradition of will theory in jurisprudence seems to resonate with corresponding notions of will and of consent at the international level (Dare 2002: 194). According to the will theory, the ability voluntarily to enforce or to waive one's valid claim-right is of the essence of the possession of such a right. It is a matter of a rights-holder's power and control over her or his situation (Kramer 1998: 99), and hence it is a matter of autonomy (Morss 2004). In strong or traditional versions of will theory, rights are inherently personal and significantly interrelated with intentionality, and perhaps with subjectivity. Hillel Steiner cites HLA Hart: 'Will Theory right-holders are small-scale sovereigns' (Steiner 1998: 239). The legal philosophy of rights offers an alternative formulation to 'will', namely an approach focused on 'interest'. The interest account is highly compatible with a collective reading of rights, and hence with the subject-matter of international law. It facilitates the recognition and the articulation of the complexities of collectives at the international level. A focus on the interests of collectives as constituting international law also generates challenging questions about the role of natural persons in international law.

It is therefore suggested that there is sufficient substance in the usage of the term 'will' in these contexts to justify the claim that the conceptual baggage of 'will' is misleading on the level of legal relationships between collectives and therefore to justify the exploration of an alternative vocabulary. That is to say, given the prima facie relationship between 'will' and the intentionality or subjectivity of an individual actor, it would seem worthwhile to investigate what an interest-based approach to international rights might look like, and what we might learn from it. It will be argued below that the interest approach to the jurisprudence of rights makes a good fit with a collective analysis of international law.

Moral Rights, Legal Rights, Group Rights

It is important to differentiate between moral and legal rights. Contemporary philosophy of international law discusses both. The relationships between them, in the global context as elsewhere, are moot. With this in mind, some general observations might first be made about the current landscape of philosophy of international law. The collection edited by Besson and Tasioulas, *The Philosophy of International Law*, is an extremely useful source (Morss 2011). Generally speaking the contributors represent a normative orientation to international law informed in particular by political theory and by the social sciences. For example

Allen Buchanan's chapter in this collection overviews his ethics-centred approach to international law. Buchanan's contribution is important to note in part because he has also written extensively on the topic of self-determination (Buchanan 2004). In his view, contemporary philosophy of international law is undeveloped; one reason being the dominance of legal positivism as against natural law in the theory of international law, and the over-extension of this leading to the exclusion of all moral aspects.

Buchanan's general position is that 'principles of justice specify the most basic moral rights and obligations that persons have' (Buchanan 2004: 1) and that international law should be designed so as to serve those principles. 'Persons' are individual natural persons overwhelmingly (2004: 7). International law is institutional, indeed it is a 'super-institution' including within itself many lesser institutions, such as those of the United Nations, and institutions are characterized by comprising 'roles, functions, procedures ... processes [and] structures of authority'. Significantly for Buchanan, institutions also embody moral principles. For Buchanan, 'the moral philosophy of international law must include *institutional* moral reasoning' (2004: 18).

Buchanan does not expressly define states as institutions in this sense, but he emphasizes that the processes by which states become recognized as such by other states are processes that are morally freighted (Buchanan 2004: 3). States may be included in Buchanan's scheme in this way. Buchanan's ethics-based approach to state legitimacy has important consequences. Thus it is important to note that while Buchanan rejects, on moral grounds, the exclusivist 'national interest' reductionism of orthodox international relations theory, as an account of the proper mission of a state, he endorses the orthodox view that 'state leaders are obligated to accord priority to the interests of their own citizens, of course' (Buchanan 2004: 8).

Buchanan's analysis of group rights in the context of international law involves a number of distinctions. Among the distinctions made by Buchanan is the argument that some group rights are to be thought of as derived from rights of individuals whereas other group rights are more radically collective in their character. An example of the former might be a right to vote, if it is held that the right is not only individualist in its manifestation (so long as individuals cast individual votes) but is based on interests that are individualistic: these interests may well be shared by most, or even all of the constituency, but are nevertheless most accurately thought of as interests of individuals (Buchanan 2004: 410). On the other hand, for Buchanan, '[t]he right of self-government enjoyed by a state ... or some other collective entity within the state' exemplifies the latter, truly collective kind of right. Such rights 'can only be wielded on behalf of a collectivity through some collective mechanism' such as voting (Buchanan 2004: 411, 414). No individual may exercise or waive such rights. Thus '[a]ll the rights of states are group rights in the sense of rights that cannot be wielded by individuals as individuals, on their own behalf' (Buchanan 2004: 412). Emphatically, however, Buchanan here rejects the view that any collective possesses *moral* rights and is in that important sense equivalent to an individual person (Buchanan 2004: 414). Elsewhere Buchanan has argued that states can act according to moral reasons, for example when implementing an international agreement by means of municipal legislation (Buchanan 2010: 87): if nothing else, this apparent inconsistency illustrates the complexity of the task of describing state conduct.

From the legal and political philosophy side, the validity of group rights, and other legal attributes of and relations between groups, has been asserted and explored by, among others, Waldron, Kramer, Tom Campbell and Joseph Raz. The main alternative position is that what may appear to be legal relations of collectives (for example legal relations in the sense articulated by Hohfeld), are no more than the aggregate of relations between natural persons. One version of this view, influenced by Raz, is that 'collective rights exist when individual interests of group members are strong enough to hold others to a duty' (Nine 2012: 47). Similarly, for political philosopher Peter Jones, mere collectives do not possess moral standing unlike corporate entities. Even group-related rights such as the rights of a linguistic minority, do not depend on or give rise to moral standing for the group as such:

> Certainly the right is a right held by the members of the group only as a group, but the right is still a right held by the individuals who constitute the group. It is simply that those individuals hold that right 'collectively' or jointly rather than independently. This idea of rights … is quite capable of making sense of rights that are commonly claimed as group rights, such as rights of national self-determination or rights relating to a group's culture. (Jones 2001: 212)

Moltchanova (2009) has explored the notion of group *moral* rights in the context of nationhood and self-determination. Moltchanova draws on a range of scholarship relevant to the current project, and develops her analysis in ways that raise questions for the approach to international collectivities that is being articulated here (Moltchanova 2009: 53). The question of moral rights in collectives will not be pursued further here, however it needs to be stressed that it remains a matter of debate as to the demarcation between moral and legal rights in groups. Current debate continues on the conceptual status of collective rights in the context of the rights of minorities (Newman 2011).

Hohfeld is the New Hohfeld

Hohfeld's scheme is routinely referred to in discussions of international law, if perhaps in an unsystematic way. In many ways this is a reflection of the ubiquity of Hohfeld's influence in legal philosophy, at least at the level of vocabulary. Devised in the early decades of the twentieth century, the formal scheme of Hohfeld was designed to facilitate the analysis of private, municipal law but has the potential to illuminate public, international law. As introduced in Chapter 2, Hohfeld's own writings were unambiguously individualistic: rights, liberties and so on are jural relationships involving private individual persons. But Hohfeld provided not merely a vocabulary for legal relations, but a grammar. He showed that a relationship such as that between a duty in one person and a claim-right in another should be thought of in such a way as to reveal underlying features, occupying as one might say different dimensions. Thus whereas the right and the duty are direct correlates, more can be said about the matrix of legal interrelationships in which right-bearer and duty-ower are positioned. For example the duty-ower does not possess an option as to the performance of the duty – it is not a liberty (or 'privilege'). Were it to be a liberty then the corresponding feature in another person – the matching pair – would be not a duty at all but something Hohfeld termed a 'no-right' (Kramer 1998: 10). The matching up has something of the quality of the matching of bases in the DNA molecule, themselves a simple set of correspondences. Just as the simplicity of the underlying formula for connections in DNA underlies immense complexity in organic structures, so in Hohfeld's scheme a simple set of interrelationships suffices to portray the complexity of obligations, norms and regimes that we encounter in the legal universe. Or at least that is the promise of Hohfeld's work.

The question of whether groups of people however defined may be bearers of rights was not discussed by Hohfeld. It would not have been surprising if Hohfeld had turned his mind to this question: jural relationships involving corporations (as legal persons) were widely discussed in Hohfeld's time and before it, for example by Maitland (Runciman 2003). In more recent decades however the question has been intensively examined within legal and political philosophy. If groups can be bearers of rights, can Hohfeld's scheme be employed in order to articulate those rights and their correlates? It is suggested that the contribution of Hohfeld is an analytic scheme that assists in the articulation of a collectivist model for international law. Hohfeld presented a scheme by reference to which the interrelationships between rights, duties and other legal connections between private individuals can be dissected. Rights and duties, as well as other Hohfeldian relationships like immunities and disabilities, arise within international law as well as within private law.

While Hohfeld's most basic formulations are routinely invoked, there are in fact many alternative post-Hohfeldian accounts in the recent and contemporary literature. Some legal or political philosophers categorize rights in ways that significantly depart from Hohfeld, deliberately developing the approach, yet remain to some extent in the Hohfeldian tradition. Generally speaking the 'default' version of Hohfeld that will be followed in this book will be as outlined by Kramer, in what would appear to be an account that remains true to Hohfeld while significantly developing the consequences of his approach (Kramer 1998). Aside from trivial errors or confusions, the ways in which other commentators would diverge from Kramer's reading of Hohfeld largely arise from assumptions being made about what might be termed synthetic or internal interconnections of legal qualities (Morss 2010). Thus for some authors a claim-right necessarily involves a liberty to exercise that right. This is Buchanan's position with respect to human rights (Buchanan 2004: 123, 333) such that if a right to secede were to be accepted, it would include a liberty in one party and an obligation in another. A purist Hohfeldian would observe that a claim-right is different from a liberty, so that if a liberty is truly enjoyed, its correlate in another party is not an obligation but something else. From an empirical point of view a party may enjoy a claim-right, and may also enjoy a liberty, but such contingencies do not undermine the distinctiveness of the jural relationships involved: they merely complicate their effect in the real world. So far as public international law is concerned, purist, analytic applications of Hohfeld as well as the more synthetic derivatives stand in need of defence. Neither self-executes as an explanation. It should also be noted that both analytic and synthetic forms of argument have long histories within international legal theory as well as within moral philosophy. The distinction between 'internal' and 'external' forms of an obligation-right relationship can be found in Vattel (Koskenniemi 2005a: 115). The Vattelian 'necessary law of nations' exemplifies internal coincidence of rights and obligations both held by one entity. The external form, corresponding in Vattel to what I have called the analytic, Hohfeldian approach, involves a right held by one party and an obligation held by another. With caution one might label the analytic approach 'objective' and the synthetic or internal form, 'subjective'.

Hohfeld set out two 'orders' of legal relationships. The first comprises the more familiar diagram of duty, liberty, right and no-right. It is this first order formulation that has become 'state of the art' and almost a cliché in legal theory, sometimes little more than an observance. Right and duty are correlates as are liberty and 'no-right'. The last term is a neologism for the status of the 'victim' or object of a liberty. The possessor of a liberty cannot trade on a duty in another, as can the wielder of a right. Liberty's 'other half' is no more (but no less) than the absence of a right against the enjoyment of the liberty. The no-right is a specific kind of vulnerability or weakness. Vulnerability – being on the 'receiving end' – is also addressed within Hohfeld's less familiar second order of jural relations. It comprises power, liability, immunity and disability. The domain of the second order is in some respects more detached from immediate relationships between parties. Thus power is defined by Hohfeld as a capacity to alter legal relations affecting others. As he does with the term 'right', that is to say, Hohfeld defines 'power' more narrowly than is usually the case. Liability is the correlate of power – a vulnerability to have one's legal relations changed about one so to speak. An immunity is a protection against a precise legal challenge (an attempted or intended changing of the legal status of the holder of the immunity) and the other party experiences a corresponding disability in relation to its aspirations.

There are connections between the two orders, although the connections are not clearly articulated by Hohfeld (Kramer 1998: 21). Power is conceptually related to liberty, and immunity to right. But second-order relations all apply directly to people's entitlements and only indirectly to their conduct (Kramer 1998: 20). This suggests that Hohfeld's second order, not his first, should be the first conceptual port of call when attempting to articulate international law as a law of collectives.

The location of 'power' in Hohfeld's scheme is another reason to prioritize the somewhat neglected second order. One pragmatic advantage of this would be to relegate to the back boiler two particularly troublesome aspects of Hohfeld's scheme, both located in the first order array: 'no-right' and liberty (privilege). The former has generated more confusion than illumination, in part as a consequence of misunderstandings by commentators. The latter, on the other hand, is in some ways all too familiar in international legal discourse. Freedom of action (and indeed of inaction) has been posited for states especially by the positivist tradition in international law, as an inherent characteristic of sovereignty.

It might be said that 'power' is also all too familiar in the language of international law although it is the discipline of international relations which most strikingly focuses upon it. Like all of Hohfeld's concepts, power is a relational matter. Absolute power – if by that is connoted true independence – is literally unknowable by Hohfeld. This is not to say that Hohfeld's scheme presupposes separation of powers or 'checks and balances' in a constitutional sense. Hohfeld's scheme could be employed to describe tyranny. Rather, it is to say that power is a feature of a whole system, not a feature of a separable component. To illustrate this, consider the phenomenon of charity or of other discretionary forms of aid. Whether deployed by an individual person walking past a supplicant on the sidewalk, or by governments deciding where to allocate foreign aid dollars, charity is a form of Hohfeldian power because it involves the capability to alter the jural relationships of recipients (debt burden, interest repayments, recourse to other forms of income generation and so on). This example suggests that the collective domain is a rich one for Hohfeldian analysis.

As noted above, Hohfeld's scheme and terminology have been employed from time to time by various authors writing on international law. For the most part this has been somewhat unsystematic, and with a variety of versions or derivative formulae being applied. One important exception is James Crawford who has commented incisively on the contribution of a Hohfeldian analysis to the question of bilateralism and its limitations. As well as noting the ways in which correlativity requirements were taken on board in the drafting of the *Articles on State Responsibility* (2002: 433) Crawford emphasizes that the Hohfeldian approach in no way supports a dyadic vision of international law as comprised of a series of bilateral relationships. Such employment of Hohfeld would be illegitimate (Crawford 2007: 432, 436–7). Hohfeld's account provides no comfort to the view that disputes in international law cannot be considered, even on occasion, the proper concern of parties only indirectly affected. Quite the reverse, Hohfeld's 'dissection' of legal relationships makes it possible to articulate the complexities with which the international community is faced in such disputes. A related point can be made about markets. Waldron has observed, also with reference to Hohfeld, that the image of the market is inadequate for understanding social life because bilateral agreements (contracts) between private individuals depend on prior collective decision-making in the community. '[C]ollective decisions define a structure of rights which *subsequently* enables individuals to deal with one another on the basis of bilateral ... decisions' (Waldron 1998: 118).

Buchanan's appropriation of Hohfeld is less successful. He accepts the broadly Hohfeldian sceptical point about unilateral assertions of rights; the consequences in terms of obligations must also be defined. '[E]xisting international law contains dangerously ambiguous references to "the right of self-determination of all peoples"' (Buchanan 2004: 333). Buchanan also adopts a Hohfeldian style in observing that he will make a case for 'unbundling ... the set of powers, claim-rights, liberties, and immunities that have traditionally been thought to define sovereignty' (Buchanan 2004: 56). Yet Buchanan defines 'a claim-right' as 'a liberty-right or permission, plus a correlative obligation' and refers to an obligation on others not to interfere (2004: 333). The virtue of the Hohfeldian scheme is the simplicity of its jural elements, from which Hohfeldian complexity may with care be constructed. Buchanan's appropriation of Hohfeldian vocabulary seeks to address the complexity of jural (and moral) interrelationships in the real world, but is not prepared to abide by the Hohfeldian discipline in order to do so (Buchanan 2004: 334). Nor is Buchanan alone in his selective appropriation of that contribution. Overall Hohfeld remains an underexploited resource in the theory of international law, moreover a resource that seems to offer intriguing possibilities in the context of a collective analysis. Here the connection with the 'will versus interest' debate is of importance.

'Will' and 'Interest' Theories of Rights: Small Sovereigns and Public Goods

Despite its somewhat antiquarian flavour, the term 'will' still has currency in international law. In his analysis of the international legal personality of international institutions, Klabbers compares a 'will theory' ('or "subjective theory", perhaps') and an 'objective theory'. The former, dominant theory 'is in conformity with positivist notions. Generally, international law is thought to be based on the freely expressed consent of states' (Klabbers 2002: 53). The will theory in this context holds that the legal personality of an organization is determined actively and expressly by the exercise of the will of each constituent. Such a nascent organization either is endowed with will, or not. Will is a kind of power, a species of sovereignty it would appear, capable of being extended at the sovereign's (or in this case sovereigns') discretion. It is important to note that the competing 'objective' explanation in this debate dissents on the origins of the will of the organization, rather than on the concept of 'will' itself. The objective theory holds that just like a state comes into being (according to one important tradition) in an immanent manner, once factual criteria are satisfied, just so does an international organization acquire a distinct will of its own, independent of the will of member states, as and when the relevant criteria are met. International legal personality follows from acquisition of 'organizationhood' (Klabbers 2002: 55).

The direct contrast of 'will' and 'interest' derives from the jurisprudential will versus interest debate in the theory of rights (Dare 2002: 194; Meyerson 2010: 132). Prominent adherents of the will theory include Hart and, more recently, Simmonds and Steiner. Prominent adherents of the interest theory include Raz, Waldron, MacCormick and Kramer. According to the will (or 'choice') theory, the ability voluntarily to enforce or to waive one's valid (claim-) right is of the essence of the possession of such a right. As observed above this comes down to a rights-holder's control over her or his situation. Rights are inherently personal and significantly interrelated with intentionality, and perhaps subjectivity.

Under the will theory, the number and variety of rights-holders envisaged is severely restricted. Thus animals, young children and the mentally incapacitated may be excluded from the class of possible rights-bearers under the rigorous application of the will theory, on the basis of their presumed lack of competence or of opportunity to lay claim to a right. The interest (or benefit) theory of rights asserts that interests subsist independently of their being asserted. From this perspective the vicarious assertion of entitlements is not only valid, but is arguably to be considered normative. For the interest theory a right-claim has a somewhat impersonal or even objective status, such that its enforcement and its waiving may in principle be implemented by a third party. That is to say an interest of X may perfectly well be protected by Y against Z. An interest is something which justifies protection and suffices to give rise to some claim-right. Under the interest theory, the advocacy, representation or protection of interests by others – for example by 'officials' – may be considered the norm, with self-representation, and self-help in general, as an extraordinary variation. Significantly for the present context, it is accepted at least by some adherents of the interest position that an interest may be held by a group and not only by a natural person (Raz 2003: 253). The compatibility of the interest position with the group rights position is one reason for favouring it in the present international law context. In contrast the will or choice theory is harder to square with a commitment to the validity of group rights, although Moltchanova has explored this possibility (Moltchanova 2009: 27). It would seem to necessitate a commitment to a group will understood in strong terms – perhaps following Rousseau (Russell 1961: 672).

Even if intentionality is allowed to play some role in the explanation, no extended or strained reliance on intentions is called for under the interest theory (Kramer 1998: 85). The interest theory emphasizes the vicarious nature of the assertion and 'prosecution' of a legitimate right and brings that characteristic to centre stage. In the words of Kramer, to ascribe a right to someone is to say that some aspect of that person's well-being is legally or morally shielded against interference or non-assistance (Kramer 1998: 2). According to Tom Campbell, 'it is hard to think of a right that cannot be justified in part by reference to the welfare of persons other than the rights-holder' (Campbell 2004: 133). In the context of international law, Tamir comments that the interest approach seems the more consistent with the concept of group rights (while rejecting the validity of the latter) (Tamir 2003: 192; Gould 2004: 120).

It seems entirely consistent with the recognition of collective rights, obligations, immunities and so on, and of collective interests with which those legal relations are to be associated, to eschew the association of 'will' with collectives as mis-directing one's attention to quasi- or pseudo-individualistic features of collectives. Conceptual difficulties with 'will' connect up with difficulties with 'consent' at the international level. There is of course no doubting the rhetorical force of such individualistic ascriptions as 'will' and 'consent' of nations or of peoples, ascriptions which also stand in complex relations with the representative functions of individual natural persons such as heads of state and UN representatives in international politics and diplomacy (and indeed with the political representation process in general).

In any event the proof of the pudding will be in the eating in that the 'interest' formulation will need to be shown to be of value in the context of international law. One may start with the term itself. Just as the use of the term 'will' is commonplace in international law, and may on occasion be little more than empty terminology, so also the word 'interest' is often encountered and weight may not always be placed on the choice of term. Some degree of precision of usage is clearly called for. Good examples may be found in the writings of former International Court of Justice judge Bruno Simma and of Andreas Paulus. Simma (1994: 217) has discussed 'community interest' and has considered the ways in which international community interests articulate with states' reciprocal obligations, obligations usually thought of in terms of a predominantly bilateral structure (Aust 2011: 423). Thus international legal theory has struggled to accommodate itself to the limitations of a bilateral orientation under which international jural relations are thought of as predominantly dyadic. Simma's own explorations of what 'community interest' might mean, as an alternative to the bilateral view, form an important backdrop to the study of the role of collective entities in international law. It should be stressed that bilateral relationships have far from disappeared. Examples are provided by the series of bilateral agreements entered into by the USA with member states of the International Criminal Court assuring the former that their military personnel would not become the subject of ICC indictment launched by the latter. But such bilateral agreements only make sense in a larger framework of legal relations. As well as the general point that such bilateral agreements would be bound by multilateral regulation (such as the Vienna Convention on the Law of Treaties 1969 or customary parts thereof), these special deals make sense only within the framework of ICC membership of the USA's partners. As Simma has forcefully argued, bilateralism is conceptually inadequate. Larger interests and contexts need to be taken into account. This is not to say however that Simma's own articulation of 'community interests' is yet sufficiently precise.

Paulus (2010: 210) notes that 'traditional' international adjudication defined its role as deferential to 'state will' (*Lotus*-style) whereas the contemporary approach demands that a balance be struck that accommodates not only the 'individual interests of states' but also interests such as human rights and environmental protection. In Paulus' words:

> 'Community interests' are common interests of states relating to public goods, whereas individual interests are those essentially selfish interests in which one state can realize its objectives only at the detriment of another, for instance in boundary disputes. (Paulus 2010: 211)

Crawford's use of the term is cognate; for Crawford, '[a]ll states are by definition members of the international community as a whole, and the[ir] obligations ... are by definition collective obligations protecting interests of the international community as such' (Crawford 2002: 278). It should also be noted that the ancient term *res publica* refers to the common good (Sellers 2006), so that republicanism as an intellectual tradition would seem to be lined up on the 'interest' side of the will versus interest divide.

Compared to the language of 'will,' the language of 'interest' is much more versatile. One aspect of this versatility is the way that different formulations of interest can be identified, corresponding to different methodologies or ideologies within the broader discipline. Importantly Paulus observes the connection between the focus on 'selfish interests' of a state and the realist tradition recently reinvigorated in the form of a 'law and economics' approach to international law (Paulus 2010: 211). The 'realist' approach within international law deals in a 'scientific' investigation of state characteristics treated as factual. It might be said that the language of interests makes it possible to contextualize and hence to interrogate the influential claims of the realist school, decentring immediate and merely instrumental interests without entirely dismissing their role. Thus, the formulation of interest highlighted by realist approaches may be seen as but one of many possible formulations, one section of a spectrum – a spectrum that ranges from complementary options to stark conceptual alternatives. To mutilate the metaphor, the 'drearily monochromatic' law and economics movement (Waldron 1998: 139) may admittedly be the 'grey' part of the spectrum. Adoption of the interest approach may facilitate the assimilation of the contemporary realist perspectives in international law into the larger context of theoretical debate in the discipline, thus putting an end to the (sometimes splendid) isolation and the 'all or nothing' character of the realist orientation. More generally, the interest approach is comfortable with pluralities of interests in tension if not conflict, indeed uncomfortable with the occlusion or suppression of such diversity. While every form of analysis of political life may be said to be reductionist, the will approach carries reductionism to an extreme of atomism or monadism.

The interest formulation is able to handle various complexities that arise in the assertion or defence of international claims. An interest even when successfully defended is not a guaranteed advantage. Thus the interests of a collective, even when properly protected by another collective, may have disadvantageous consequences to the holder of the interest. Minority group cohesion might provide an example. A minority group whose ability to freely associate (which may well be considered a legitimate interest) is assisted or enabled by another collective, might develop bizarre social arrangements. Less dramatically, it might suffer economic loss as a community because of its relative isolation from a mainstream population. Again, paternalism is a recognized pitfall for the implementation of the interest approach. There are undoubted political and ethical difficulties (if not legal difficulties) in the practice of protection either of individuals, of nascent states (Wilde 2008), of people or of peoples. The recently proclaimed 'Responsibility to Protect' (Arbour 2008) raises such issues and the importance of teasing apart individualist and collectivist concepts in that context are indicated by Arbour's use of the phrase 'duty of care'. The difficulties are closely related to what David Kennedy has called the 'dark sides of virtue' (Kennedy, 2004). Will, sovereignty and the consent of states seem to offer inadequate conceptual analysis for such debates.

Further aspects of the interest theory should be noted. Importantly, the interest theory seems able to accommodate the situation in which a right when honoured turns out to be disadvantageous to the sole beneficiary or to some of many beneficiaries (Kramer 1998: 94). This notion may sound paradoxical, and it is certainly hard to understand under the will theory. It is however of relevance to the aims of this book. One example in relation to rights of a natural person is for X to inherit a rundown house or rundown horse. It is entirely consistent with an 'advocate' for X, including a bureaucratic one who may execute the inheritance without relying on instructions from X, to be insisting on the inheritance right of X, that the item inherited might be more trouble (cost) than it is worth. Examples can also be found in larger contexts. In Kramer's example, a social policy like a minimum wage might well benefit the majority of workers and yet turn out to be disadvantageous to some workers who (now) cannot muster the skills required to earn that minimum. They may therefore have no income at all, whereas in a free-for-all market they might at least have earned something. Again, a duty to financially support some person or group of people, such as a community, might give rise to negative outcomes for the person or persons thus supported – for example through 'dependence'. Evaluation is inevitably complex and potentially involves political judgement, as the example of dependence illustrates. The interest theory is complex enough to account for such situations, notwithstanding the predominance of advantage (benefit) to the defence of interests.

There are some limitations or possible weaknesses in the interest theory that should be noted. It may be hard in practice to determine the existence of a legitimate interest. Determining which persons or entities are capable of having a legitimate interest might sometimes be difficult. Precision may be a problem in other respects. For example the role of the state in prosecuting criminal matters on behalf of the victim and of the community as a whole can be treated as an illustration of the interest theory at work but at the same time the interest-rights connection perhaps loses its precision if the whole state apparatus is considered to be an instance of the defence of an interest. There is also the problem of paternalism (Kramer 1998: 286). Generally speaking then the interest theory of rights is in need of articulation and development, not least in the group or collective context. But there is no reason to be pessimistic about the prospects of that enterprise and exploration of the collective interest argument may in fact assist in the understanding of the interest theory more widely.

For the present purposes, it seems clear that of the two contenders 'will' and 'interest' in that jurisprudential debate on rights, the latter is by far the more promising in the context of international law. It should be stressed that this provisional conclusion does not derive merely from the terminology, notwithstanding that given a framework of critique of 'will' in international law, the rejection of 'will' in rights theory may seem something of a set-up. There would seem to be some substantive ways in which the usages of the concept of 'will' across the contexts complement each other and indicate some larger conceptual resonances, relating to intentionality and to the subject. For Kramer, the will theory is 'strangely remote as a means of shoring up the dignity of the individual' (Kramer 1998: 76) and this remark would surely apply 'in spades' to the collective context.

It is important to note the argument made by Moltchanova for the applicability of a (Hartian) will theory of rights in the international context. While noting that collective rights of a legal kind such as self-determination are widely accepted, Moltchanova argues that 'the opposition between the "interest" and "will" accounts of rights does not manifest itself when we deal with the rights of human groups' (Moltchanova 2009: 27). The will approach, Moltchanova argues, is adequate to this context. A 'capacity condition' must be satisfied, that is to say by groups as collective agents. Thus,

> [t]he constitution of a collective agent is defined for its members by its members in the context of the collective good around which the group is organized ... groups organized around the shared good of self-determination have the capacity to relate to other collectives as free equals and can possess primary rights ... religious, linguistic, and cultural communities derive group rights from individual rights to collective goods that do not require such equal freedom. (Moltchanova 2009: 26)

For Moltchanova, interest and will approaches come together because 'group rights belong to sets of individuals who organize as collective agents around the shared characteristic that requires protection' (Moltchanova 2009: 26). Thus for Moltchanova, a shared interest is at the same time the ground for protection (and hence a right), as under the interest theory, and the characteristic that generates the collective agency that can wield choice in relation to that interest, as under the will theory. In other words the individualism of Hart's account of rights is overcome without abandoning the important dimension of agency.

Moltchanova's analysis is important but does not seem to deal comprehensively with the difficulties that a will approach causes. In this context, it can be argued that Hart's thinking about international law if it had been followed through, and integrated in certain ways with his views on rights, may well have led him to a refinement of the will theory and hence to a position more friendly to the interest approach in the international law domain. Hart's identity as a will theorist therefore requires scrutiny. In several ways Hart qualified and constrained his will approach. Thus while Hart emphasized the control exerted by a rights-holder, for example to waive or extinguish an obligation arising in another, he accepted that such power can be delegated by a rights-holder to another (Steiner 1998: 247). This moves so to speak in the direction of interest theory in which legitimate actions are detached from personality. More significantly, Hart owned that the pure or traditional will approach applies most adequately to private natural individuals in their dealings with other private natural individuals: Squire Smith and Squire Jones wrangling over title to Blackacre and so on. (This of course is also the 'home' domain of application for Hohfeld's scheme.) If there is a larger, 'constitutional' framework under which officials play a substantive role then significant alterations to the theoretical account are required. To put it starkly, for Hart constitutional provisions can overrule will-theory rights. It seems to be the case that public law in general is exempt from, or in various ways exceeds, the explanatory boundaries of will theory.

It is unlikely that Hart's hypothetical development of international legal theory would have led him to endorse the more grandiose of the international constitutionalist claims of recent decades. In any event there are no grounds for Hartian will theory to be presupposed in the context of public international law. The adjustments to that account that Hart recognized in public law may well be required in the international legal domain. Some of those adjustments might move toward a Waldronian-inspired interest account, some may move in directions to which the latter would itself need to respond. It may also be possible to link across to the exciting developments in the international law of state complicity (Aust 2011). It may be that the 'interest' alternative as extrapolated from the jurisprudence debate is not so valuable as anticipated. After all the 'interest of the state' is not an entirely unfamiliar concept; it already has baggage in its international law context. In particular it has connections with the so-called 'realist' approach to international relations and to international law. Care will have to be taken in working through the possibilities opened up by the analogy. At this point, however, some other aspects of group functioning need to be addressed. These turn on questions of identity.

Waldron's Warning

As well as many writings on the classic issues and themes of analytic jurisprudence, Jeremy Waldron has pursued a number of specific projects in legal philosophy that relate to the law of nations. Other major research topics touch on international jurisprudence less directly but still substantively; these have included the legal and political philosophy of property (as in the writings of Locke) and the philosophy of rights; the critique of undemocratic powers of constitutional courts able to overrule parliaments by judicial review; sovereignty and the executive powers; the role of constitutional norms; and the validity of indigenous claims. Events following the US-led invasion of Iraq in 2003 and the consequent detention of combatants in Guantanamo and elsewhere, and related questions of extreme interrogation techniques, gave rise to significant contributions to public policy (Waldron 2005).

Many aspects of these topics themselves overlap with, and offer challenging perspectives on, issues in the jurisprudence of international law. With respect to the latter Waldron has written on sovereignty, on an international rule of law and on the problems created by a reliance on identity in the analysis of political communities. In this connection, Waldron's recent analysis of self-determination focuses on the identity-based conception of self-determination such as advocated by Kymlicka. In Waldron's words, the identity-based case for self-determination 'is predicated on the assumption that the members of an identity-group have an essential investment in the integrity of their culture and that they need empowerment to protect it from being overwhelmed or unduly influenced by other cultures' (Waldron 2010: 405–6). This is 'the philosophy of identity politics' (2010: 408).

Where Kymlicka's argument thus finds legitimacy for self-determination in the preservation of a distinct cultural identity, Waldron argues that legitimate self-determination is a much more humble and, so to speak, a ragged business, a political arrangement for the governance of a particular piece of territory by which self-government by the inhabitants (in all their multicultural diversity) is to be assured. Waldron argues that it is not just that extreme forms of cultural 'purity' and hence intolerance give rise to problems when allied to self-determination. Rather, it is identity politics as such that is the source of those problems. For as Waldron has argued in the context of cosmopolitanism, 'we are always likely to find ourselves alongside others who disagree with us about justice' (Waldron 2000: 240) so that the tendency of some political thinkers like Rawls as well as some communitarian writers to presuppose shared values on such matters seems misplaced. In Kant's image of the global world community we are all alongside such others in a sense, sharing a limited space. Thus the identity-based conception of self-determination is 'inapposite to a world of mingling and migration, a world of fluid and compromised identities' (2010: 398).

As Waldron describes, the orthodox approach to self-determination and to minority rights is strongly associated with affiliation with, and defence of, cultural identity (Waldron 2010: 401). Moreover it is more than a logical nicety that the 'self' of self-determination is opposed to an 'other': as with the Palestinians in Israel, being identified by the Israeli state as 'other' brings with it a variety of disabilities (2010: 400). It should be noted that 'existing non-Jewish communities in Palestine' were thus defined (by exclusion so to speak) as far back at least as the Balfour Declaration of 1917. Waldron has issued a warning on identity politics which, it will be argued here, is (among other things) a warning about the hazards that arise from treating states or peoples as if they can express a unitary, quasi-subjective general will. For Waldron, 'identity politics is a misbegotten evil in all its manifestations, whether it is the politics of individual identity or the essentialist politics of group identity' (Waldron 2008: 28). I have called this 'Waldron's warning' (Morss 2012).

Waldron thus issues a warning against a conceptual slippery slope that leads to nationalism or to 'tribalism' thought of in a cognate sense. Identity claims, Waldron suggests, tend to obliterate political differences and political connections. For Waldron, political collectives are characterized by at least some degree of internal diversity and tension rather than by internal homogeneity. It might be observed that the internal diversity, even if limited (and the extent of diversity must have its limits), prevents the collapse into tyranny of one kind or another – or the extreme conformity of 'sheephood' (Waldron 1999a).

Waldron's concerns about 'identity politics' may thus be understood as a warning about the susceptibility of *properly* collective accounts to be reduced to accounts of uniformity. Properly collective accounts recognize the internal diversity and complexity of collectives. For various reasons, including human frailty in attention span, accounts of collectives sometimes tend to be reduced to accounts of monoliths. Such false uniformity transforms the collective into a quasi-individual; that is to say, into the kind of entity to which a 'will' may be plausibly attributed. Waldron's well-known celebration of the noisy dissension within a parliament demonstrates this point (Waldron 1999b). The result of decision-making by an assembly, such as by a majority vote, may be colourfully expressed as 'the will of the parliament' or of the people – just as the overall result of a general election may be so termed. But if we treat such descriptions as anything other than rhetorical flourishes, we overlook the only aspects of the process that give the outcome its legitimacy – its pluralism, or to put it another way, those aspects that put the *pluribus* in its *e pluribus unum* character. This is what one might call its truly collective character as against a pseudo-collectivity such as any dictator might lay claim to in seeking to justify his actions as being on behalf of the people. And legitimacy is as much conceptual as it is political. The intercourse of sovereigns is just inadequate as a model of international legal governance, and enlarging the scope of 'sovereigns' to include peoples, perhaps INGOs and multinational corporations and so on, does not in itself fix the problem.

It might be thought at first glance that Waldron's critique of identity politics aligns him with an individualistic liberal tradition in political theory. As Paulus observes in the context of international law, the liberal perspective is individual-centred and relatedly, 'liberals display a certain disregard for "collective" legitimacy in favour of a more pragmatic concept of international tribunals as service providers to individuals' (Paulus 2010: 216). But the opposite is the case. Waldron has explored the consequences for political life of 'taking group rights carefully' (2002: 203). While strongly advocating respect for group rights, he warns of the dangers of nationalism, tribalism and similarly intolerant ethnocentric movements, movements which might seem to be validated or provided with oxygen so to speak if group rights are highlighted. How can the 'groupness' or community of people in affiliation be properly recognized and appreciated without too high a price being paid – for example by indiscriminately licensing or endorsing whatever shared dispositions or projects may emerge from such collectives? What Waldron calls for and adumbrates therefore is a formulation of group rights within international law that will avoid the pitfalls of identity politics: 'group dignity without identity' (Waldron 2008: 29). One way of contributing to the overall project of the collectivist analysis of international law, while remaining aware of Waldron's warning, is thus to call upon the above jurisprudential distinctions (between 'will' and 'interest') with a view to clarifying the conceptual underpinnings of rights and other jural relations in international law. This assists in the consolidation of the status of collectives. Thus informed and in many ways reassured by legal philosophy, attention can now be focused again on international law.

Chapter 5
Statehood, Consent, Complicity: Defining the Collective

The Hollow Crown: Will and the Withering Away of the State

It is now possible to turn more directly to the part played by the state in the discipline of international law. In many ways the state as now understood – as often loosely referred to by the term 'the nation state' – plays quite straightforwardly the role of sovereign monarch in the law of nations of earlier times. This is the case at least to the extent that sovereign monarchs may be seen as the source as well as the embodiment of international legal regulation. This smooth conceptual transition from King to Country is highly compatible with the account of international law's history encapsulated in the word 'Westphalia' as discussed in a previous chapter. A modern state system, as exemplified in the General Assembly membership, is very easily seen as the progressive political development of a pluralized monarchical scheme supposedly established in that Westphalian era. Although the grammar is inconsistent, 'the state' is, in many ways, in the discourse of international law, the successor to 'will' as examined in the previous chapter.

As previously observed the vocabulary of 'will' is ubiquitous in international law whether within its textbooks or in the decisions of its tribunals. Convention-based international law, in particular, is commonly said to represent the express will of states, perhaps by analogy with a contract between two natural persons. This is often expressed by the term 'consent'. According to the discipline's textbooks the 'consent theory' is intimately connected to a 'positivist' view of international law dominant in the nineteenth century and still a significant, conservative tradition, not least because of its influence over the infrastructure and the institutions of international law. Critical scholars have pointed to the persisting effects of this positivism. According to post-colonialist international law scholar Antony Anghie, '[t]he late nineteenth century was ... the period in which positivism decisively replaced naturalism as the principal jurisprudential technique of the discipline of international law'. Anghie continues: 'The sovereign is the foundation of positivist jurisprudence, and nineteenth-century jurists sought to reconstruct the entire system of international law as a creation of sovereign will' (Anghie 2007). Sovereignty itself seems to be implicated in this question of the relationship between international law and the personality of the international legal subject (the state). Clearly, much is at stake in the inquiry into the 'will of the state' and into the related concept of 'consent'. The collectivist project offers, it is hoped, a new perspective on this tangle.

It is helpful to look beyond international law for understandings of the state. It is commonplace in disciplines such as sociology to treat the state as an institution, as a complex node of bureaucratic power. This approach is best known as a contribution of Weber. Weber's critical analysis of bureaucratic power was itself in part a response to a 'Hegel-like idealization of state bureaucracy in Wilhelmine Germany' (Merquior 1980: 121). For Weber as for Hegel, the problem of the state is the problem of legitimacy. While some states may take the form of constitutional or even absolutist monarchies, and may be to be favoured or disavowed because of such characteristics, statehood is not a consequence or an appendage of monarchical sovereignty. Just as Hobbes recognized that the sovereignty of an assembly is at least theoretically valid, so Hegel and Weber would both have agreed that the state is conceptually speaking 'bigger' than individualized monarchy. At least from the point of view of legitimacy, the state is a complex machine. Its typical official needs to be seen as 'giving orders he did not originate from a room which was not his own' (Merquior 1980: 117). The phrase is for legal scholars reminiscent of Hart's sociologically inspired analysis of legal obligation as something immanent in the activities and decisions of a cadre of officials, collectively implementing a legal system. In both cases the conceptual contrast is being made with a simplistic account of individualized domination. All of this is to make the point that a simplistic view of the state is a conceptual non-starter in many disciplines. It would seem that international law has been satisfied with a highly reductionist account of the state. Positivism as an attitude to methodology in the human and social sciences could easily be linked to this analysis.

It may be that this judgment is too hasty. A simplified view of the state may be pragmatic or strategic rather than a sign of sloppy thinking. One way of approaching this is to consider the notion of 'dualism'. According to this view, which is itself closely connected with the positivist orientation to international law, there is a qualitative divide between the level of the national legal system and the level of international regulation. Thus the 'external' simplicity or opaqueness of the state, that is to say from an international law perspective, is an entirely different matter from its rich, 'internal' character. The former standpoint is not inconsistent with the latter. Just as a family may be extremely complex, yet count as a single unit for statistical purposes or for some forms of taxation or voting under patriarchal models, so it is argued the face of the state that looks inward is quite a different face from that which looks outward, towards other states. Some (early) forms of dualism in the theory of international law would espouse a simplistic view of both 'faces': the 'internal' face might be thought of as the face of the monarch who commands or speaks law. But more sophisticated versions of dualism should not be neglected. In many states around the contemporary world it remains the practice that international legal agreements (conventions) reached by international representatives of the state's executive do not become applicable law domestically until and unless transformed by domestic legislation (see Nollkaemper and Nijman 2007).

Elsewhere the incorporation of such agreements is conditional on consistency with a written constitution. The rationale for such practices can itself take several forms: appeal may be made variously to the democratic process, to ethnocentrism, to 'checks and balances' and so on. Dualism in action is entirely compatible with complex understandings of the role of the state 'internally' and this supports the view that a unitary actor-like picture of the state when seen externally might be, so to speak, a legal fiction, a deliberate style or expression. Clearly there is an important sense in which its place in a scheme of representation, at the United Nations for example, imposes a *de facto* singularity on the state. Put crudely, one vote means one chair. Making a related but more general point, Runciman has suggested that 'it is precisely because it is so hard to understand modern state action as a form of collective action that states need representatives to act for them' (Runciman 2003: 41).

Despite the possibility that some aspects of international law's theory of the state are driven by convenience or even by the political necessities of representation, it remains the case that statehood is the weak link in the theory of international law. Instead of being the common core uniting all the other levels and varieties of international legal regulation, statehood is more like a conspiracy theory or the latest outfit for the Emperor: only from a distance, or if examined superficially, does it present an appearance of substance. Statehood as an analytic or as an explanatory entity is threatened from all directions. Levels of analysis and of policy implementation which appear to be 'above' the level of statehood, such as regional, quasi-federal and global arrangements, seem to have much more substance than statehood itself (Walker 2010). Processes and constituencies that seemed to occupy a lower level on the state-centred hierarchy turn out to have as much or more significance, if not validity, than the state. As Klabbers observes, 'infranationalism' is an increasingly important dimension of European regulation, exemplified by international conversations between judges, between civil servants and between financiers (Klabbers 2002: 339). In Europe's past the Hanseatic League of cities was a major feature of the international trading landscape, a collective that was able to disregard geopolitical boundaries to a significant extent. In our own time international retail corporations, such as coffee vendors, are able to minimise the tax liabilities that arise within particular jurisdictions because of flexibility over the geographical attribution of functions of the corporation (choosing how to define where costs are said to have been incurred, where profits are said to have been made and so on). The characteristic mobility of capital thus involves a permeability of state boundaries by fiat, so to speak, just as much as it involves permeability in the form of capital flows as such. Thus processes and institutions that cut across the statehood level of analysis push the state further to the background of theoretical analysis. Systems theory and autopoiesis are called upon to inform structural understanding of international regulation (Teubner 2012). Thus the state as unit of analysis is dissolved from above and from below, from within and from without. Any solidity to the state, in an international law sense, can be seen as constructed by those surrounding processes.

In exploring the legal personality of organizations, Klabbers cites the observation of Bederman that organizations are much more 'communities' than they are 'persons'. As Klabbers comments, 'to use the metaphor of "personality" fails to do justice to [the] complexity' of the interplay between organizations and states, 'and may even be misleading' (2002: 58). This suggests the question: are states organizations? States and organizations can 'hide behind one another, in fact even to become indistinguishable. And this is no coincidence, as they stand for the same thing: politics in accordance with the law' (Klabbers 2002: 343). Klabbers' explanation for this phenomenon seems preliminary at best. But as he says elsewhere, '[s]tates as well as organizations represent organized political life; both ultimately represent the idea that we can make and control our surroundings, and that we can conquer both nature and human nature' (Klabbers 2002: 337).

Statehood in International Law

Given the above considerations it is important to examine how international law has understood statehood. The theory of statehood has had a central role in international law for several centuries even though there has always been more to international law than state conduct, state regulation and state interaction. This 'apologetic' state-centred genre of international law has at times purported to constitute the entirety of the discipline but this hegemonic move has always had its resistant margins. Broadly speaking the 'resistance', or alternative candidates for explanatory status, have come either from 'above' or from 'below'. Above would include normative or ethical principles of the law of nations supervening on state conduct. Below would include the rights and obligations of individual persons. But the problem of statehood requires more radical surgery. Statehood needs to be addressed in some detail in the context of the present project. The claim has been made above that states are kinds of collective, and this claim needs to be substantiated and explored.

The nature of international statehood, the processes by which new states emerge and old states disappear and the delineation of the diversity of variants of statehood are authoritatively discussed by James Crawford (2006). Crawford's approach emphasizes effectiveness of territorial governance, coupled with some carefully delineated dimensions of legitimacy, in contrast to a traditional focus on a formal analysis. In many ways it is the grey areas of contested statehood that reveal the theoretical underpinnings of these matters. 'Contested statehood' can be taken to cover such cases as newly emerging candidates for statehood, such as Kosovo and Palestine in our times, as well as cases where states seem to be 'failing' or going 'rogue' or breaking up in other than respectable ways. Alongside such 'critical' cases, there are also many international entities whose status has been considered marginal on a chronic basis for reasons such as small size, such as Monaco and the other European 'microstates', or for other reasons such as the Vatican City/Holy See. It is important to observe that states whose status as such is broadly uncontested, such as the typical Security Council member state, still depend on the continuation of processes and mechanisms that are ultimately contingent ones, such as geopolitical and democratic processes, so that every state might be thought of as a contested state. Somewhat grandiosely, it could be said that if any state is contested, then each and every state is contested: any examination of a particular case raises some questions about general criteria, however formal or informal. In that respect, irrespective of geography, no state is an '*Iland*, intire of it selfe', but rather 'a peece of the *Continent*, a part of the *maine*'. It remains the case that the conceptual questions are thrown into sharp relief by the more dramatic or pressing examples of contested international status.

So far as international law of statehood is concerned, some broad trends over time can be detected in what is inevitably a complex picture. These will be presented ahead of bringing to bear the collectivist contribution and in order to provide a context for that. First, legitimacy has taken an ever greater role in international debates on contested statehood over the last 100 years. Legitimacy has never been absent from such debates. In early centuries conquest, that is to say successful deployment of force internationally, was not infrequently taken to connote legitimacy and there were a variety of accounts of the 'justness' of a just war. It should also be noted that questions of legitimacy were of express concern for the diplomats assembled at the Congress of Vienna, following the final defeat of Napoleon. But it is a much more recent development for legitimacy to take such a central role and to be scrutinized as such by scholars and by practitioners of international law. The role, and the concept itself, remain imprecise. There are of course close ties, both conceptually and empirically, with notions of self-determination and notions of independence and of 'sovereignty'. Relatively democratic and relatively tolerant forms of governance are increasingly being taken as default requirements in the context of new states emerging, for example, out of former Communist regimes. It is significant that legitimacy in anything other than the most oblique sense is absent from the most influential of formal or 'objective' templates for statehood: that located in the Montevideo Convention of 1933.

This is one illustration of, and perhaps one reason for, the second trend: an increasing focus on functional rather than formal criteria for recognized statehood. States play various roles within international law, for example as parties to international agreements, and such roles, which encompass rights, duties, privileges and so on, thereby in a sense constitute statehood. As Crawford observes, the 'hackneyed formula' of Montevideo does not assist with such an approach (2006: 437). The orientations are not entirely distinct: as well as pointing to such factors as territorial sovereignty and stable population, Montevideo includes criteria that refer to effectiveness, and effectiveness remains perhaps the key term in a contemporary (Crawfordian) account of statehood. But the criterion-based approach of Montevideo has proved irrelevant. Various microstates such as Monaco and San Marino seem to squeeze the Montevideo criteria to a minimum in relation to geography and population and in terms of economic or political independence. In the advocacy of a collectivist view of international law, there is no mileage in an extended critique of the Montevideo analysis of statehood which would be to flog a dead conceptual horse.

A third trend worth noting is the decline of the strong theory of state recognition as an account of the legitimacy of states. There is no longer any plausibility, if there ever was, in the theoretical position according to which statehood could arise as a consequence of 'recognition' in and of itself. This is not to overlook the important role played by express decisions on recognition for example by the European Union in relation to former components of Yugoslavia in the 1990s. But it is to say that the picture of an inchoate entity achieving uncontested statehood as a direct and sufficient consequence of such state conduct by other states no longer has credibility. It may never have been seriously asserted that statehood might emerge irrespective of all factual circumstances, all considerations of legitimacy, effectiveness and so on. But such a theoretical position of 'pure' recognition was certainly 'on the books' in earlier decades. It was in a sense a constructionist theory, a theory of 'collective invention' so to speak. By foregrounding a constitutional recognition by pre-existing states, this theoretical position sufficed to marginalize those other factors of effectiveness and legitimacy. At the same time, the existence of this extreme recognition theory may have helped to clarify what seemed to be its alternative, a declaratory theory according to which all that is involved in the recognition of a new state is a reflection or a representation of a factual matrix (Beard and Noll 2009: 469). This alternative theory was then a 'collective discovery' theory, in contrast with the 'collective invention' account: 'we have taken note of the factual existence of this place as an international legal subject'.

This 'meta-theory' of a debate between two rival accounts – of collective invention versus collective discovery – can be said to have evaporated. Before dismissing it however it should be noted that both alternatives that it comprehends are collective ones in the restricted sense that collective conduct or agreement on behalf of the international community of states is being described. Contemporary approaches to statehood therefore focus attention neither on the 'pull' of existing, uncontested states' formal declarations of recognition of new or otherwise contested entities; nor on the 'push' of non-negotiable facts of geopolitics. Instead a range of functional factors are taken into account. This approach lends itself to connection with the collectivist analysis.

Complicity and Collectives of Collectives

It has been observed that legal theorists are 'generally ill equipped' to explain the co-operation of states. This has usually been left to scholars of international politics (Klabbers 2002: 34). For international law, it is co-operation in relation to wrongdoing that presents the biggest problem both theoretically and practically. In this connection an important contribution to our understanding of collective state responsibility has recently been made by Helmut Aust (2011; also see Nolte and Aust 2009). Aust focuses on complicity between states, especially in the context of the definition of wrongfulness in state conduct. State complicity is a chronic symptom of geopolitics, and can be traced in the context of customary international law over many decades. Some key aspects of complicity, such as the definition of neutrality in times of war, have been recognized and to some extent regulated for centuries. But complicity in wrongfulness is an especially pressing question in the contemporary era when co-operation between governments may extend to the facilitation of illegal acts such as those implicated in the 'rendition' of terrorist suspects. Further, the analysis and articulation of complicity opens up theoretical possibilities that go beyond such current matters. In Aust's words, 'the concept of complicity ... offers answers to problems which are community-related: it determines the degree of necessary international solidarity in the face of violations of international law' (Aust 2011: 425).

It would be possible to locate the notion of complicity in relation to Simma's framework of an evolution from the bilateral toward community interests. It certainly contributes to a more nuanced understanding of that model (Aust 2011: 49; 423). But for Aust complicity is a notion that more significantly captures and helps to articulate the value of a rule of law orientation in international law. As he notes, such interventionist formulations as the currently trumpeted 'Responsibility to Protect' (or 'R2P') bring with them the practical temptation for abuse by more powerful states (Aust 2011: 424). It might also be said that the R2P carries with it conceptual temptations, such as the temptation to focus on states as individuals. This would be to draw something of an analogy with the situation of the bystander to the needy under Civil codes of law on the continent of Europe to whom, unlike their Common Law counterparts, some duties of offering assistance to a needy compatriot may apply (Kroslak 2003). As Aust emphasizes,

> The magnitude of the catastrophes often coincides with the grandeur of the legal concepts in which refuge is sought: humanitarian intervention, the responsibility to protect or countermeasures in the collective interest. (Aust 2011: 426)

The focus on complicity is by comparison, bathetic:

> If States scrutinise their connections with wrongful conduct at an earlier stage, the need for recourse to more intrusive mechanisms may be reduced ... [B]efore States take positive enforcement action, they should have scrutinised possible complicity with the situation they wish to affect ... In this light, a prohibition of complicity could become part of a larger principle of proportionality in the enforcement of the community interest. (Aust 2011: 426)

As Aust adumbrates here, a grammar of complicity offers the opportunity of making tangible progress toward the honourable but poorly articulated protective ideals that have received so much recent attention. Complicity is about the quotidian conduct of states, that everyday level at which, as more optimistic international jurists point out, much of states' conduct is in fact usually compliant with international norms and expectations. And of course the quotidian is the very stuff of rule of law, whether 'municipal' or international. The extraordinary, it might be said, has played too great a part in both thinking and practice in international law. Aust's contribution is, so to speak, to reassert the Kelsenian spirit against the still lingering Schmittian.

More broadly, an 'international rule of law' orientation, informed by the writings of Waldron among others, enables Aust to introduce a series of important theoretical perspectives to the discussion of complicity. For example, Georges Scelle's notion of the dual role (*dédoublement fonctionnel*) is called upon to suggest one way in which states may serve plural functions thus offering a theoretical escape from the circularity of states both regulating, and being regulated by, each other. As Aust emphasizes, Scelle, like Hohfeld, thought of law as a form of relationship among individual persons, and extrapolation of his formulation to the international domain must likewise be tentative and carried out with caution. Paradoxically, the 'personological' commitment of the original formulation can assist in the theoretical work needed to reconfigure the ideas in the global domain. It serves as a reminder that the mere transposition of the original formulation from the domain of persons, to states thought of as kinds of person, is entirely inadequate, not least by its violation of the ontology of the original. Also, to focus on consequences, such applications may be said to do no more than consolidate the inadequate state-as-individual formulation. The theoretical work is more demanding. So far as Hohfeld's contribution is concerned, as will be discussed further below, a direct transposition of his scheme from the context of individual rights-holding persons to the context of individual rights-holding states would simply reinforce the bilateralist orthodoxy as cogently expressed by Roberto Ago, in his earlier writings (Aust 2011: 91).

As Aust also discusses, the question of state complicity intersects with interrelated questions of the completeness of international law as a regulatory system, and of the freedom of states to act independently as a default whenever positive and relevant regulation is absent. The latter question or problematic is often tagged by the name of the Permanent Court's decision in 1927 on the *Lotus* incident. The *Lotus* dispute arose when a collision on the high seas between the French ship *Lotus* and the Turkish ship *Boz-Kourt* gave rise to fatalities from the crew and passengers of the latter. Once arrived in Istanbul, Turkish authorities sought to prosecute the naval officer of the *Lotus*, a French national, whom they considered to have been responsible for the fatalities. Criminal jurisdiction was disputed by the French government which argued the case for jurisdiction based on nationality of the accused person in such circumstances. A customary basis was claimed for this practice. On that occasion the Permanent Court, direct antecedent tribunal to the International Court of Justice [ICJ], found there were no grounds on which to discern such a customary rule. It was stated that international law does not provide default obligations so far as the conduct of states is concerned: obligations are to be found in positive international law, including customary as well as conventional (treaty-based) variants among others, or nowhere.

It is unlikely that the Permanent Court intended its decision on the facts of this dispute to be interpreted as providing states *carte blanche* to pursue independent policy (Aust 2011: 69). Further, an early decision of the ICJ in 1951 gave a significantly different expression to the issue (Aust 2011: 67). More to the point perhaps, as Aust describes, the so-called *Lotus* principle, the principle of an inherent freedom of action for states, would not make sense as a statement of international law even if it makes theoretical sense as a formulation in political theory. It comes down to a matter of jurisdiction. International litigation, at the Permanent Court, was a process that defined the dispute as well as, and as an essential step toward, attempting to resolve it. There were always other options for the parties involved. The issue between Turkey and France could have been addressed by diplomatic communication behind the scenes, like the *Caroline* incident of a century earlier. Diplomatic exchanges between US and GB around the destruction of the *Caroline* gave rise to formulations on the criteria for international use of force even more important than the ideological principles that seemed to be endorsed by *Lotus*. In some respects the destruction of the US-owned ship *Caroline* by British naval forces was a more serious incident in terms of the deliberate application of military force: in effect an act of war against a neutral neighbour of a troublesome colony, Canada. At the other extreme, of course, Turkey and France could have gone to war over the *Boz-Kourt*. When a dispute is treated as a dispute between states, as this was, then it is defined as a clash between the rights, obligations or interests of the parties. No clash, no dispute. An intrinsic license for untrammelled action is by definition unregulated and unconstrained. For the Permanent Court or the ICJ to purport to identify or endorse such a phenomenon would be simply beyond its jurisdiction.

It is important to clarify here that liberties or privileges in Hohfeldian terms, that is to say as correlated with Hohfeldian 'no-rights' in others, may of course be matter for such a tribunal. They are among the jural relationships that may be in conflict in a dispute. They might even correspond in some limited degree with the liberal freedoms referenced by the *Lotus* principle. Now it may turn out on the facts, and according to the decision-makers on the bench on the day, that one particular jural relationship is decisive. This might be a privilege. But if so, it will be a privilege that is such by reason of its structural relationships in the jural network within which the parties are located. Radical political freedom of conduct, of the kind sometimes claimed by superpowers, is by definition unilateral and unregulated other than by the subjective will of the sovereign: in other words, not regulated at all but merely whimsical. Political theorists of earlier centuries would have said 'tyrannical'. The Hohfeldian formulation employed here needs to be made good by further discussion, but it is important to indicate at this point that the *Lotus* principle as usually glossed is an ideological or political principle at best, not a principle of international law. James Crawford is dismissive of the orthodox invocation of the *Lotus* decision; he refers to 'that imagined *Lotus* land in which the State is free of all law' (Crawford 2007: 400).

As Koskenniemi has observed in this connection, 'there is no essential limit for … a reading of international law as a set of wide-ranging authorizations for the use of power and privilege' (Koskenniemi 2005a: 614). In Aust's words,

In these situations of conflict of interests, the *Lotus* principle does not work. Bilateralism defeats itself: the question remains whose sovereignty is to gain the upper hand. (Aust 2011: 66)

It is somewhat like the *Monty Python* 'argument' sketch. An interchange of sheer repudiation and denial ('No it isn't' ... 'Yes it is') is qualitatively different from a structured dialogue in which opposing points of view are set out, with both parties obeying some shared regulatory practices. A community of interpretation is being manifested and called upon. Consistent with this interpretation of the outcome of the *Lotus* dispute, it should be observed that international jurists of the between-wars period were actively engaged with the question of interdependence of states, and of an 'international community' (Aust 2011: 75). Although regionalism in international law is not entirely a new phenomenon (Obregón 2006: 263), the emergence of regional polities that are not empires has recently given rise to tangible manifestations of interdependence. Thus the supranational entity that is now 'Europe' has in some respects developed a federal style for the administration of international agreements among its members. It is of course at the same time one facet of the diverse phenomenon known as 'fragmentation' in international law by which regimes, levels and regional structures all multiply and appear to race apart from each other as if in a kind of jurisdictional Big Bang. This multidimensional plurality in international law, which at the same time indicates the richness of the concept of state complicity, is a reminder of the ubiquity of the collective. The notion of complicity facilitates both analysis and intervention. It is engaged with the nuts and bolts of international law.

Here it is important to consider the matter of 'subjectivity'. Aust suggests that

it is ... possible for international practice to ... develop the rule [against complicity] further in the direction of a more objective form of responsibility for complicity. Arguably, such a more objective form of responsibility would presuppose progress on the institutional side of the law as well. (Aust 2011: 427)

However, Aust argues, 'the current state of the law requires the finding of a subjective element on the part of the complicit State, i.e., its intent'. The challenge here is to establish some purchase for 'intent' within the language of complicity, without falling back on orthodox concepts of the 'will' of states.

Koskenniemi has commented that 'even non-intervention is intervention – namely intervention on the side of the *status quo*' (Koskenniemi 2005a: 614). As the Bolsheviks used to remark, 'if you are not for us you are against us'. Omission is commission, and omission can amount to complicity. It would do no service to Aust's project to over-extend the formula. Its precision is correlated with its conceptual circumscription. But it can certainly be said that the language of complicity opens up the plurality of the role of the state, a plurality which is an essential dimension of its collective character. For the relationship of a state to its citizens is not the only, and perhaps not the most important of its collective characteristics or roles. Another is the plurality of its loci within networks of legal relationship. If there is any conceptual value in the notion of legal personality for states at the international level, then that personality has to be seen as multiple – and not in the least pathological. In the words of *Yes, Minister* it is 'a question of hats'. To understand the state as a collective is to recognize the displacement of its functioning.

As noted above, a bilateralist understanding of international law has been shown by Simma in particular to be profoundly inadequate to the explanatory task. International law does not, at a useful level of analysis, consist of a universe of dyadic relationships between self-contained states. Issues such as the effects of climate change, and other environmental concerns, are good examples (Quirico 2012). And yet many relationships between states are indeed reciprocal, and are structured as such (Paulus 2011). The notion of a community interest calls for greater articulation. In order to achieve this, the conceptual framework of the traditional bilateral approach needs to be dismantled in an even more comprehensive manner than indicated by Simma. Aust's work is a major contribution to this program because it demonstrates that community can be articulated with precision in the context of state conduct. Clearly, then, the concept of a community of states, a collectivity of states, is workable. Not only is it consistent with the current understanding of international wrongful acts and their consequences, as laid out in the *Articles on State Responsibility* (Crawford 2002), it also contributes to a deepening of the understanding of that regime. This does not in any way presuppose that the constituent states are thought of in traditional ways. In other words one possible interpretation of the community of states, engaging in such diverse conduct as complicity, competition, domination, hegemony and so on, is as a collective of collectives, a community of communities. Nor should this vision be thought of as a neat hierarchy of nested entities, of 'big fleas having little fleas'. It is important to stress that the instability of the state must be in some sense captured within the explanatory framework. The domain of complicity and of its cognates is among other things a pointer to the ways in which collectivity may be articulated.

Consent, Custom and the State: Why States Are Not Like Persons

The functioning or effectiveness of a state is often expressed in terms of 'consent'. Consent is said to represent the expression of the sovereign will of a state, of its sovereign or of its people. In Hohfeldian terms consent may be thought to be some variety of power, by the deployment of which (including by its withdrawal) international legal relationships may be altered. The orthodox understanding of international law is consistent with a generic notion of will and thus the 'consent' of states as a conceptual foundation. Reference to 'the will of states' is a commonplace especially in accounts of convention-based (treaty-based) international law. The 'consent theory' itself supposedly underpins a 'positivist' view of international law (Capps 2004: 16). As Capps has pithily expressed this view, state consent is treated as generating 'law-creating fact' (2004: 16). Positivism in international law 'has often been equated with a rather crude empiricism' manifesting no attempt at serious engagement with normativity (2004: 14). Positivism need not be crude; Besson frames her conceptual project in terms of a positivist (and democratic) basis for international law (Besson 2010: 166) and, more broadly, Kramer (1999) has demonstrated the relevance and cohesion of the legal positivism approach.

It is however widely recognized that 'consent' is conceptually problematic as an explanation in international law. The collection on the philosophy of international law edited by Besson and Tasioulas illustrates this, although it also includes some attempts to salvage the concept. For example Pettit argues that consent has no explanatory power in relation to the legitimacy of states (Pettit 2010: 144). The social contract tradition in political theory (Gilbert 2006: 55), to the extent that it relies on (and in effect provides a definition for) consent, has proved inadequate. Raz concurs: consent provides no general basis for understanding law's authority (Lefkowitz 2010: 192). Besson, in seeking an adequately contemporary and democratic account of the sources of international law, makes somewhat the same point (Besson 2010: 175). Elsewhere, Allen Buchanan describes why it is implausible to place much weight on 'state consent' (2010: 307). He is critical of the proposal that consent is some 'super-norm' or constitutional principle. For Buchanan state consent is neither necessary nor sufficient for system legitimacy (Buchanan 2004: 307).

Treaty-based forms of international law are the most susceptible to description in terms of consent. This would apply for example to states parties to the compulsory jurisdiction regime at the ICJ, or of course to membership of the United Nations as a whole. Consent as a model is not exhausted by its seemingly more express forms as in conventional agreements between nations. Customary International Law [CIL] as currently understood would also seem to involve consent in significant ways. It is of the essence of CIL that it be held to bind a 'non-consenting' state just as much as a 'consenting' one, so long as the existence of the relevant custom can be shown to the satisfaction of the tribunal. But a constructive kind of consent seems to be part of the rationale. The customary practice itself is generated by the conduct of those states that observe it, by their exhibiting the relevant actions or prohibitions and by treating their observance as legally required. The latter criterion, the *opinio juris sive necessitatis*, is consent by another name; it represents a subjective, voluntarist assent, a manifestation of the will of the sovereign. The recognized 'loopholes' in the effectiveness of this form of law also point to a consent-based rationale. The 'persistent objector' under CIL – the state whose dogged protestation may suffice, in theory, to immunize it from the reign of an otherwise non-negotiable custom – is a patently will-ful actor (Baker 2010; Lepard 2010: 119, 234). Similarities with conventional international law in terms of a common rationale of 'consent' are also indicated by the supposed customary origin of numerous conventions (whereby a treaty is said to codify a custom). Also, the argument that international conventions are themselves reliant for their reciprocally binding quality on an underlying and prior understanding of a customary character – *pacta sunt servanda* – might seem to suggest that customary and conventional forms of international law are indeed conceptually linked in terms of a consent model (Morss 2008; Tasioulas 2010: 114).

It is important to note that circumscribed or modified senses of consent or will in states are sometimes defended. Lefkowitz warns against too quick a dismissal of consent as an account of legitimacy (Lefkowitz 2010: 193). Having indicated that consent is often rejected on the basis that states rarely give consent in a 'free and informed' (thus a truly voluntary) manner, Lefkowitz proposes a qualified form of consent that in his view survives that critique. For Lefkowitz, state consent sometimes may indeed be voluntary. Lefkowitz thus endorses a somewhat 'anthropomorphic' and subjectivist account of states. Further, and consistently with that position, states are said to be capable of belief: thus state practice is said to be a route to, or evidence of, a shared belief. State practice can contribute to 'the communication necessary to create a shared belief' in the normativity of a norm. As Lefkowitz notes (2010: 201), the writings of 'collectivists' in political theory on such notions as 'plural intention, group belief, joint commitment' are of relevance here (see Fox 2007: 138; Sanchez Brigido 2009). Lefkowitz's position converges with that of Buchanan (2010: 87) for whom, as previously noted, states can sometimes be moral agents (agents capable of moral reasoning). Consent and its cognates are not unsophisticated concepts, and Lefkowitz's warning about too broad and hasty a dismissal should be heeded; however it remains clear that consent on the part of states is a very tricky notion (Klabbers 2002: 64).

As observed above there is a close connection between complicity and the 'international rule of law' (Aust 2011: 95). In a discussion on the related notion of 'rule of international law' Waldron compares the nature and function of the rule of law in the municipal and in the international settings. In the municipal setting, Waldron takes a strong liberal position on the freedom of the individual person under law. Except where constrained by properly enacted (and properly promulgated) law, there is a valid case to be made that the citizen may exercise unlimited freedom (Waldron 2006: 17). She has a legitimate interest in doing so and the rule of law must be consistent with that. In contrast the municipal government has no such residual or immanent legitimate interest. There is no freedom residue for the state, Waldron argues. It is possible that the contrast is too sharply drawn and that the radical liberal viewpoint on individual liberty may not be essential to the argument. But Waldron's point is to use the dichotomy in order to articulate the question of rule of law at the international level. For a traditional view might align the state, as an international legal subject, with the individual citizen in the municipality and hence might advocate a corresponding role for freedom under the rule of law. If this were a valid line of reasoning, then the sovereignty of independent states would be built upon this inherent and radical freedom which an international rule of law should complement but not undermine. In other words, a *Lotus*-style interpretation would emerge. Waldron roundly rejects this view:

> This way of looking at international law is a mistake and the analogy on which it is based is misconceived. In fact, the state is quite unlike an individual [person];

certainly it is quite unlike an individual when it comes to the value of its freedom of action. (Waldron 2006: 21)

In this important statement Waldron continues as follows:

> [A] state's sovereignty is an artificial construct, not something whose value is to be assumed as a first principle of normative analysis … In its international aspect, the sovereignty and sovereign freedom of the individual state is … an artefact of international law. What its sovereignty is and what it amounts to is not given as a matter of the intrinsic value of its individuality, but determined by the rules of the international order.

As Waldron notes this argument is supported by Kelsen's analysis of the state from a municipal perspective, and by Hart's observations on the nature of sovereignty in international states. It is also consistent with Kelsen's approach to international law. According to Covell, as we have seen, it can even be discerned in Hobbes.

Thus for Waldron it is from within its role (or rather roles) within a network of regulation that the international state derives any 'respect' that may be due. Such respect would include the kind of expectations over independence, freedom from outside 'interference' and so on, that are usually connoted by the term state sovereignty. Again Waldron's words can hardly be bettered: the state is a 'law-constituted and law-governed entity. It is not to be regarded in the light of an anarchic individual, dragged kicking and screaming under the umbrella of law for the first time by some sort of international social contract' (Waldron 2006: 21). The image of a set of individuals existing in a pre-societal state of nature has been applied to the international realm since the time of Rousseau and Kant if not before, as discussed in Chapter 2. As Waldron observes, this application of social contract theory to the international sphere was roundly rejected by Kant.

Relatedly Waldron rejects the argument for the equality of sovereign states based on the state of nature argument. For Waldron then the notion of inherent rights to freedom in a state, that is to say some residue of absolute autonomy vis-à-vis the international order, is a nonsense. Borrowing from Bentham one might want to say, 'nonsense upon exceptionally long stilts'. For Waldron, '[i]n the international realm, the state remains a creature of law, a tissue of legality that is imbued with the idea of law' (Waldron 2006: 23). Therefore the relationship to law of the state in its international context is very much like that of the state in its municipal setting. There is no sequestered space for a personal freedom to inhabit. Like any machine, one might say, however similar in some respects its functioning to the functioning of a person, it remains a machine. While states are properly said to be subjects of international law they are not subjects in the way in which individual citizens are subjects of municipal law (2006: 23). They are also 'much more like legislators than most legal subjects'. Moreover the state is also 'an *official* of international law'.

The form of Waldron's argument is thus to set up a hard and fast boundary between individual human persons on the one hand, and states on the other. The distinction is, so to speak, ontological: these are just different kinds of thing and it would be a category mistake, at least, to blur those boundaries. One way of paraphrasing this in the context of the theory of international law would of course be to suggest that international law is all about the needs and rights of individual persons as such (as in the notion of universal human rights) and any other levels of organization such as governments, states and so on are merely so many means to the end of delivering services and protecting human dignity thus understood. As Waldron notes, authority for this view can be found in Kant. What is important here is the message that the state is conceptually cut down to size; the state as sovereign subject, issuer of commands, is shown to lack legitimacy. It has been suggested by David Kennedy that states are merely 'disaggregated social functions in a broad civil society' (Kritsiotis 2004: 47). In a similar vein Koskenniemi has pointed out that 'it is not evident why liberals [such as Hart and Rawls] should be entitled to treat such collective entities as States as simply so many individuals' (2005a: 90).

The familiar clothes of the state are, so to speak, no more substantial than the new clothes of the Emperor. Such sceptical standpoints on statehood are not universal among the critical community however. Treating the state as a kind of individual retains its intellectual attractions. Thus Beard and Noll (2009: 469) seek to explain state recognition in terms of 'an ethical turn to the self performed by the agent seeking recognition'. Beard and Noll suggest that the standard options for understanding state recognition 'are incapable of capturing the interplay between the agent seeking recognition and the interlocutor recognising her'. This line of reasoning is sophisticated, and is consistent with the Hegelian traditions on which these authors draw. Yet the assertion of subjectivity of this kind on the part of the state – with its connotations of will, sovereignty, autonomy – seems at best anachronistic. Appealing to such questionable formulations in the context of refugee law, as these authors do, is problematic. It is hoped that the sceptical reframing of statehood facilitated by the shift to a collectivist viewpoint reduces the likelihood of such difficulties. But dissolving the system of states into a matrix of collectives gives rise to questions about self-determination. These questions are addressed in the next chapter.

Chapter 6
From Peoples to People?
Self-determination, Identity, Territory

Compromises of Place

In some ways self-determination is the international law of collectives *par excellence*. This chapter explores the implications of the collectivist orientation for understanding the interrelated topics of self-determination, cultural rights and the rights of minorities and the question of indigenous peoples. These are topics where international law already takes an approach that could surely be said to be collective. It is therefore important to examine what contribution if any is made by the reorientation to the discipline suggested in previous chapters. A collectivist emphasis in international law may well highlight such processes, and urge their centrality for the discipline, but it should aim higher than this. What does it add that is new or that challenges current orthodoxy?

To anticipate, what will be argued is that the collectivist approach to international legal theory helps to clarify and to articulate certain approaches to self-determination and to the rights of minorities that are already being explored within the wider literature. These newer approaches are innovatory in striving to think beyond identity as the central characteristic of such issues. In the words of Sergei Prozorov, they are moving away from a commitment to 'identitarian pluralism' (Prozorov 2009: 215). There is therefore a need to pay attention to the variety of perspectives on these issues that are currently available in the literature of international law and of cognate disciplines, since debate on these topics has been lively and productive in recent times. As against the more orthodox essentialist or identity-based approaches, these alternative approaches cluster around such ideas as function, fluidity, hybridization, construction and denizenship. Pressing these approaches brings to the foreground some significant challenges for international law but also suggests some lines of possible theoretical development. Identity has often been seen as the heart of any collective analysis or collective experience in the context of international law and international relations. The 'law of people' might readily be articulated as a genre of identity politics. As discussed in Chapter 4, this would be a mistake. It is precisely in offering alternatives to international law as politics of identity that the collectivist project is innovatory. But at the same time the political dimensions that the vocabulary of identity seeks to capture need to be addressed. This is cosmopolitanism, to which we return at the end of the book.

In contemporary international law, the concept of the will of a people finds its most significant expression in the notion of self-determination. The International

Court of Justice [ICJ] has considered matters relating to self-determination in two recent Advisory Opinions. In 2004 it strongly affirmed self-determination on behalf of Palestinians in territory affected by the Israeli Government's security barrier. In 2010 it much more cautiously affirmed that the leaders of Kosovo had not breached international law in issuing their unilateral declaration of independence (Aust 2012). A definition of the principle of self-determination offered by the ICJ in the *Western Sahara* Advisory Opinion of 1975 provides that self-determination consists in 'the need to pay regard to the freely expressed will of peoples' (para 59). Much may depend on what sense is made of, and what weight is placed on, the word 'self'. An intellectual tradition goes back at least to Rousseau according to which national law may be said to represent 'the general will' (Oklopcic 2009: 684). 'Identity' is a closely related concept. Moltchanova's sophisticated approach to self-determination as a matter of international morality may be said to be focused on group identity (Moltchanova 2009: 30). In contemporary legal theory, as already noted, Waldron's approach to self-determination confronts the identity-based conception of self-determination as embodying an impoverished and dangerous 'identity politics' (2010: 408). It is not of course that the *de facto* division of the earth's liveable surface into a particular pattern of territories is itself unproblematic, nor that the connections between particular groups or sets of individual inhabitants, and particular 'soils', are unproblematic. Within international law, the doctrine of *uti possidetis juris* brings together issues of territory, colonial and post-colonial governance, and self-determination, in a problematic mix (Lalonde 2002; Oklopcic 2009: 679).

Any discussion on the international law of self-determination needs to grapple with the concept of a 'people'. As noted in an earlier chapter, my proposal is that the term 'people' (in the 'singularist' sense of 'one people, two or more peoples') is frequently used in imprecise ways. In some ways it thereby resembles terms such as 'nation state' and in law more widely, terms like 'duty of care' and 'informed consent'. These are terms that give the appearance of technical precision while generally speaking lacking it. It is not clear whether the term 'nation state' can be defined with sufficient precision to be useful but it is unusual to encounter it, in writings on international law or international relations, conveying anything beyond the sense carried by the word 'state' or perhaps the phrase 'modern state'. 'Duty of care' is a term of art within the law of torts, and the 'consent' part of 'informed consent' can also be defined with some degree of precision in its proper sphere. This is not to digress as much as may appear. The 'Responsibility to Protect' is conceptually related to the tortious notion of the 'duty of care'. 'Informed consent' is a term most encountered in the context of individual autonomy but as we have seen, consent is a central term in public international law and these usages while dissimilar in application are closely related in conceptual ways. Of course conversational levels of precision are often quite adequate, but there are many occasions when the conversational standard is just not high enough. Unfortunately use of the term 'peoples' in international law rarely meets that precision requirement of going beyond the conversational. Examples may be drawn from the legal response to the Kosovo Declaration (Aust 2012).

Who Lives in Kosovo?

Like all disputed questions of self-determination, the proclaimed independence of Kosovo from Serbia, itself the rump of a former Socialist entity of Yugoslavia, involves claims about history as well as geography. As Noel Malcolm observes, it has proved too tempting for those way beyond the region to resist thinking of the disputes in the Balkans as 'the bubbling up of obscure but virulent ethnic hatreds among the local populations' (Malcolm, 1998: xxvii). Yet ancestors of the Albanians and of the Serbs fought side by side in the famous battle of Kosovo in 1389 – perhaps even side by side on both sides of that battle. At times of foreign invasion in later centuries, the local populations fought together (1998: xxix). As elsewhere, it took the efforts of political leaders to transform cultural distinctions into racial hatred. For 'between low-level prejudices on the one hand and military conflict, concentration camps and mass murder on the other, there lies a long road' (Malcolm 1998: xxviii).

Famously, the International Court's Advisory Opinion on the Kosovo Unilateral Declaration of Independence [UDI] of 2008, was *not* about self-determination. The Court has been criticized for adopting an extremely narrow stance on the issues raised by the Kosovo UDI, an event which on its face generated both legal and political claims relating to self-determination. Yet in the circumstances this seems to have been the correct approach at least in the Churchillian sense of being the least worst. The Court thus limited its discussion to the question of whether the UDI *per se* had breached international law. On this point, both particular facts and general principles were salient. As to the latter, no international law was breached by a statement of this kind being made by a representative assembly of the kind that made it. As to the former, some fine distinctions were made concerning the status and identity of the authors of the Declaration. This was important because Kosovo was already the scene of direct United Nations intervention, with which the Declaration was in many ways inconsistent. UN governance structures and related processes for representative participation precluded certain officials from unilaterally compromising that international agenda, as UDI declared by those officials would have done. The Court found that the authors of the Declaration were in fact representatives of the local population, not officials under the provisional UN-backed governance arrangements as such. Here I wish to address some conceptual matters raised by Judge Cançado Trindade in a lengthy Separate Opinion.

Cançado Trindade presents his Opinion as providing an independent rationale in support of the majority position (*viz* that the Kosovo UDI was not in breach of international law). Cançado Trindade emphasizes the centrality of 'the *conditions of living of the "people" or the "population"*' (para 65). Cançado Trindade's point is to de-emphasize considerations of territory as such, and questions of territorial sovereignty, in favour of a focus on the inhabitants of the territory in dispute. Cançado Trindade refers to 'the people-centred outlook in contemporary international law' which focuses on the 'most precious' constitutive element of statehood – 'the "population" or the "people"'. He attempts to be more precise, acknowledging that debate has been inconclusive on the conceptualization of 'people' in this sense. Cançado Trindade refers to 'the difficulties of international legal thinking to arrive at a universally-accepted definition of what a "people" means' (para 170). Despite Cançado Trindade's wariness of the term 'peoples', he does not seek to distinguish with any precision between 'peoples' and 'populations'. Thus he observes that 'juridical institutions [such as mandates and trust territories] ... were conceived and established ... to address, and respond to, the needs (including of protection) and aspirations of *peoples*, of human beings' (para 65). The 'common denominator' of characterizations of these institutions is for Cançado Trindade, 'the basic considerations of humanity'.

Cançado Trindade uses the term 'peoples' in the context of earlier centuries (specifically the 1500s) in which context it seems somewhat anachronistic. Thus '[p]eoples assumed a central position in the early days of the emergence of the *droit des gens*' (para 71). As noted earlier, Charles Taylor has emphasized the vicissitudes of the term 'the people' across history: one cannot so blithely read a twenty-first century sensitivity into the writings of the sixteenth century. People, peoples and populations are for Cançado Trindade all ways of talking about the same thing, so to speak; thus '[w]hat has happened in Kosovo is that the victimized "people" or "population" has sought independence' (para 176). It is probably fair to say that Cançado Trindade's position is a variant of the Lauterpachtian monism of international law according to which all international law is directly or indirectly concerned with the rights of individual persons. As Cançado Trindade remarks later,

> [t]he conception of fundamental and inalienable human rights is deeply-engraved in the universal juridical conscience; in spite of variations in their enunciation or formulation, their conception marks presence in all cultures, and in the history of human thinking of all peoples. (para 199)

The term 'peoples' does not add precision to the discussion here. If there is fog in the Peace Palace, visibility is affected across the world of international law.

It is noteworthy that in the General Assembly Resolution, as well as discussing populations in terms of ethnicity, reference is made to 'the people *in* Kosovo' (para 113; emphasis added). Thus the persecution of 'ethnic Albanians in Kosovo' by Yugoslav state officials and military is discussed as well as frequent instances of persecution 'of ethnic Serb, Roma and other minorities of Kosovo by ethnic Albanian extremists' (para 111). Without suggesting that the definitions of 'ethnic Albanians' or 'ethnic Serb' or 'Roma' are themselves unproblematic, the absence of reference to 'the people of Kosovo' is to be noted. When push quite literally comes to shove, reference to 'the people' seems not to work. This is despite the fact that before the break-up of the former Yugoslavia, Kosovo had the status of an autonomous province with something close to the (of course limited) autonomy of the Republics such as Croatia and Slovenia (para 43). Yet when the ICJ gave its Opinion on the Kosovo UDI, it referred to 'representatives of the people of Kosovo' (para 109).

Self-determination in International Law

Self-determination is both an old and a new idea. As a defined right or principle in international law it is perhaps less than 100 years old, but as a political principle it has been defined and understood in a variety of ways since the end of the eighteenth century when the French and American Revolutions brought it to prominence (Crawford 2006: 115; Panayi 1999: 100). Closely related concepts may also of course be traced back to the political theorists of the seventeenth century if not earlier. John Locke's statement on the collective rights of 'Grecian Christians' is a good example. Writing in 1690, Locke argued that 'Grecian [Orthodox] christians, descendants of the ancient possessors of that country, may justly cast off the Turkish yoke, which they have so long groaned under, whenever they have an opportunity' (Bass 2008: 55). One hundred and thirty years later, in the decades after the fall of Napoleon, British foreign minister Castlereagh used the same form of words. He asked '[o]ught the Turkish yoke to be for ever rivetted upon the necks of their suffering and Christian subjects ...?' (Bass 2008: 63). Castelreagh steadfastly opposed intervention on behalf of foreigners however much they might be oppressed, which makes his statement especially noteworthy.

Of course, a key word in both Locke's and Castlereagh's impassioned remarks was 'Christian' since the sympathy was with co-religionists rather than with a foreign nation as such. The genealogy of self-determination as a concept in Western thought has a great deal to do with the story of Christianity and, more generally, with Judaism. The collective entitlements and collective responsibilities of God's chosen people were precisely those of a nation under a foreign yoke: 'When Israel was in Egypt's land'. The messianic aspect of self-determination has been of long standing. In many ways it can be thought of as emblematic of messianism in international law as a discipline (Grbich 2006). It should also be observed that more than one religious tradition includes strands that could be described as charitable or even as cosmopolitan, in reaching out beyond co-religionists. The point was well made in 1696 by William Wake, chaplain to Britain's William III: 'True religion desires the welfare and happiness of those who are at the greatest distance from its own persuasion' (Pincus 2009: 457).

Alongside the sense of a right of nations not to be oppressed by tyrannical foreign regimes, especially those of a heathen disposition, the modern sense of 'a people' as a political entity was emerging. The Declaration of Independence of the United States of America of 1776 was made 'in the Name, and by Authority of the good People of these Colonies'. It stated that from time to time it becomes 'necessary for one People to dissolve the Political Bands which have connected them with another'. This usage of the term people in the singular, meaning something like 'nation' but with a much stronger emphasis on popular or even democratic processes and on 'the Consent of the Governed', was commonplace by the middle of the next century. Liberal theorist John Stuart Mill, writing in 1859, was sympathetic to intervention on behalf of 'a people in arms for liberty'. Mill referred to the events of the revolutionary year of 1848 when Hungarians collectively attempted to assert independence from the political domination of the Austrian Empire (Bass 2008: 355). It is important to note also that Mill's enthusiasm for self-determination (and hence for a kind of equality between nations or peoples) did not extend to 'barbarians', so that the proper rules and customs applicable between civilized nations were not relevant to dealings between the latter and the barbarians (Mégret 2006: 279; Mill 1974: 69).

At the time Mill was writing, British authorities were contesting for territorial control in Southern Africa. From the sixteenth century onwards, the area now known as South Africa had been extensively settled by a farmer population ('Boers') of Dutch descent. The Boers had conquered indigenous people such as the Zulu, and the British initially tolerated that state of affairs: they 'saw no reason to play Pharaoh to the Boers' Israelites' as a historian has quaintly expressed it (Van Hartesveldt 2000: 3). During the South African War of the turn of the century, settlers of Dutch descent were rounded up in *laagers* by the British military headed by General Kitchener. This was an early, and perhaps the first, form of concentration camp technology. A visitor queried, 'Since Old Testament days, was ever a whole nation carried captive?' Adumbrating attempted resettlements in later decades, General Kitchener proposed the large-scale resettlement of these civilians to South America in order to make space for British arrivals (Everdell 1997: 121). The 'Boers' probably thought of themselves collectively in national terms. As with the emerging USA in the 1770s, indigenous populations were a marginal note to such settler-based national or 'people-hood' identities. In 1776 the Declaration of Independence had referred to 'the Inhabitants of our Frontiers, the merciless Indian Savages, whose known Rule of Warfare, is an undistinguished Destruction, of all Ages, Sexes and Conditions'. This description was given in the context of listing King George's delinquencies (which included fostering the depradations of these savages), that is to say in building the case for the legitimacy of the secession. The strong language used was presumably influenced by that context. But the Declaration was unambiguously made on behalf of the settler society. In South Africa, the British built camps for 'Kaffirs' as well as for the Dutch settler population. Self-determination was not yet understood as incompatible with the colonial program.

Self-determination was widely referred to as a general principle at the time of the break-up of the Ottoman Empire after World War I and in the inter-war years. It was influential on League of Nations protection regimes over minorities from the former German, Austro-Hungarian and Ottoman empires (Morgan 2011: 93). This is not to say that it was treated as a rule or principle that would overrule other considerations in international law (Cassese 1995: 27). Self-determination is not mentioned as such in the Covenant of the League of Nations. It was not until the founding of the United Nations that the term came to be used in international agreements such as the Charter itself. While absent from the Universal Declaration of Human Rights of 1948, a right of self-determination (of 'all peoples') is affirmed in Common Article 1 of the two Covenants that were derived from the UDHR in the 1960s. It can now be said that the concepts of self-determination and of a people are reciprocally defined in international law. As Ralph Wilde notes, '[i]n the parlance of the law on self-determination, a particular population grouping enjoying an "external" self-determination entitlement is sometimes referred to as a "people" and its territory a "self-determination unit"' (Wilde 2008: 155). It remains unclear how much weight can be placed on self-determination, and what consequences are to be anticipated from its recognition, against the often competing interests of the integrity of existing state territories. This tension between the aspiration to support self-determination and the imperative of maintaining peace was already clearly evident at the time of the creation of the UN and is manifested in the Charter.

Theories of Self-determination: Buchanan, Young, Waldron

It is clear that a working account of self-determination has a place in contemporary international law. Yet conceptual analysis seems to have lagged behind pragmatic and reactive developments. While self-determination in practice is inevitably a law of collectives, there seems no coherent articulation of this. In this section attention turns to contributions from contemporary legal and political philosophy.

In contemporary debate on self-determination, across a range of overlapping disciplines, a broad orthodoxy can be identified, within which there are in turn many variants. Following Waldron I will label this broad orthodoxy the 'identity-based' approach. This approach focuses on shared identity as a stable characteristic of a well-defined population. For Waldron the alternative conception of self-determination would not focus on identity. 'Waldron's warning' is precisely a warning about identity politics. Rather, an alternative scheme would focus on functional and practical matters, in particular the characteristics and democratic needs of the inhabitants of a territory, whoever they happen to be. Waldron's 'territorial self-determination' is described and evaluated further below. The negative moment of Waldron's argument – the critique of the identity-based approach – is adopted in order to discuss some further aspects of the conventional view.

An important question to be considered is the location on Waldron's scheme of other influential accounts of self-determination. These include the proposals of Allen Buchanan from philosophy and of Iris Marion Young from political science. Is Buchanan's approach, or Young's approach, 'conventional' in the sense of being identity-based? This enquiry will make it possible to evaluate these alternative schemes in a manner that focuses attention on the role of identity and that therefore maintains attention to Waldron's important questions.

More should first be said on the identity-based approach. It is a broad church. One could locate a group of simplistic, 'essentialist' perspectives on self-determination as fitting within the identity-based approach. This is the kind of position Iris Marion Young criticized in observing that 'peoples are not natural kinds, clearly identifiable and distinguishable by a set of essential attributes' (Young 2007: 41). In turn an essentialist grouping could be said to include expressly racist varieties. Some forms of racism might thus assert that all the people of the world naturally and biologically fall into genetic groupings, bloodlines that separate every tribe, clan or nation from every other ethnic unit. Such a framework could be taken as the explanatory basis for a kind of self-determination theory; 'England for the English' and so forth. Here racism and nationalism intersect, and to put it generously, as Waldron observes, the identity-based approach 'has to constantly battle [the] tendency ... [of the] pull towards outcomes that might only be achieved by unacceptable methods' (Waldron 2010: 413).

Racism and nationalism also intersect with indigeneity, raising further complexities. For example, the political domination of others by an indigenous population that is a numerical minority within an independent state, as has been the case in Fiji, illustrates the inadequacies of current articulations of 'self-determination'. But some non-racist formulations might converge on the view that the natural way of things, the prototype or default position perhaps, comprises separable populations which reside in correspondingly separate physical spaces. This is the view critically described by Young in this way:

> A self-determining people dwells together in a relatively large territory in which only members of their group reside, and this homogenous territory is contiguous and bounded. (Young 2007: 58)

This essentialist vision can take the 'thin' form of a working model of convenience, a deliberately simplified first approximation that is adopted in the interests of theorization of other matters or of articulating practical policy in a conceptually messy world. John Rawls' version of this in *The Law of Peoples*, described previously, might generously be thought of as an example of this. However the liberal tradition in political thought has not, in general, adequately addressed the difficult conceptual issue of the role of boundaries of political communities (Waldron 2010: 409), preferring perhaps to take such matters somewhat for granted. It is important to stress that the identity-based approach includes sophisticated versions that avoid many of the deficiencies and objectionable features noted here. However Waldron, Young and other critics are surely correct to point to the inadequacies of any model that places such a premium on homogeneity and on what are in effect cultural readings of nationhood. As Waldron has expressed it, '[w]e need cultural meanings; but we don't need homogenous cultural frameworks ... We need culture, but we don't need cultural integrity' (Waldron 2010: 402). Indeed, as Schwartz notes with reference to Waldron and also to Gerald Postema, 'interpretive disagreement is not a peripheral problem that interferes with or complicates integrity – it is the basis for integrity in the first place' (Schwartz 2011: 525).

The debate here is over the status of cultures as packages of lifestyle, to which individuals commit themselves and with which they form identity-based attachments. The notion of what amounts to the purity of a culture may play a role. As Waldron notes,

> The case for self-determination is predicated on the assumption that the members of an identity-group have an essential investment in the integrity of their culture and that they need empowerment to protect it from being overwhelmed or unduly influenced by other cultures. (Waldron 2010: 405–6)

Self-determination is, in this sense at least, a conservative principle. When the essentialist claim is made in terms of indigeneity and connectedness to land, then a very 'thick' version is of course being deployed. Even if not, self-determination is treated as an outcome or expression of a pre-existing bond, as of kinship writ large. Self-determination becomes somewhat like marriage in the modern Western tradition, that is to say the legalistic and political manifestation and recognition of a pre-existing, affective fact. To look at this another way, self-determination thought of in this orthodox way becomes the legitimate project of any group that properly identifies as such: 'because we are the people of country X, X is rightfully ours to dominate'.

Allen Buchanan's influential approach to the legal philosophy of international law has been introduced in earlier chapters. Buchanan argues for the necessity of a moral theory of the international legal system, a systematic philosophy of international law to be based on a 'Natural Duty of Justice' (Buchanan, 2004: 28). Self-determination is the 'conceptual heart' of such a moral theory of international law. Buchanan considers and rejects two versions of an approach under which self-determination, as connoting a right to secession, is a positive rather than a reactive (remedial) entitlement. These comprise the 'ascriptivist' and the 'plebiscitary' versions of such a 'primary right' approach. The familiar ascriptivist version asserts that such characteristics as nationality or other ethnic distinctness (as in 'peoplehood') in themselves generate a right of secession. Buchanan stresses that it is a mistake to treat self-determination as a direct consequential entitlement based on ascriptive status, as for a 'people' (Buchanan, 2004: 405). '[E]xisting international law contains dangerously ambiguous references to "the right of self-determination of all peoples"' (2004: 333). Quite the reverse should be promulgated: '[I]nternational law should unambiguously repudiate the nationalist principle that all nations (or "peoples") are entitled to their own states' (Buchanan, 2004: 331).

The less well-known, plebiscitary version of the primary right approach is also rejected by Buchanan. This approach asserts that any majoritarian preference for autonomy in a particular territory should be respected by means of independence (Buchanan, 2004: 353). In principle this plebiscitary process need not pay any regard to history, culture, identity, language or ethnicity. Neither prior ascriptive connection among the population nor cultural coherence are required. The plebiscitary viewpoint is a radically democratic, or at least a populist proposal. Common to both the ascriptivist and the plebiscitary viewpoints, which are different in many other ways, is the position that neither injustice nor inadequacy of protection of human rights is required to generate the legitimacy of secession. Such 'remedialist' factors are neither sufficient nor necessary. The legitimacy is called forth either by the inherent characteristics of the community (the ascriptivist version) or by the ballot-box (the plebiscitary version). In either case a strong sense of self-determination is posited, that is to say a sense that connotes independence on a par with pre-existing states: what in international law is usually referred to as 'external' self-determination.

Relationships between self-determination rights and territory are discussed by Buchanan in the context of the (rejected) plebiscitary theory. Buchanan points out (2004: 374) that if taken literally as a license for full secession, the plebiscitary theory would generate catastrophic instability in state boundaries since any ephemeral majority could elect for further secession at any time. The gerrymandering dimension should also be noted: Nine observes that any majoritarian argument is circular since definitions of territory (within which some plebiscite is envisaged) may determine an outcome, at least on a crude analysis (Nine 2012: 47).

On a more principled level Buchanan objects that the plebiscitary theory neglects the whole-state dimension so far as rights to territory are concerned. For Buchanan, the doctrine of popular sovereignty 'which lies at the core of liberal political theory' correctly identifies rights in the territory as being held by 'the people as a whole'. For Buchanan, 'the right of the people as a whole to the whole territory of the state is not unconditional'. Human rights violations may undermine that right. But there is a default presumption of a legitimate state as having a valid claim to its territory. This default presumption is uncontroversial, if only on pragmatic grounds, and is not contested by Waldron or other scholars, but its role in Buchanan's argument needs to be commented on. For while the default entitlement to the prevailing territory of a state is said to be held by 'the people as a whole', Buchanan offers no analysis of what he means by 'the people' or its legitimacy in that context. For Buchanan, full-blown 'external' self-determination – the final step to independence – should be available only when other mechanisms fail. More usually, the principle of self-determination is served by the maximization of intrastate autonomy for vulnerable populations within existing states, that is to say 'arrangements for self-government short of full sovereignty' (Buchanan 2004: 331) in the interests of the protection of human rights. If such arrangements fail as a consequence of state repression then full-on 'external' self-determination through secession may be justified. For example Buchanan proposes that such was the case in Chechnya (2004: 357).

The main reason Buchanan rejects both versions of the primary right argument is its neglect of the responsive or remedial dimension. But he has supplementary reasons. There are he says empirical difficulties with the ascriptivist account, if it is taken to be the claim that national groups have a right to seek statehood on the grounds of cultural cohesion. Buchanan states that such political aspirants as Scottish Nationalists 'are not united by anything that could reasonably be called a distinct Scottish culture'. Nor is nationalism in Northern Ireland 'based on a distinct Catholic or Irish cultural identity' (Buchanan 2004: 381). Buchanan is certainly correct to suggest that neither of these examples manifests the kind of holistic and encompassing, even monolithic forms of shared identity that may be demanded by the ascriptivist model. But Buchanan misfires here. His casual dismissal of cultural dimensions to either Scots or (Northern) Irish nationalism seems uninformed. These movements are in both cases of course conglomerations and alliances, drawing on cultural fragments and traditional life-worlds of various kinds as well as on contemporary socio-political formations. In addition, the Scots and Irish 'questions' overlap with each other in significant ways given the historical connections across the Irish Sea (only rowing distance across at its narrowest points), as well as the shared experience of Westminster rule in recent centuries (Carty 1996). But the larger mistake is that Buchanan differentiates these United Kingdom examples from what would presumably be genuinely encompassing cultural groups. The inadequacies of the cultural-group version of the ascriptivist theory are surely conceptual, as Buchanan himself shows, rather than merely empirical.

In contrast to the rejected 'primary right' notion, for Buchanan 'the central idea is simple':

> Individuals are morally justified in defending themselves against violations of their most basic human rights. When the only alternative to continuing to suffer these injustices is secession, the right of the victims to defend themselves … makes it morally permissible for them to join together to secede. (Buchanan 2004: 354)

Several claims in this admirably straight-talking proposal call for comment. The notion of self-defence for individual persons over human rights violations is hardly 'simple'; there must for example be some nexus with prevailing regimes of criminal law. In any event the move from such an individualistic right, even if granted, to the supposed rights of a collective ('the victims') raises many complex issues. It is also hard to see that secession will ever be 'the only alternative', even if it is the best alternative, to the continuation of suffering. Joining together to secede is a big step from the first premiss, even if that first premiss be accepted. The whole argument (as cited above) might be thought more appropriate for a retrospective justification than as a positive moral argument applicable to future circumstances. Of course, the US Declaration of Independence makes out a very similar argument. It is important to observe that Buchanan is attempting to grapple with the collective aspect of self-determination. He describes a situation in which collective autonomy plays a central role. But his analysis is individualistic: it is based on the moral rights of individual persons. He is not equipped, by his own theoretical apparatus, to deal with questions of collectives (Buchanan 2004: 333).

From political theory, a significant contribution was made to contemporary debate over self-determination by the late Iris Marion Young. Young had explored her own take on 'two concepts of self-determination' some years before Waldron's essay was published (Young 2007: 39). Young's starting-off point was the foregrounding of non-domination, as articulated in the neo-republican theory of Philip Pettit. She thus defined her project as 'a quest for an institutional context of non-domination' (2007: 108). As noted above Young criticized essentialist claims, holding instead that 'the relations among peoples and their degrees of distinctness are […] fluid, relational and dependent on context' (Young 2007: 41). Young sought to refine our conceptions of self-determination so as to align them more closely with aspirations for global justice. Young's approach is influenced by feminist theory and post-colonial theory as well as by the more traditional schools of political theory. As indicated above, Young shares much with Waldron in respect of the more orthodox positions that they both reject. Yet it is not clear if Young avoided the problems of identity-based analysis. Young's approach tests Waldron's dichotomy and his definition of the identity position, and if her work still falls into the latter camp then much is learned about the contribution to the self-determination debate of those wider intellectual movements on which Young has drawn. Alternatives to the identity-based approach to self-determination would then be challenging to a range of disciplines.

Young is cautious about the stronger forms of 'external' self-determination on the basis that such models are committed to outdated conceptions of sovereign independence in the international sphere. With other scholars in the political sciences as well as within international law, Young is sceptical about sovereign independence in an absolute sense: what Young like many others refers to as the 'Westphalian' idea of sovereignty. Her scepticism is both conceptual and pragmatic. From a conceptual standpoint the account of freedom presupposed by the 'splendid isolation' of absolute sovereign independence is faulty. For Young the neo-republican approach of Philip Pettit provides a more appropriate formulation, under which freedom is defined as non-domination rather than as a positive attribute that entirely, and so to speak ontologically, excludes interference from outside. Young is also sceptical about the notion of 'self' in self-determination, cautioning that it must be thought of in terms of a unity achieved and maintained only through deliberation and representation. In Young's words, '[s]uch a discourse of group agency and representation of agency to wider publics need not falsely personify the group or suppress differences among its members'. As Waldron would surely agree, '[t]his capacity for agency is the only secular political meaning that the "self" of collective self-determination can have' (Young 2007: 50). Young's emphasis on 'secular' is a reminder that earlier versions of the collective 'will', especially in Rousseau, were strongly influenced by religious doctrine (Damrosch 2007: 350).

As to pragmatic grounds, Young warns against the political goal of independent statehood, that is to say independence as non-interference. For aspiring groups of indigenous people, for example, Young suggests that a federal model of governance both regionally and globally is preferable to statehood in the pure, absolute sense or even in the watered down sense which we experience in today's globalized world. Relevant models of federated systems of governance include for Young the historical example of the Iroquois nation in North America in the seventeenth and eighteenth centuries. As Young points out this example has indeed played a part in political thinking in the West for some while. John Locke's discussion of the forms of society open to those in a state of nature, and the contributions of his contemporaries to this debate, owed much to reports of sophisticated social organization among these tribal groupings (Young 2007: 20). Clearly the reference to 'merciless Indian Savages' in the United States Declaration of Independence as noted above, was a deliberately provocative one.

Young thus distances herself from the more familiar form of the conventional conceptions of self-determination. One reason is the inadequacy of the assumption of homogeneity in self-determination units. Young stresses the ways in which groups or communities of people with varying collective identities and affiliations find themselves, generally speaking, mixed in among each other. Homogeneous cultural communities are, for Young, at best an ideal type with no practical significance because of rarity; at worst a politically loaded vision closely associated with nationalism and with racism. In many ways this is Waldron's point too: people are mixed together, sharing some affiliations and alliances, differing or clashing on others. The emphasis on 'hybrid democracy', on republicanism and on federalism is in the same ballpark as Waldron. This convergence is reinforced by Young's phraseology of 'being together-in-difference' and 'differential solidarity'. But Young's account retains the presupposition of identity-based groupings as the substrate of legitimate self-determination aspirations. In her discussion of the Israel/Palestine situation, the status of both Jewish Israeli people, and Palestinians, is described as 'a people'. Young is agnostic about whether Jewish Israelis or Palestinians can properly be termed 'indigenous' (Young 2007: 62) but 'peoplehood' is granted. For Young the intermingling of Jewish and Palestinian identities within the geographical terrain points towards a federated solution, perhaps along the Swiss lines as suggested by Edward Said (2000: 320). The shared identities of the two communities generate, in both cases, legitimacy for such aspirations as self-determination. Thus,

> [p]eoples, such as the Jewish people and the Palestinian people, have a legitimate claim for a social and political means to govern themselves in their own ways and to enact public expressions of their history and culture as a people. (Young 2007: 73)

However '[t]he humanist vision of a secular individualist state conflicts with these goals'. An important point to be noted here is the role played in Young's account by the analogy between individual human persons and collective entities treated as kinds of individual. Consistent with her nuanced discussion of a collective 'self', Young makes it clear that the analogy, or extension of argument, is deliberate. Clearly it is no mere figure of speech or rhetorical flourish. Thus Pettit's account of freedom for individual persons, as non-domination, can be extended so as to 'conceptualize autonomy for peoples' (2007: 193). Elsewhere, Young discusses the implications of this move, with its problematic treatment of the notion of 'self', in the following way:

> Extending any ideas of individual freedom and autonomy to peoples ... raises conceptual and political issues. Extending political theoretical concepts of individual freedom to a people appears to reify or personify a social aggregate as a unity with a set of common interests, agency, and will of its own. In fact, however, no such unified entity exists. (Young 2007: 49)

Young's gloss on this point is that the 'people' is a collection of individuals, with 'diverse interests and affinities' (Young 2007: 50). This she says is all that the 'self' in self-determination can mean' (2007: 59). This liberal viewpoint contributes to but falls short of the collectivist analysis of international law that this book is attempting to articulate. It does not suffice to dissuade even someone as politically insightful as Young from treating 'the people' as some kind of individual entity. The applicability of Pettit's account of freedom and of the philosophical alternatives to it, to collectives, is a key question for any attempt to articulate a collectivist account of international law. However the step from the individual level of analysis, as in the liberal traditions, to the collective level of states, peoples or communities needs to be examined. If the step involves treating those collectives as if they are quasi-individuals then conceptual warning bells should sound. Young's analysis might be said to be limited in this respect.

This limitation is conceptually related to the limitation that appears from comparison with Waldron's account: the focus on shared cultural identity. Young's approach is thus to be included in the category of the 'identity-based' theories of self-determination. This shows how broad and diverse the category is. It should be observed that this step therefore significantly 'ups the ante' for Waldron in the sense of further raising the bar of explanatory adequacy and comprehensiveness for his 'territorial' alternative. Waldron's positive formulation, outlined as a response to the inadequacies of the identity-based model, is driven in part by a pragmatic acceptance of the territorial divisions more or less as we currently find them in the world, state boundaries in particular. It treats the *de facto* resident population of a territory thus defined, such as 'the inhabitants of Australia', as the people to whom a kind of self-determination rightly applies. That is to say, the occupants of Australia are held to be functioning under some appropriate political structure, enabled to avoid such forms of external control as colonialism or other form of inappropriate domination. There is a kind of contingency to the subdivision of the world's population, not arbitrary but workmanlike. There is a cosmopolitan sensitivity to Waldron's analysis, and also a bathetic lightness of touch which suggests as it were that 'the music has stopped' in a global game of musical chairs: current boundaries may well reflect conquest, colonialism and other geopolitical delinquencies of the past, but here we all are, and we need to make the best of it. But territorial self-determination is not merely pragmatic or, in Koskenniemi's terminology, 'apologist'. It is also based on a principle of political philosophy according to which the very purpose of political communities is to provide frameworks for diversity and for antipathy. Such tensions or at least differences are to be thought of as concomitants of the human occupation of territory. This robust pluralism is an important if sometimes overlooked strand of the Hobbesian social contract tradition. This is thus the opposite of the identity approach, according to which political communities are the collective expression of sets of individuals who are already well disposed to each other (Waldron 2010: 409). Importantly, of course, Waldron's position raises questions about the status of the attachments to land that typically characterize indigenous populations.

At this point the collective aspects in Waldron's account need to be examined. Waldron's 'territorial' self-determination is not assumed to be vested 'in a "people" with a distinctive identity of its own'. It is not even strictly speaking a group right; 'instead it comprises the rights of individuals participating in a common exercise of collective decision, under conditions of equality and fairness'. It is 'like the right to democracy' (Waldron 2010: 408).

Now Waldron is of course correct to be precise on this matter and this in turn helps to render more precise an understanding of collectives in international law. But sight should not be lost of the fact that Waldron's account of the territorial approach is in important respects much more sensitive to the collective dimension than is the more conventional identity-based approach. The latter has a tendency to treat self-determination units as relatively homogenous cultural blocs. These are in effect nations, tribes or clans by any other name. They have a monolithic character in the way remarked upon by Young. In rejecting the identity approach, with its fantasy of aligned and consistent definitions and attachments, Waldron shows how the complexity of overlapping and of hybridity must be foregrounded (Waldron 2010: 403). Territorial self-determination is indeed comparable to a right to democracy and is likewise held collectively even if it is not a group as such that is thereby understood to be protected.

This account of Waldron's views has served to introduce many of the key aspects of the difference between the two broad camps as well as to examine Waldron's own contribution to elaborating an alternative to the conventional approach. Waldron's contribution is based on the literature in political and legal philosophy more than on the literature of international law as such. From political philosophy Anna Stilz has recently described an approach to territorial sovereignty that in some ways complements but in some ways challenges Waldron's account. For Stilz the constitution of some grouping of people as 'a people' in the sense of a self-determination unit emerges from a shared history of political co-operation. Stilz's contribution facilitates a further dissection of the important relationships between territory, self-determination and the collective project in international law (Stilz 2009: 209).

Stilz first describes a set of orthodox nationalist approaches to territorial legitimacy, very much in line with the Waldronian critique of identity-based approaches to self-determination. 'Nationalist theories hold that territorial jurisdiction is a collective right of cultural nations and that a nation bases its right on formative ties between the group and a particular territory' (Stilz 2011: 575). In addition to describing the more familiar 'identity' argument for such formative ties, Stilz discusses the suggestion of Miller and of Meisels that settlement and development may generate formative ties in a somewhat different manner (Stilz 2011: 576). In this argument, settlers who, having arrived from elsewhere, work on the soil, build, exploit resources and so on, by those very activities generate a right to the territory. Stilz demonstrates the inadequacies of this basically Lockean analysis and her critique is instructive especially when brought into contact with Waldron's proposals. It should be emphasized that Stilz classifies this 'argument from settlement' as a version of the nationalist theory of territory and distinguishes her own proposed scheme from it, as discussed below.

Stilz examines the collective dimension of territorial possession under statehood. For example even if the Lockean argument were given credence for an individual settler (that is to say gaining property rights over land as a direct consequence of her or his own labour), there would be considerable difficulties explaining group rights over a given territory, on this basis. Nor could territorial claims over the undeveloped parts of a geographical territory be readily understood on this application of Locke. Instead unexploited sections of a territory would remain *terra nullius* in the sense of being 'up for grabs' by any future settler from anywhere. More significantly, because less fantastical, the Lockean proposal would seem to suggest that sustainable and culturally cohesive settler communities would acquire territorial rights – rights just as good as those of any state. Statehood would be immanent in such settler communities, to be manifested in an inexorable secession. 'Little Havana' in Miami would be able to claim independence from both Florida and the USA, and there might arise a whole franchise system of 'Chinatowns'. Moreover the comparative recency of significant cultural influence across what are at present international borders might seem under the settlement approach to generate entitlements to territory, irrespective of those international borders. Cultural affinity would trump territorial sovereignty of states. An example might be culturally 'German' influence in, and cultural attachment of some German people to, parts of what is now western Poland. The Lockean trope of earning title through the working of the land is even to be found in the context of modern-day Israel. '[F]or the earliest Jewish settlers in Palestine, the right to a state would emerge as much out of the up-building of the land as out of the mists of time'. Jacqueline Rose cites Chaim Weizmann, first President of Israel who stated: 'It was the service to the soil which determined the right in our favour' (Rose 2007).

Settlement and settlers of course raise enormous difficulties both politically and legally, not to speak of the conceptual complexities (Gover 2010). The Lockean settlement theory for territorial legitimacy would appear to be something of a non-starter, not least because of its apparent disregard of the collective dimensions of settling. Yet it at least has the virtue of highlighting the importance of the settler process. Settlement is not a marginal or occasional phenomenon but a component of the ubiquitous phenomenon of population movement. Thought of somewhat broadly, settlement is of the essence of human connexion to territory, that is to say of association of any kind between people and places including the most ephemeral contingencies of who happens to be where at any particular time: migrant workers, tourists, refugees, 'ex-pats'. Waldron's approach of territorial analysis is consistent with this thin and pragmatic sense of association which implies little more than the observation that people's bodies occupy space, and so do their buildings, vehicles or beasts of burden. Of course in many circumstances the effects of settlement are much more intrusive than this stipulative, baseline footprint. Loyal Protestant families and soldiers were settled in the north of Ireland (approximately, 'Ulster') under the policy of Elizabeth I. Many were Scots or of Scots descent. This 'plantation' was remarkably successful from the point of view of the English Crown, that is to say in implementing English domination over the most troublesome quarter of Ireland,

and of course it continued to generate conflict and tension for many generations. Settlement generally speaking implies the displacement or domination of an indigenous population. It is therefore important to note that like Waldron, Stilz rejects special status (in respect of rights to territorial sovereignty) for 'the very first occupants' of any piece of land, even if firm evidence can be found for such historical claims. These kinds of historical issue are largely irrelevant for Stilz as for Waldron. But recent history is not at all irrelevant for Stilz, as discussed below.

Stilz's proposal is that a set of criteria may be identified by which territorial legitimacy for a state may be ascertained, irrespective of formative ties 'between [a] group and a particular territory'. These criteria comprise first, effective implementation of a legal system on that territory, especially with respect to property rights; second, a legitimate claim of the subjects of the state to occupy that territory; third a sufficiently participatory and representative legal system; and fourth the requirement that 'the state is not a usurper'. The first and third of these criteria are relatively familiar and here attention will be focused on the second and fourth criteria. In general terms Stilz emphasizes that in her view, 'the "people" are made into one collective body by being subject to state institutions and by participating together in shaping those institutions' (Stilz 2011: 579). Like Waldron, at least at this point in her argument, Stilz rejects the causative or temporal sequence of cultural coherence taking precedence over statehood. 'The state instead defines the citizenry that is subject to it ... [P]eoples are brought into being by states' (Stilz 2011: 579-80). Stilz's theory 'does not invoke a prepolitical nation independent of the state' (2011: 590). This is an important proposal.

Stilz indicates the theoretical basis for her argument above and beyond the identification of inadequacies in the alternatives that she has identified:

> What is truly the heart of the matter is individuals' need for a stable legal residence: their need to live under a legitimate state that allows them to exercise personal autonomy in a particular place. I might require occupancy of territory in this sense in order to sustain the integrity of my plans and pursuits even if I haven't settled it or identified with that territory in any more robustly cultural way. (Stilz 2011: 584–5)

This claim is not novel but it is noteworthy in its commitment to individual, personal autonomy, very much in a Kantian tradition. Thus Stilz goes on to state that 'the morally significant feature of the situation is that I am present on the territory without wrongdoing (perhaps by having been born there)'.

In broad terms Stilz's 'legitimate state theory' relies on the provision or maintenance by the state of an adequate legal system in the relevant territory. But Stilz makes it clear that in her account (2011: 595), self-determination 'trumps' the baseline requirement that states provide adequate protection for citizens or other occupants of relevant territory. This latter consideration, often referred to under the rubric of a 'fiduciary' duty of the state towards its nationals (Criddle and Fox-Decent 2009), is a commonplace of liberal political theory. Compared to a status quo, the tasks of '[p]rotecting individuals' basic rights and providing essential public goods' might after all be better delivered by some foreign regime that annexes a given territory and its inhabitants. If the delivery of the services, however high or low the threshold for adequacy, is the key criterion for legitimacy of a state, then self-determination becomes a secondary consideration at best. It is not necessary to descend to the level of the punctuality of trains in considering such an annexation scenario. It is a challenging question for the fiduciary (or more widely the Kantian) approach.

But for Stilz no level of fulfilment of rights would suffice to displace self-determination. For Stilz, to argue that it might do so would be to ignore 'the political histories that would be destroyed' by such annexations (or 'mergers') (Stilz 2011: 595). The particular local scheme of law and of governance more generally that prevails in a particular territory has a value that arises from that connection. Most important, for Stilz 'it is because this particular scheme of rules is the one that a people has produced together that it has a special value for them' (2011: 595). But this argument seems to move too quickly and to step out of the framework of criteria that she has previously defined for legitimacy.

The argument for local control of decision-making and other political processes is, broadly speaking, the argument for democracy. It would seem to be covered by Stilz's own third criterion (participatory governance). Having one's governance structures changed from being ruled by X to being ruled by Y may well have implications for democratic participation, although the change may be for better as well as for worse. But this is not the same as a 'political history' understood as a scheme 'that a people has produced together'. Waldron's cautionary points about identity-based approaches to self-determination need to be referred to. Stilz's political history is an identity shared by a collective but it is inaccurate to say that it has been produced by 'a people', if by that is meant that there exists 'a people' in a strong, as it were causative sense – a sense apparently rejected by Stilz in the earlier phase of her argument. This seems to ground territorial claims of 'a people' in peoplehood itself. Thus if a state 'fails, becomes illegitimate, or is usurped', annexation would still be wrong because this may run up against the residual claim 'vested in the people ... to reconstitute legitimate political institutions on their territory' (Stilz 2011: 591). Stilz's proposals seem to fall short of what is called for by a collectives-sensitive analysis of self-determination. Elsewhere, in the literature of international law, other avenues have been pursued that in some ways converge with Waldron's project. Benedict Kingsbury's (1999; 2000) approach to self-determination adopts a constructivist position from international relations theory in order to escape from formalist, state-centred thinking. For Kingsbury, conventional understandings of self-determination within international law tend to exaggerate stability and to place too much emphasis on the cohesiveness and integrity of territorial units. Instead, Kingsbury argues for fluidity.

Peoplehood in relation to Palestine and Israel is no less complex. In its earlier Advisory Opinion, issued some six years before the Kosovo Opinion, the International Court of Justice had with near unanimity declared the illegality of the construction of a security barrier within the Occupied Territories. The impact on self-determination of the Palestinian people was one important consideration. Without attempting to definitively articulate the territorial dimension of that entitlement, the Court was clear that the conduct of the Israeli Government in its activities well beyond its internationally recognized borders was in violation of this entitlement. As the Court observed, the Israeli Government was among those regimes that had recognized a Palestinian people as such (para 118). More recently, the attempt has been made by representatives of Palestine to accede, as a state party, to the Rome Statute of the International Criminal Court. The statehood of Palestine has been recognized by enhanced status at the UN.

Some other issues of the Palestine/Israel conflict are taken up in the chapter that follows. Overviewing the above, it seems clear that self-determination as traditionally understood in international law, needs to be radically rethought. The close connections to nationhood, as connoting cultural homogeneity, need to be dismantled. It may well be that 'peoplehood' stands or falls with nationhood. Collectivity may seem a very poor conceptual (and affective) substitute for these idols, but erring on the side of theoretical parsimony seems indicated. Those suggestions that have been made from time to time concerning heterogeneity within cultures, the deep interdependence of nations, are pointers to the conceptual vocabulary that is needed. As Derrida has observed:

> What is called the political can no longer be bound in its very concept, as it always has been, to a presupposition of place, of territory – and of what pertains to the state … Some would like to continue to think – but this is more and more difficult – that the political necessarily takes the form of a state, and that is bound to an irreplaceable territory, to a national community. But this is exactly what is being *dislocated* today. (Kellogg 2010: 8)

Chapter 7
Cultures, Attachments, Minorities, Movements

States Within States

Four years before the establishment of the state of Israel, Hannah Arendt wrote as follows:

> [I]t was precisely because of this nationalist misconception of the inherent independence of a nation that the Zionists ended up making the Jewish national independence entirely dependent on the material interests of another nation. (Rose 2007: 44)

Arendt was surely referring to Great Britain here, as guarantor of a homeland to be located within Palestine, although by extension her comments could perhaps be applied to the role of the USA in later decades. The point in any case is a general one. Neither states, nations nor 'peoples' are independent planets or universes. With respect to Israel, it is relevant to observe that the vision of one of its Zionist advocates, Herzl, was a profoundly Eurocentric one. In *Der Judenstaat* Herzl argued that a Jewish state would be 'a rampart of Europe against Asia, an outpost of civilisation as opposed to barbarism' (Rose 2007: 47). Herzl was of course seeking European-wide support for his political cause, so that his appeal to European self-esteem in this manner was no doubt strategic as much as anything else. But clearly the state of Israel can be described as 'a European project'. It was never (or never again) going to emerge from the wanderings of a tribal community in hostile desert lands. Indeed local resistance was to be anticipated; as Herzl himself had drily put it, 'only the desperate make good conquerors' (Rose 2007: 47). This trope was shockingly revived by US President Bill Clinton who in celebrating 50 years of the Israeli state in 1998, praised the 'small oasis' of Israel for 'making a once barren desert bloom' and for 'building a thriving democracy in hostile terrain' (Said 2000: 266).

The worldwide political efforts to secure a Jewish homeland in the 'near Middle East' took place alongside first the continuing existence of the Ottoman Empire, with its own internal administrative structures including regional divisions, and then alongside the disposal of the region by the victors of World War I following the collapse of that empire. The Western European powers took responsibility for different sections of the region, most notably so far as Palestine was concerned by the British under a League of Nations Mandate. Various proposals were entertained within British Government circles in the inter-war period for territorial settlements comprising the demarcation of a proto-Israel. For example one proposal comprised a coastal strip comparable in size to present day

Gaza, that is to say a geographical area very much smaller than either the area proposed under subsequent UN leadership, or the larger again area claimed by Israel's founding Government at UDI in 1948. Immigration of Jewish people from Europe and beyond into the region was to some extent regulated by the occupying powers in the inter-war period and even minimal immigration, of anyone and from anywhere, inevitably raised questions concerning the developing political structure of the region. It seems undeniable that the emergence of Israel as an independent political entity was associated with large-scale depopulation of the claimed territory in relation to the previous, Palestinian inhabitants (according to Jacqueline Rose, at least 700,000; Rose 2007: 43). As with many other situations of mass relocation and polarization based on ethnicity or religion, it is difficult to quantify the roles played by voluntary if reluctant relocation and of coerced relocation going to what is now called, at best, ethnic cleansing. Matthew Lister has emphasized that large-scale involuntary population movements routinely accompany the process of self-determination. What might be called the dark side of self-determination thus contributes to the global phenomenon of displaced populations and people in flight (see Lister 2012).

Retrospective attributions of self-determination are the preferred variety. If the inhabitants of a geographically well-defined territory have expressed an overwhelmingly majoritarian view on national affiliation, and if such a position corresponds to current actualities, then international law has been reluctant to respond to alternative proposals. This has at least been the case for the past 100 years. The term self-determination tends to be used by political leaders in such contexts. Thus the territorial sovereignty status of the Falkland Islands/Islas Malvinas, and of Gibraltar, are understood by the United Kingdom as sustained straightforwardly by the expressed wishes of very large proportions of their respective populations to be 'British' in some significant sense. This is thought of as 'self-determination'. Any territorial dispute that might come to an international tribunal such as the International Court of Justice, for example a dispute with Argentina over the Malvinas, would be presented by the British officials as straightforwardly a matter of self-determination. Yet the outcome of such a hypothetical dispute is not so easy to predict.

The states whether real or imagined of a united Ireland, Israel, Palestine and Kosovo share some important characteristics especially in terms of history, while the differences are of course equally striking. Only the first is geographically bounded in a way that suggests natural borders, a feature that is technically of no concern to international law but which is often of considerable significance in its practices (as well as being of great concern to nationalist thinking of many kinds). The first three share the history of direct control by England or Britain, either by conquest in the late Middle Ages in the case of Ireland or by internationally sanctioned regimes of protection in the case of Israel and Palestine. Kosovo is a proto-state emerging, like Israel and Palestine, from the consequences of the break-up of the Ottoman Empire 100 years ago. Ireland unilaterally declared independence in 1916; Israel in 1948; and Kosovo in 2008 (Aust 2012). It may be said that self-determination was thus asserted in each case. But it is important to observe that continuities in terminology may obscure significant differences in meaning. 'The people' has not always been thought of in democratic ways:

> What seems to us flagrant inconsistency, when eighteenth-century Whigs defended their oligarchic power in the name of the 'people', for instance, was for the Whig leaders themselves just common sense.
>
> In fact, they were drawing on an older understanding of 'people', one stemming from a pre-modern notion of order ... where a people is constituted as such by a Law which always already exists, 'since time out of mind'. This law can confer leadership on some elements, who thus quite naturally speak for the 'people'. (Taylor 2007: 163)

Thus '[t]he tribal unit was seen as constituted as such by its law, which went back "since time out of mind," or perhaps to some founding moment which had the status of a "time of origins" in Eliade's sense' (Taylor 2007: 208). Now Taylor's analysis of historical change with regard to these conceptual frameworks can be challenged, and the brush may turn out to be a little broad. But the key point is that a twentieth- or twenty-first-century sensibility concerning 'peoples', even if it affords precision in the contemporary era, cannot be assumed to have purchase on events and examples in earlier times. As it turns out the precision question and the anachronism question are both stumbling-blocks for international law.

Freud and the Return of the Suppressed

If there is such a thing as a people, then every people is by definition unique. Any kind of comparison between peoples is fraught with risks including the giving of offence, as is the questioning of the reality of 'peoplehood' in general or in particular. But it can in any case hardly be an exaggeration to say that if the concept of peoplehood means anything, then 'the Jewish People' is and has been one of the most significant of peoples for world history in the last few millennia.

As well as other connections, the meaning and understanding of law worldwide has been in large part, although of course not in its entirety, the consequence direct or indirect of the cultural traditions of that people. The figure of Moses looms large over Western culture, including its legal traditions, as well as looming not a little over much of the rest of the world. The interweaving of Judaic and Islamic traditions across the centuries, and the conflicts and collaborations between Judaism's Christian offshoots and the world of Islam, shaped the history of much of the Old World. Moses stands in the company of patriarchs and visionaries who reveal or deliver law to their people or to the world at large: 'Moses, Solon, Lycurgus, Plato, Zarathustra' (Douzinas 2006: 44). Sigmund Freud speculated that Moses was an aristocratic Egyptian who gave laws and religion to the Jewish people. In his own way Freud himself was of course one who revealed or delivered the law (Rose 2007: 87).

The story of Moses and the Jewish people, as provided by Sigmund Freud's account published on the eve of World War II, is a study of the interactions between collective identity, law and resilience. By resilience I am referring to the persistence of ancient processes, as claimed by Freud, just as much as to the dedication of succeeding generations to maintain their community. The frankly speculative account given by Freud of Moses and his role in the adoption of monotheism by the ancient Jewish people is therefore of interest for a number of reasons.

Freud's identification with Judaism as a faith and with the Jewish people as something like a race was a matter of complexity both in personal and in scholarly terms. Much earlier, in 1913, Freud had written to his brilliant young Russian colleague Sabina Spielrein about their common identity. Responding to the news of her pregnancy, Freud wrote: 'We are and remain Jews. The others will only exploit us and will never understand or appreciate us' (Morss 1990: 147). In *Moses and Monotheism* Freud defines himself as 'someone who is one of' the Jewish people (Freud 1964: 7). The book was written in the last few years of his life, shortly before Freud left Vienna for London in 1938. According to James Strachey it presents the 'analysis of a national group' (Freud 1964: 5). In *Moses and Monotheism* Freud proposed that 'of all the peoples who lived around the basin of the Mediterranean in antiquity', the Jewish people 'is almost the only one which still exists in name and also in substance' (Freud 1964: 105).

It is still shocking to see Freud using the phrase 'a State within a State' in this book, in his account of this ancient history (1964: 76). The phrase was commonly used in anti-Semitic propaganda, and is employed by Freud in what appears to be an almost casual manner (but probably is anything but). If communities, as 'peoples', can threaten states from within, and can be seen as subversive or even treasonous in that capacity as a 'fifth column' for an enemy, then at least this is a pointer to the complex forms of explanation that international law is going to require. The speculative chronicle of the man Moses having been a disappointed monotheistic Egyptian aristo looking around for a congregation may be put to one side except as metaphor. More significantly, as later emphasized by Edward Said, Freud's account of Jewish religious history and cultural identity describes it as not merely entwined with that of Egypt but reliant on it. This account, Said suggested, inscribes the Jewish people in a non-European heritage, 'carefully opening out Jewish identity toward its non-Jewish background'. In Jacqueline Rose's words,

> This is a plea for a model of nationhood that would not just accept the other in its midst, nor just see itself *as other,* but that grants to that selfsame other, against which national and political identities define themselves, a founding, generic status at the origins of the group. (Rose 2007: 80)

Displacement may be taken as the key term here. Freud's writings on Moses provocatively displaced Moses as founding Jewish father of his people. The cultural identity is itself displaced from within; it is derivative, the collateral effect of some other process. And it is important to emphasize, even if Rose does not, that 'Egyptian-ness' is surely subject to the same corrosive critique here. Said's intervention here may well attest 'to the fundamental importance of Egypt in the history of mankind' (Rose 2007: 80). But equally, the role of Egypt may be scorned as it was by the poet Heine, when he deplored his Jewish religion as 'the unhealthy ancient Egyptian faith'.

Egyptophilia and Egypt-blaming are two sides of the same coin. 'Egyptian culture' or nationhood can no more be seen as foundational and absolute than can Jewish or indeed Palestinian nationhood. The displacement runs deep. Displacement is the diachronic counterpart to hybridity in the synchronic register. As the term hybridity may more patently connote, it is not just a matter of two entities defining themselves in opposition to the other. Otherwise 'Israel' and 'Egypt' become twinned and thereby in a sense unified, like matter and anti-matter. The empirical communalities should not of course be overlooked. In the case of Israel and Palestine, the common experience of 'a diasporic existence' might optimistically be thought of as grounds for solidarity (Žižek 2008: 128). Yet the displacement is multiple not merely reciprocal. If self-determination depends on peoplehood then it is built on shifting sands. Of course there are dimensions to the Israel/Palestine conflict that are intensely reciprocal, such as the incompatible territorial claims currently being made. But the reciprocity is only part of the picture. Relationships with Russia, with the USA, with the global Jewish-identifying and Palestinian-identifying diasporas, with Iran, with the international intelligentsia, are all involved. These dimensions are all political and they are all collective.

Rethinking Culture

Christine Schwöbel has argued that '[c]ultural identity, determined through cultural affiliations, is itself fluid and open to change … Identities are as fluid as the plurality in the world' (2010: 545). Culture is not about irreducible difference nor about the consciousness of or the display of such uniqueness (Waldron 2000: 233). As Waldron has shown, this conventional approach overlooks several important, inclusive dimensions of culture such as the sharing of worldwide practices: Roman Catholicism being a good example of this. Waldron criticizes the view that there is some inherently or primitively homogeneous local connectedness of people in the sense conveyed by some forms of cultural relativism and identity politics (2000: 241). This view might be thought of as sentimental, with its 'talk of community in the nostalgic first-person plural of belonging' (Waldron 1992a: 777); or as an ur-nationalism (756); or of course, as racism. A version of this myth of the origin of culture, if one could call it that, might seem to emerge in Rawls' *The Law of Peoples*. This problem is related to the imprecise sense of 'community' used in the writings of communitarians and others (1992a: 755). While it picks up something extremely important, indeed something central to the argument of this book, reference to communities as providing context for or even constituting identity and subjectivity can remain imprecise. The scale is undefined – a village or a state? States are not natural kinds. Nor are small-scale national communities. 'Ethnic nationality is an idea which postulates or dreams its own naturalness, its own antiquity, its immemorial cultivation of a certain patch of soil' (Waldron 1992a: 781).

An emphasis on collectives in international law adds weight and urgency to the questions over territorial sovereignty and associated senses of self-determination. Weak senses of self-determination in international law, which reduce to the honouring of individual rights to culture and association, evade the issues raised by the collective analysis. But strong senses of self-determination make presuppositions about the coherence and cohesiveness of territorial communities. Societies that are for the most important purposes homogeneous are in effect treated as the canonical form of territorial community. As we have seen this 'nation state' template is central to John Rawls' *The Law of Peoples*. Models of self-determination that break away most rigorously from this orthodoxy, such as that described by Waldron, emphasize the pluralism and other forms of complexity that characterize the populations of territories. It would be consistent with Waldron's approach also to lay stress on the forms of association that cross territorial borders, including regional and bilateral agreements between governments as well as informal or cultural affiliations. This approach does not in itself resolve the puzzle of territoriality. Waldron's approach is to be pragmatic about territory in the sense that it is those people who currently reside in any particular geographical location whose political needs, as a complex population, are to be met by governance structures and by international regulation.

In some ways this aspect of Waldron's argument on self-determination converges with aspects of Stilz's proposals. As will be recalled, for Stilz the constitution of some grouping of people as 'a people' in the sense of a self-determination unit derives by and large from a minimal, shared history of political co-operation. 'The bond that constitutes a democratic people can thus be quite thin'. For Stilz this approach is Kantian. Again, it seems satisfactory at a descriptive level but lacks precision when applied to problematic cases. Political co-operation, which may be taken to include mutual respect for legal processes, takes place across territorial borders and can be manifested by negative as well as positive conduct in the sense that non-interference is 'negative'. Political co-operation is often regional. It appears that geographical boundaries, as defined at some particular time, are playing the kind of 'master' role that we have seen in Rawls and to some extent in Waldron. Territorial enclosure is a 'bright line'. This status is much more than pragmatic.

Yet from a conceptual point of view it is difficult to defend such a strong role for geographical territoriality. For example the history of colonization and its aftermath in the emergence of new state entities shows just how complex is even such an apparently simple idea as retaining colonial administrative boundaries as default state boundaries (the principle of *uti possidetis juris*) (Lalonde 2002: 238). These complexities operate in relation to relevant chronology (what year should serve as the baseline, and why?) as well as in relation to the administrative structure of the colonies which in the case of Spanish America, for example, was Byzantine in its hierarchies. *Uti possidetis* turns out to be a way of retrospectively legitimizing certain options for territorial boundaries. One of the contributions of the collectivist analysis to this problem is to put territorial boundaries into perspective. Their ephemeral character cannot be over-emphasized (Davies 2011). As Florian Hoffmann has observed in the context of human rights, our world is 'a world which is increasingly marked by global communication streams and material exchanges, a world in which the "trans-", the "cross-" and the hybrid has, at least in part, replaced what was previously assumed to be the co-existence of discrete, bounded formations such as nation-states, cultures or identities' (Hoffmann 2006: 227). Among other challenges, the challenges that this orientation presents for minority and indigenous populations have to be faced up to.

Minorities and Indigenous Populations

Gaetano Pentassuglia has suggested that minority protection under international law has moved in waves, the first wave being the post-World War I machinery put in place under the aegis of the League of Nations. Certain racial, religious or linguistic minorities, newly vulnerable or exposed as a consequence of the break-up of pre-war empires, were protected by machinery that included both direct and indirect supervison by the League. As commentators have noted, exploitation of minority issues by the Nazi regime played a part in the discrediting of this style of minority protection (Morgan 2011: 94). The regime claimed in some circumstances to be acting on behalf of oppressed minorities in other states as a pretext for military occupation. The policy switched to an approach based on universal, individualized human rights after the end of World War II. To some extent this second wave downplayed or even disallowed 'minority identity claims and their concomitant collective dimension' (Pentassuglia 2009: 3). Collective protection did not entirely cease, as instruments such as the Genocide Convention of 1948 demonstrate, manifesting a third wave. As observed by Morgan, notable international collective rights protections of later decades include the African Charter on Human and Peoples' Rights 1981 (the Banjul Charter).

The United Nations Declaration on the Rights of Indigenous Peoples (UNDRIP) was adopted by the UN General Assembly in 2007. It has been said to constitute 'the only specifically collective human rights instrument recognized by the UN' (Morgan 2011: 17). This description is debateable, but it highlights the question of the relationships between minority protection, collective rights and indigeneity. In this connection Kymlicka has commented that the distinction between minorities as such, and indigenous communities as such, is too sharply drawn. There is, says Kymlicka, a 'firewall' mentality in which the promotion of indigenous rights can coexist with 'resisting the rights of minorities' (Kymlicka 2011: 199). There has been a 'total rupture at the level of international law' as a consequence of the perceived urgency of indigenous claims, whereas national minorities have been 'lumped together with visitors, immigrants and diasporas ...' (Kymlicka 2011: 201). For Kymlicka, national minorities or 'stateless nations' include 'Scots, Catalans, Kurds ... Tibetans' all of whom are 'culturally distinct groups living on their traditional territory, who think of themselves as a distinct people or nation' (Kymlicka 2011: 199).

An important dimension of the regulation (including self-regulation) of indigenous communities is the role played by express constitutional documents and arrangements. In a comprehensive analysis of constitutional arrangements among indigenous populations in settler societies, Kirsty Gover observes that '[t]ribal constitutionalism introduces a new legal pluralism to the constitution of the Western settler societies that is necessary for the continuance of tribal self-governance' (Gover 2010: 209). Gover discusses the role of 'public indigeneity'. Public indigeneity 'is a pan-tribal concept that allocates indigenous status to individuals' in the public law of settler states such as Australia or Canada. It arises in the context of policy implementation (Gover 2010: 1). As Karen Engle has emphasized, difficulties arise from essentialist understandings of indigenous culture, even (or especially) when the essentialism is 'strategic' (Engle 2010: 4). In this connection Gover introduces Nancy Fraser's notion of 'relational pluralism', a term that emphasizes the fluidity rather than the fixity of shared identity or membership. In the context of indigenous identity, this connects with the idea of an 'indigenous cosmopolitanism in which individual indigeneity can be constituted by more than one set of local cultural practices' (Gover, 2010: 25).

These somewhat radical, pluralistic ideas on indigeneity contrast with more familiar notions of membership based narrowly on descent and on family structures. The latter are in many cases legally prescribed in the context of rights to land and resources. Thus there is a serious risk that fluidity in cultural definition 'may undermine indigenous claims based on historic continuity' (Gover, 2010: 22). It should also be observed however that indigenous definitions of descent and of group membership by descent may themselves be much more flexible and negotiable than their formulaic assimilation into European legal systems may suggest (2010: 33).

These points illustrate the complexity of indigenous status in relation to contemporary legal systems. While indigeneity is a special form of collective community in many important respects, it cannot be treated as entirely distinct from other dimensions and manifestations of collectivity, some of which flow beyond state borders. Phrased more positively,

> [n]ew norms of indigenous peoples' rights ... represent the bridging of a paradigmatic gulf between [on the one hand] traditional liberal conceptions of human rights and the privileging of individualism and [on the other] the collective claims of historically grounded associations. (Morgan 2011: 2)

Morgan has also observed that '[c]ollective rights offend the traditional liberal paradigm whereby rights are entitlements held by individuals and individuals alone' (Morgan 2011: 89). The legal status of indigenous communities is among other things a clear signal of the inadequacy of that traditional individualistic paradigm.

Moving Toward Justice: Social Movements

In many ways the argument of this book is that international law should be thought of as the study of mass movements: people on the move. Political expression is mass movement of a kind, so that geographical relocation of populations is not essential to this idea. To put it another way, mobilization is a central concept. Within many democracies, mobilizing voters to turn out on election day is of very great significance. That kind of mobilization is at one end of a spectrum, towards the other end of which is forced relocation of populations. The extreme of that pole is the genocidal death march of which the twentieth century saw several episodes. Short of that extreme is the phenomenon of 'ethnic cleansing'. Further back again, and correspondingly more common, can be found a range of situations in which populations move with a complex combination of volition and duress. As observed above this is in many ways the dark side of self-determination (Panayi 1999: 103). Somewhere in the middle of the whole conceptual spectrum might be placed historical examples such as the invasions of early Europe by central Asian tribal populations, and the invasions of the Americas, and of Australia and the Pacific, by Europeans themselves. 'Plantations' of loyal or merely respectable and hard-working populations into the northern part of Ireland, or the southern part of Chile, would also be part of the picture. A comprehensive theory would consider a dimension of intensity among other dimensions. International law is about people in motion even if they are not going anyplace right now.

Social movements, and their articulation with international law, are therefore of considerable relevance to the current project. Some comments were made in Chapter 3 above on the recent literature in post-colonial perspectives on international law. The authors discussed there focused on historical analysis. In a cognate vein, but with a different research agenda, Balakrishnan Rajagopal has explored the interrelationships between human rights discourse and social movements in the context of 'Third World Resistance' (Rajagopal 2003: 204). Rehearsing a familiar argument, the mainstream of international law is said 'to function within specific paradigms of western modernity and rationality, that predetermine the actors for whom international law exists. These include political actors such as state officials, economic actors such as corporations and cultural actors such as the atomized individual who is the subject of rights'. Rajagopal continues, 'This actor-based approach of international law simply privileges what happens in certain institutional arenas. [But] most of the people in the Third World live and interact in non-institutional spaces: in the family, the informal economy, and non-party political spaces' (Rajagopal 2003: 2).

Importantly, Rajagopal affirms the theoretical as well as the political significance of 'the resistance of mass action' (Rajagopal 2003: 11). In a variety of ways this work both illustrates and contributes to the current project. For Rajagopal, social movements 'seek to redefine the "political" in non-institutional, non-party, cultural terms [and] "law" in radically pluralistic terms' (Rajagopal 2003: 293). Castells' notion of 'resistance identity' is apposite here (Morgan 2011: 61). Rajagopal observes that international law tends to step aside in the face of disruptive social and political events until such times as stable statehood is established or re-established, so that the victor may be welcomed 'as the legitimate representative of state sovereignty' (Rajagopal 2003: 11, 166). Such events will often be defined as 'emergencies' by which a suspension of various procedures and protections may be legitimated. Resistance in this sense is so much 'noise' which, until it gives way to 'signal' again, cannot be comprehended. This is of course an important indication of the significance of collective phenomena such as social movements. As Rajagopal notes in this connection, '[t]he sanctioned language of resistance in international law' is the language of human rights (Rajagopal 2003: 21). And while state-centred international law and universalized human rights discourse are in substantial respects alternative paths for international law, as previously discussed they meet up in certain theoretical as well as practical respects. Human rights as 'the sanctioned language' relies on state-centred international law, and the implementation of such rights 'require[s] an active role for the state, [and sometimes] state-building' itself (Rajagopal 2003: 21). As Rajagopal (2003: 189) observes, it is a mistake to think of human rights as 'an anti-state discourse'.

Rajagopal therefore sets out some of the reasons why individualized human rights, and an overarching understanding of international law that centres on states-as-individuals, provide an inadequate conceptual apparatus. He scrutinizes the role of 'modern human-rights discourse as the sole approved discourse of resistance' (Rajagopal 2003: 165). Individualized formulations of human rights are a reflection of a liberal view of politics and a liberal conception of the 'unity of the social actor, and the sharp divide between public and private' (Rajagopal 2003: 167). A focus on social movements as such offers for Rajagopal new ways of thinking about 'how to redeem the emancipatory promises of the liberal rights discourse without succumbing to its sovereignty-property [Lockean] roots' (Rajagopal 2003: 253).

Importantly, for Rajagopal, the influence of liberalism is also more diffuse and subtle than this. The Working Women's Forum (of India) [WWF] cannot be reduced to the roles, the conduct or the rights of its members as individuals, but nor can it be reduced to a mere exemplar of a women's movement 'or an NGO or a trade union'. The WWF 'defeat[s] the liberal categories currently in vogue. In fact, it is the very heterogeneity of its multiple forms that gives the WWF its unique character as a social movement' (Rajagopal 2003: 167). While problematizing individualism in the description of social movements, then, Rajagopal's critique extends much more widely. This is an important cautionary note for the present project. Mere reference to group phenomena, or a collective level of description, may not ensure that adequate levels of complexity are being recognized. Rajagopal sums up the position as follows:

> The international legal discourse is inadequate ... in explaining [the] complex interactions with the state structures, or in exposing the ideological framework within which ... identity formations [for the members of the movement] resist and sometimes assist the neoliberal project. (Rajagopal 2003: 167)

Without neglecting the caution, it might be observed that Rajagopal's critique could be extended to cover 'peoples'. It seems consistent with Rajagopal's approach to define that term, although he does not do so, as another of the 'liberal categories currently in vogue'. If so, 'peoples' might be seen as a term that represents an attempt to conceptually cut the masses down to size. For fear and distrust of the masses (in Western elites) is an important component of the ideological framework that Rajagopal describes. Thus:

> [T]he present human-rights corpus, which incorporates the concept of emergency
> ... perpetuates the same fear, contempt, and loathing of the masses, the same legal
> void that enables governments to take extreme measures ... (Rajagopal 2003: 182)

Governments of course manipulate the masses at the same time as despising them. They 'organize a repulsive mixture of power and opinions' characterized by 'the blind confrontation of communities' (Badiou 2003: 53). As Gerry Simpson observes, the modern state coerces its whole population in time of war along the lines of the *levée en masse* of Revolutionary France, but in such a manner that 'war's modern hierarchical impulses ... meet its romantic counterpart (the possibility of a politics of resistance without or outside the state)' (Simpson 2011: 82). The state, so to speak, enlists the whole community in a performance of *Les Mis*. This is a salutary reminder of the romantic aspects of collective resistance and of its representation, consistent with Rajagopal's cautionary remarks noted above. For academic discussions of international law as inherently violent seem to fall prey to this temptation. According to Beard, '[a]ny population that attempts to challenge the Westphalian system, including contemporary ways of understanding state governance, must do so violently' (Beard 2011: 26). Despite the sophistication of Beard's larger argument, drawing from Butler and Benjamin among others, this is a problematic suggestion in my view, whatever may precisely be meant by 'violently'.

Social movements of various kinds, including those comprised of indigenous communities, have in their thinking and self-presentation undergone something of a 'turn to culture' which

> has emphasized rights to identity, territory, autonomy and alternative conceptions
> of modernity and development. This has brought [social movements] into direct
> conflict with the discourse of private property, which has acquired a principal
> place in international development policy, and, therefore, in liberal theories of
> international law. (Rajagopal 2003: 263)

Rajagopal thus distances himself from the 'liberal internationalism' of Anne-Marie Slaughter who has attempted to define a 'disaggregated sovereignty' characteristic of relationships within and between modern liberal states (2003: 255). Liberal internationalism has an understanding of law that 'is almost ethnocentrically narrow and is built on significant exclusions of categories of marginalized peoples'

(2003: 293). Reference is made instead to group rights and to 'the actual struggles of the people' (Rajagopal 2003: 169, 170). Thus the 'praxis of many social movements attempts to articulate an embedded, place-based cosmopolitanism' (2003: 256) inconsistent with this Slaughterian distinction between liberal and non-liberal states (Rajagopal 2003: 256). Ironically the axiom of equality of states is called upon to show the deficiency of Slaughter's analysis. It is not clear why Rajagopal would think that so much weight can be placed on what might be thought of as a liberal shibboleth (Rajagopal 2003: 266). In any event, mainstream human rights discourse is described as conservative, such that its effects have included the 'taming' of 'group rights such as self-determination' (2003: 247).

It is consistent with Rajagopal's approach, while extending his claims, to suggest that all human rights protections should be thought of as protections of collectives: of communities, of pluralities, of the vulnerable. With this in mind, the next chapter shifts focus by considering sovereignty and governmentality, especially through the lens of a discipline cognate with international law.

Chapter 8
International Relations and International Law: Rethinking Statehood and Sovereignty

Leagues and Nations

The topics focused on in this book are meeting places for many disciplines and the perspectives of those disciplines other than international law 'itself' must not be entirely overlooked. Indeed valuable insights may be gained from the ways in which scholars in sister disciplines define the place of international law in the larger conceptual landscape. Some examples of this will help to clarify the challenges, and the opportunities, to which this book is intended as a response. In addition this wider perspective enlivens the question of sovereignty which is central to all these disciplines. Questions about international law may well, at least at times, be too important to be left to the international lawyers.

It is not clear whether international law should be thought of as a distinct academic discipline. It is certainly possible to treat it that way, and historical accounts of international law generally take a narrow and somewhat technical view of the dots that are to be joined in constructing such a narrative. There has undoubtedly been professional cohesion and shared intellectual traditions among practitioners of international law over the centuries. The writing of textbooks has been a professional, just as much as a scholarly pursuit, so that generations of students have been presented with an account of international law that emphasizes and perhaps exaggerates its distinctiveness. However the connections between international law and other academic disciplines are at least as significant as its singularities or its communalities with other kinds of legal study including legal philosophy. For the topics that international law deals with are also of key concern to disciplines such as international politics and international relations as well as to history and to the interdisciplinary studies of sovereignty or of national identity. With reference to writings by scholars in international relations, Klabbers has observed that 'outsiders tend to look at international law as either descriptive sociology (and thus of little practical effect in terms of constraining states' behaviour) or as a branch of ethics (and therewith equally of little practical effect)' (Klabbers 2002: 335). Cultural and literary studies are also relevant. It might be also argued that international law is fundamentally about hospitality, in which case a variety of scholarly traditions knock on the door.

International law as currently articulated involves an uneasy cohabitation of two formulations: the state-as-individual-centred and the individual-person-centred. Issues relating to the responsibilities of states, their immunities, privileges and other forms of interrelationship, such as obligations based on customary international law, speak to the former. Universal human rights, international humanitarian law and international criminal justice all speak for the latter. The former is characterized by a detached, quasi-scientific attitude; the latter by reference to ethics and to subjectivity. Of course some areas of concern within international law manage to yoke together these two disparate domains. So-called 'peremptory norms' involve moralistic arguments, more closely associated with subjective approaches, but are couched in terms of the objective conduct of states (Orakhelashvili 2006). Such observations serve to demonstrate the tensions between these two approaches to international law, the state-centred and the person-centred. But both take an individualistic stance. What is needed is an approach which treats collectives as the central topic for the discipline. In a previous chapter it was suggested that the state must be seen as a collective entity. This perspective enables an opening up of the 'unsplittable atom' or 'monad' (Bowden 2011: 59) of the state, as theorized in various disciplines. In this chapter, this proposal is clarified and to some extent tested out by examining the similarities and differences between international law and one of its neighbour disciplines: international relations.

This chapter thus articulates and discusses the implications of the collectivist viewpoint on international law in relation to a discipline that borders on international law. It focuses on international relations, a discipline that has historically intimate connections to international law. The state as actor in a political world is the common ground of international law and its neighbour disciplines of international relations and international politics. There are of course many concepts and themes that are of common interest, chief among which is sovereignty. But the state has a special status. There are many ways in which significant variants or schools of these disciplines virtually coincide in their understanding of statehood, even if each discipline also embraces variants that substantially diverge from that interdisciplinary consensus. Within international relations theory for example, as in international law, innovative contemporary contributions are problematizing this account of the state and seeking to articulate alternative frameworks. Some of these alternative viewpoints may illuminate the question of the state in international law. In turn, it is possible that scepticism toward the theoretically unitary and individualistic state in the latter discipline may provide some insights into the theoretical options opening up in international relations and international politics.

International Relations: So Near and Yet So Far

International relations is a discipline that in an institutional sense split away from international law. The deficiencies perceived in the parent discipline of international law by the offspring discipline played a key part in its own differentiation and subsequent theoretical development. Within the discipline of international relations, international law sometimes takes the role of straw man in that it is taken to represent, anachronistically, an outdated theoretical standpoint on relationships between nations. It is identified as the embodiment of a 'formal-legal' viewpoint on authority relationships among nations. This viewpoint is defined as heir to a long tradition in political philosophy going back at least to Hobbes, according to which the natural state of affairs as between nations is one of a 'state of nature' or 'anarchy' (Lake 2009: 1). That is to say, international law is, for international relations, the discipline which implements this particular, minimalist account of legitimate authority as between states. In turn this 'formal-legal theory' is itself described as having had hegemonic status within the larger academic debate (Lake 2009: 34). From this standpoint international law becomes a discipline that persists in mistaken beliefs about its subject matter, beliefs which international relations theory has shed and to which it offers competing alternatives. Of course correspondingly dismissive and ill-informed views about international relations theory could be found in the writings of international law. Although such disciplinary disputes are largely professional identity matters, rather than matters of substance, the understanding of international law within international relations theory is of some interest. The subject matter of the two disciplines does overlap and a genuine contribution to theoretical development in one would also contribute to the development of the other (Aalberts 2012). Reconsiderations of the state-as-quasi-individual account may therefore give rise to some new perspectives on the larger conceptual package of which international relations and international law are a part.

International relations theory has been, and has continued to be, strongly influenced by social science disciplines such as political theory and, to a lesser extent, sociology. It is, one might say, an unambiguously social science whereas the larger affiliation of international law is less easy to assign. The major theoretical orientations within international relations are briefly examined in the course of this discussion. In significant ways the major contemporary approaches within international relations correspond to dominant approaches in international law. Standard overviews of the discipline divide it up into two main approaches: 'realism' and 'constructivism'. Both in turn take different forms. In particular the well-established realist tradition in international relations can be divided into (at least) two streams: a classic approach as set out by the discipline's founders such as Morgenthau, and a more recent neo-liberal, institution-focused version which Reus-Smit labels 'rationalist'. The realist approach takes an objectivist view of states and their conduct. In Erskine's words, 'much work within IR is premised on (often uncritically accepted) assumptions of the ontological status and idealized capacities of those institutions known as states' (Erskine 2003b: 3).

'Constructivism' is a more recent approach, being first articulated in the later 1980s, although it too already takes different forms (Reus-Smit 2004a). In contrast with the realist approach, the constructivist approach focuses on somewhat subjective or meaning-based forms of analysis. The influence of the behavioural sciences in particular has been such as to reinvent an individualistic account of the state – a state-as-actor account according to which states interact on the basis of meanings and intentions. This at least is one of the versions of the constructivist approach in international relations theory. The constructivist approach finds space for considerations of ethics and for norms, whereas the realist approach is characterized by an instrumental or Machiavellian orientation focusing on naked power. Realism understood in that way is itself of course an ethical position, of a dogmatic kind. In any event questions of ethics are integral to world politics (Booth, Dunne and Cox 2001: 6). Both approaches are more complex, more diverse and of course more sophisticated than this summary suggests, yet the correspondence with contemporary international law remains viable (Koh 2005: 18).

Morgenthau and Realism

The relationships between the two disciplines of international law and international relations include both complementary and antagonistic elements. Early scholars of what might now be termed international law, such as Hobbes, Grotius and Pufendorf, were at least as much concerned with what would now be called international relations (Nussbaum 2007: 230). It is still unclear whether any of these early writers should be aligned with the realist tradition that came to dominate international relations theory in the twentieth century. Hobbes is often categorized in this way but it has been strongly urged that Hobbes was part of a natural law tradition in this respect (Covell 2004: 6). To some extent the independent discipline of international relations arose out of debates within international law, broadly conceived as an extended discipline, in the early decades of the twentieth century (Koskenniemi 2001: 473). The discipline of international relations arose in part as a reaction to certain forms of international law discourse, perceived as having failed the world in its times of greatest need. The League of Nations was itself a response to related concerns and both in its intentions and in its realization it formed an essential background to the development of the discipline in the 1920s. But it was E.H. Carr and Hans Morgenthau, writing in the decades around World War II, who set out the manifesto for the modern discipline of international relations as the study of state interests understood as primitive and entirely egotistical; such that states were to be seen as entities that in the words of Kenneth Waltz, 'at a minimum, seek their own preservation and, at a maximum, drive for universal domination' (Waltz 2005: 27).

As Reus-Smit shows, Morgenthau's approach treats states as 'the key actors ... engaged in a continuous struggle with each other' (Reus-Smit 2004b: 15). They are 'rational unitary actors' whose interests are well defined (Buchanan 2004: 108). What is important to stress is the reliance of realist international relations theory on notions of the state as actor. The theory 'is built up from the assumed motivations of states and the actions that correspond to them' (Waltz 2005: 43). According to Covell 'the claims of the realists concerning international politics ... are claims that imply a limited role, or indeed no role at all, for law, and for the principles of justice and morality associated with law, in the conduct of states and rulers and in the overall organization of the international sphere' (Covell 2004: 7).

Morgenthau distinguished international law from international relations thus conceived, such that international law is to be understood as a secondary and by no means a necessary effect of the clash of states. It is however clear that statehood within international law has itself, at some times at least, been understood in ways that are very close to Morgenthau's sense of the state, that is to say as a unitary actor whose relationships with other corresponding actors is fundamentally competitive. It may well be that Morgenthau was correct to argue, as in effect he did, that if the state for international law is understood in such ways, then international law reduces to international relations; international law 'is thus epiphenomenal' (Reus-Smit 2004b: 16).

For Morgenthau, international relations, understood as power politics, underlies all international dealings. Even if international law remains descriptively adequate to certain spheres, an understanding of international law as in any sense normative is ruled out as conceptually inadequate. Indeed it would be utopian and self-deceptive. International law is at best secondary to power-politics. For example international law is called in to articulate the effects of war, 'to formulate in legal terms the shift in power which victory and defeat in the preceding war have brought about, and to ensure the stability of the new distribution of power by means of legal stipulations' (Morgenthau 2005: 37). Koskenniemi has argued that Morgenthau's conceptual development of the political 'as a quality and not a substance, capable of penetrating every realm of international life' was influential on international legal theorist Carl Schmitt in the form of 'the political as an intensity concept' (Koskenniemi 2005: 436). Conceptual contributions to international law include a variety of responses to the trans-disciplinary notion of realism in international affairs. Allen Buchanan (2010) has argued that realism in international relations theory has had a deleterious impact on international legal theory. Buchanan rejects realism, in relation to the international conduct, for example, of states, as having no substance. Its nihilism extends to any moral aspect of international law and hence clarifies the need for a moral theory of international law (Buchanan 2004: 34).

It is true that international law for Morgenthau is in some respects more than the above (Jütersonke 2010). Perhaps grudgingly, Morgenthau agrees that much of international law is usually complied with. This compliance arises in economic, territorial and diplomatic applications of international law, rather than in those areas more directly concerned with competition for power and with attempts to keep the international peace (Morgenthau 2005: 39). Moreover so long as the price is not too high, compliance is in nations' interest for example in the context of reciprocity (Morgenthau 2005: 42). In general for Morgenthau international law is characterized by poor enforcement as a consequence of the supreme importance of power relations. 'When push comes to shove', so to speak, when 'compliance with international law and its enforcement have a direct bearing upon the relative power of the nations concerned … considerations of power rather than of law determine compliance and enforcement' (Morgenthau 2005: 42). And the whole process is an inevitable because a natural one: for Morgenthau the struggle for power is the driving force of international relations. 'The drives to live, to propagate, and to dominate are common to all men'. These are the 'elemental bio-psychological drives by which in turn society is created'. International structures and arrangements are not 'social arrangements and institutions created by man' (Morgenthau 2005: 34).

While Morgenthau's writings are only part of the corpus of the discipline, and in many ways an historical part, realism in international relations remains a significant school. 'Realism' in international relations theory includes the assertion that 'the state is the most significant actor in international relations' (Erskine 2003c: 37). In Erskine's words,

> For those who focus on 'agents', employing rational choice and Game Theory models, states are unproblematically independent, unitary and rational actors – a depiction based on an analogy with individual human beings drawn from microeconomics. (Erskine 2003b: 3)

One way of thinking about realism in international relations is to accept its own evaluation; that is to say to accept its fundamental presuppositions. Thus Walt has written as follows:

> By identifying the core problem of international politics – the insecurity and competition induced by the existence of independent states in anarchy – the realist tradition has set the terms of debate even for those thinkers who do not accept its generally pessimistic conclusions. (Hathaway and Koh 2005: 48)

According to Walt the phenomena discussed by realism in international law are themselves in effect natural phenomena like gravity. But as we have seen in previous chapters and as other contributors to international relations theory point out, the presupposition of anarchic, independent states as the factual substrate is itself questionable, if indeed it is even coherent as a formulation. An awareness of the limitations of the realist approach is what drives the search for alternative formulations within international relations theory, so these other traditions should be examined.

From Anarchy to Constructivism in International Relations

Alternatives to the early realist orthodoxy may be said to include other 'interest-based theories of state behaviour', such as institutionalism and liberal theory, as well as 'norm-based theories of state behaviour' including 'constructivism'. For example, the 'English School' international relations scholar Hedley Bull, writing in the decades after World War II, had described how 'a group of states, conscious of certain common interests and common values, form a society in the sense that they conceive themselves to be bound by a common set of rules ...'

(Reus-Smit 2004c: 274–5). This is a social contract approach writ large, expressed in the language of the subjective, will-deploying actor. According to Christian Reus-Smit, 'pluralists and solidarists' within the 'English School' of international relations differed over how to unpack Bull's proposal. For the pluralists, each state 'may pursue his own purposes'; for the solidarists, according to Reus-Smit, international society is not 'a society of states' at all but 'a society of individuals and peoples' (Reus-Smit 2004c: 276). It is 'a world society … [T]here is an ethical universe beyond the state that is … constitutive of international society and its law'. Contemporary scholars within international law are attempting to improve the precision of this kind of claim (Capps 2009; Lepard 2010).

Martha Finnemore's approach is a version of constructivism in international relations theory, focused on norms and structures of 'meaning and social value'. Interests for Finnemore are 'constructed through social interaction' (Finnemore 2005: 113). Thus '[s]tructures of shared knowledge and intersubjective understandings may … shape and motivate actors' such as states and individuals. 'We can understand changes in [the] normative fabric of international politics only if we investigate the shared understandings that underlie it'(Finnemore 2005: 116, 119). Finnemore uses the language of states being 'socialized', for example socialized 'to want certain things by the international society in which they and the people in them live' (2005: 113). As for international law, Finnemore calls upon international law's acceptance of norms as support for her constructivist approach and identifies a common focus on norms as an avenue for dialogue 'foreclosed under realist domination of our discipline' (2005: 118). The *opinio juris* is quite correctly cited by Finnemore as an example of normative conduct being determined in international law by recourse to statements of shared belief among states. It may be however that Finnemore here has identified common problems in the two disciplines, rather than a common avenue to solutions. The 'sociological' or socio-psychological approach adopted by Finnemore is in many ways a much more sophisticated framework than realist theory, yet it remains in its own ways problematic. Similar caveats apply to the approach of John Ruggie, for whom 'constructivism is about human consciousness' (Ruggie 2005: 120). For Ruggie, the social constructivist approach to international relations is above all characterized by its recognition of the importance of constitutive rules at the international level. States are individual actors: '[A]t the level of individual actors constructivism seeks, first of all, to problematize the identities of and interests of states and to show how they have been socially constructed' (2005: 126).

In a similar tradition, Alexander Wendt seeks to draw ideas 'from structurationist and symbolic interactionist sociology' (Wendt 2005: 127). Wendt states that a 'fundamental principle of constructivist social theory is that people act towards objects, including other actors, on the basis of the meanings that the objects have for them. States act differently toward enemies than they do toward friends because enemies are threatening and friends are not' (2005: 128). Thus '[a]ctors acquire identities – relatively stable, role-specific understandings and expectations about self – by participating in … collective meanings [such as "the cold war is over"]' (2005: 129). Wendt is clear that states are like persons: 'states are people, too'

(Erskine 2003c: 19). Thus '[t]he distribution of power may always affect states' calculations, but how it does so depends on the intersubjective understandings and expectations ... that constitute their conceptions of self and other' (Wendt 2005: 129). Similarly, 'self-help' in the international sphere is one of the 'structures of identity and interest that may exist under anarchy' (Wendt 2005: 130). The language of anarchy and the language of intersubjectivity do not seem to go together. More to the point, neither seem helpful in analysing the interrelations of collectives (Prozorov 2009: 223).

From the point of view of the current project, some useful formulations can with difficulty be derived. For Wendt, states have multiple identities just like persons, and likewise, these arise from institutional roles. Thus 'a state may have multiple identities as "sovereign", "leader of the free world", "imperial power", and so on' (Wendt 2005: 129). It is so to speak 'a matter of hats'. This pluralistic or perspectivist notion has been discussed above in Chapter 5 in the context of state complicity and of *dédoublement fonctionnel*. Wendt's approach might in this sense contribute to the collectivist project. But the price seems very high to pay. Wendt's position is radically subjectivist:

> The commitment to and the salience of particular identities vary, but each identity is an inherently social definition of the actor grounded in the theories which actors collectively hold about themselves and one another and which constitute the structure of the social world. (Wendt 2005: 129)

Consistent with this approach, institutions for Wendt are 'cognitive entities that do not exist apart from actors' ideas about how the world works' (Wendt 2005: 130). The discussion switches from the motivation of individual persons (such as professors) to the 'identity confusion' of the US and former USSR, states which 'seem unsure of what their "interests" should be' (Wendt 2005: 129). This anthropomorphic approach is diametrically opposed to the agenda of the present work. Wendt directly addresses the question of anthropomorphism:

> I assume that a theoretically productive analogy can be made between individuals and states ... states are collectivities of individuals that through their practices constitute each other as 'persons' having interests, fears and so on. A full theory of state identity-and-interest-formation would nevertheless need to draw insights from the social psychology of groups and organizational theory, and for that reason my anthropomorphism is merely suggestive. (Wendt 2005: 133)

So what do these explorations tell us about the discipline of international relations? One purpose of the present book is to argue that international law needs a more nuanced understanding of statehood, and the lurking threat of reduction to a realist theory of international relations is one reason for this. At the same time and for the same reasons, the alternative traditions in international relations need to be examined. Unlike the Morgenthau tradition, those alternatives may contribute to the project of developing international law and in turn may be themselves assisted by that process. However the neo-liberal, institution-focused version of realism retains its focus on states as rational actors, while expanding the account of co-operative co-ordination among such states. It is the constructivist alternative (Morgan 2011: 51) advocated by Reus-Smit and others that attempts a radical shift away from realism. This approach treats political action as fundamentally social and as governed by norms just as much as by material interests. There is a focus on 'actors' [social] identities', their 'intersubjective beliefs' and reasons for action (Reus-Smit 2004b: 21). Identity and purpose are understood as socially generated or even 'learned'. The language here is the language of 'socialization' and meaning for actors. There is a marked influence from psychology and from forms of sociology most influenced by psychology. Just as for Reus-Smit international law in contemporary times is increasingly oriented to the rights and agency of individual persons (Reus-Smit 2004a: 7), so a constructivist international relations treats international political actors as exhibiting (or, at least, reflecting) human characteristics such as the search for meaning.

The orientation brings to bear a humanistic, subjectivist orientation to international relations, emphasizing belief structures and moral agency. It also brings to bear, secondarily as it would appear, a discursive orientation, emphasizing social practice. These two orientations are in tension with each other in other disciplinary contexts, which may be a warning sign. Within international relations the implementation of these perspectives includes an unpacking of the forms of reason that are said to characterize political deliberation. For Reus-Smit political deliberation is carried out by social actors pursuing goals relating to self-identity. Thus 'the politics of identity … necessarily accompanies the mutual recognition of sovereign statehood' (Reus-Smit 2004b: 32). Reus-Smit refers to 'the complex of intersubjective meanings that constitute international law as a distinctive social practice' (2005c: 274).

In thinking about international law from a constructivist international relations perspective, there does seem to be a model of interaction between individual human persons at play – perhaps an image of a parliamentary debate, or even a Rawlsian summit meeting of the representatives of 'peoples'. The question arises as to the adequacy of the approach when extrapolated to international politics or law. Reus-Smit says that 'international actors reason with analogies' and indicates that states can 'feel obliged' (Reus-Smit 2004b: 41–2). The obvious danger is that a model of individual persons in communication with one another is transposed to the international sphere so that states are treated as person-like actors, not only competing, co-operating and otherwise interacting with corresponding others but also 'feeling' and 'believing': setting off all the familiar concerns of such tropes. The model may or may not be adequate to describe the interaction of individual humans – psychology presents us with a range of options. Even if it is adequate to that context, the shift of context calls the model into question. In a related manner, Waldron's warnings on identity politics are also, of course, extremely pertinent. This issue becomes particularly significant in relation to sovereignty; Tanja Aalberts has referred expressly to 'the constructivist conceptualization of sovereignty as identity' (Aalberts 2012: 84). Before turning to that issue, some final comments should be made on conceptualizations of the state in contemporary international relations theory.

In the context of an examination of states as institutions, Toni Erskine makes a distinction between groups or collectives that can be identified as 'institutional moral agents' (Erskine 2003c: 29) and those that cannot. Mere crowds for Erskine clearly cannot. States clearly can be so identified unless their statehood is severely compromised. Erskine emphasizes that institutional moral agents must have an identity that is internal, not merely ascribed from the outside. Thus she asserts that states 'are institutional moral agents' because they meet a set of criteria of which the most notable is as follows:

> [T]he state has a conception of itself as a unit. This feature is distinct from the juridical identity that it is granted by international society and is perhaps most evident in the constitutional framework by which it defines itself. (Erskine 2003c: 27)

Erskine comments that attempting to assign duties 'to a collective that is *not* an agent is an incoherent exercise' (Erskine 2003c: 35). She argues that formal organizations can be moral agents and 'can therefore be bearers of duties' (2010: 262). As well as states, the category of institutional moral agents includes for example 'Hamas, Amnesty International, Microsoft, the Catholic Church and the World Bank' (Erskine 2010: 265). Other examples for Erskine are 'the UN' and 'the US military'. Generally speaking 'nations' as such are not institutional moral agents, nor is the 'international community'.

Erskine discusses Robert Jackson's model of states and quasi-states, in which the latter category include weak, recently emerged post-colonial states that while formally recognized as such by the international community, are highly dependent on powerful states. Erskine notes that Jacksonian quasi-states are still, in her account, institutional moral agents, so long as they possess the capacity for collective purposive action and can be said to constitute a 'distinct organized unit through time' (2003c: 29). Erskine likewise claims that institutional moral agents, under her theory, have internal identities, and in effect, are thus 'self-conscious entities'. The subjectivist tone should be noted. Except for adjustments over the margins of statehood, where a mere collectivity has failed to meet the criteria of subjecthood, the account reaffirms a picture of the state offered by Wendt and by Reus-Smit. The true state is a kind of person.

Statehood, Sovereignty, Governmentality

The main forms of explanation in international relations theory are therefore familiar ones. The more traditional forms are versions of realism based on states as self-contained actors. The main alternative theories, generally labelled as 'constructivist', concern themselves with intersubjectivity and meaning-making between individuals. The 'plague on both your houses' attitude seems to cover these options. This should be borne in mind when discussing the topic of sovereignty.

Tanja Aalberts offers a critical overview of sovereignty as understood in contemporary international relations and international law. Aalberts' project to some extent converges with one of the projects of the current book: an account of states that keeps in focus their collective character. She criticizes Wendt for being too individualist in his account of the origins of sovereignty (Aalberts 2012: 78). For Wendt, as Alberts describes, what critically emerges from co-operation is 'collective identities'. Thus 'as a result of interaction and shared meanings' between states as actors, 'a sort of "super-ordinate identity" can develop, above and beyond the state, blurring the boundary between Self and Other and generating interests being defined on account of "us as a team"' (Aalberts 2012: 74). Aalberts suggests, again glossing Wendt, that the European Union may be an example of such a 'tangible collectivity' and that 'membership of the "society of states", with the accompanying norms and institutions [such as sovereign equality], constitutes a collective identity if states adhere to them … because they have internalized the norms and identify with them' (Aalberts 2012: 74).

As Aalberts shows, Wendt thus treats a corporate identity as an essential or inherent ('primordial') aspect of statehood, prior to interaction. Aalberts argues, against this view, that states' individuality is not so much inherent or primordial, but constructed out of the larger processes of regulation. Aalberts is thus critical of the express anthropomorphism of Wendt, for whom as we have seen above, 'states are real actors to which we can legitimately attribute anthropomorphic qualities like desires, beliefs, and intentionality' (Aalberts 2012: 84). For Aalberts, in contrast, 'the state is a legal fiction much like a person is'. Citing Raič, the state 'has to be treated in international law as a subject separate from the individuals comprising it, that is, as a legal construct: a legal person'. More succinctly, quoting Ngaire Naffine, the state is a 'contingently constructed socio-legal complex' (Aalberts 2012: 85).

Among other intellectual resources from the social sciences and philosophy, Aalberts explores Foucault's analyses of governmentality in the context of statehood and sovereignty. Thus Aalberts suggests that

> if governmentality can be described as a form of power/knowledge, a particular way of imagining the world for the purpose of demarcating a realm of governable conduct, then sovereign statehood can be conceived as both a 'principle of intelligibility of reality' and a 'regulatory idea' … the Westphalian template itself can hence be seen as a governmental project … (Aalberts 2012: 137)

It should be stressed that in general Aalberts is careful to avoid the fetishization of Westphalia, its overvaluation as origin point or as watershed. By 'the Westphalian template' she refers to an accepted formulation without necessarily endorsing its veracity. In the Foucaultian context, Aalberts points to a contrast between two viewpoints: on the one hand 'traditional Westphalian conceptions' of sovereignty according to which 'an immanent status of absolute freedom and self-determination' is posited; and on the other a 'more ambiguous position of sovereign subject-hood, which at the same time constitutes an object of knowledge and a subject that knows' (Aalberts 2012: 141). Thus, for Aalberts, states are not only 'bearers of power and authority in the international realm' but also 'subject to international protocols and regimes of knowledge that empower them as subjects' (2012: 141).

This statement needs careful analysis. The double use of the word 'subject' at the two ends of this clause, both for a process and for a product so to speak, is a little inelegant but consistent with the Foucaultian framework being explored. Subjectivity in Foucault's vocabulary is complex and sophisticated, and the sense of 'them as subjects' has to be understood in that light. However, it seems difficult to avoid the conclusion that Aalberts has failed to entirely disenchant herself of the traditional viewpoint of states as person-like subjects. A thorough-going Foucaultian analysis of international relations as a form of governmentality might well yield new insights into the construction of statehood on the international stage, but Aalberts has not yet developed that project.

Some possibilities are offered by the more extensive discussion of Foucault's ideas on governmentality by Golder and Fitzpatrick (2009). As these authors discuss, Foucault's writings on this topic included an analysis of 'pastoral power', the development of which he characteristically traced from ancient times up till modernity. 'Foucault's lecture course is hence the narrative of the progressive "secularization" of the Christian pastorate and the adoption of many aspects of pastoral power by the institutions of the modern European nation-state' (Golder and Fitzpatrick 2009: 30). Significantly, Foucault's 'pastoral power' is manifest in the doctrine of *raison d'état* in modern times – 'reason of state' as an overriding caretaking or welfarist policy – and in its 'individualizing power, in that the pastor must care for each and every member of the flock singly' (2009: 30). What Foucault was suggesting then was that individualization in modern life, a topic of considerable significance to the project of international law as a law of collectives, was over-determined: as well as the more strident claims of reformed Christianity, less patent but perhaps even more pervasive forces were pressing in that direction. If the modern state is modelled on a shepherd (to phrase it crudely) then the image of state as person is not limited by personalized monarchy. Princes come and go, and the epoch of monarchies has come and gone, but the pastoral state perdures. The pastoral state cares for its flock, the population. Some reasons for the tenacity of the personalized image of the state, as a subject that is to say, are thereby indicated. But while important pointers can be found (Koskenniemi 2005a:614), a Foucaultian analysis of the theory of international law remains a barely commenced project.

If polities are defined as independent, like pre-Socratic 'atoms' so to speak, then it would appear that the pragmatic task of international law is primarily one of seeking some kind of communication and *rapprochement*, or even co-ordination, as between those 'sovereign' entities. This is the mission apparently manifested in the daily activities of the world's diplomats. The project of one of international law's most influential writers, the eighteenth century Swiss diplomat Vattel, has been treated as the construction of a systemic account of international law on this basis (Lake 2009: 38). To the extent this is accurate, Vattel's account stands in a line of descent from the theoretical analysis of sovereignty due to Jean Bodin in the late sixteenth century. Bodin had asserted that sovereignty is an all-or-none affair; it must be absolute in the sense of not being shared or compromised (Koskenniemi 2005a: 78).

Of course it might be argued that if states were indeed independent, absolutely sovereign and (so to speak) cognitively isolated, then neither communication nor co-ordination could ever be possible. This model of plural, independent sovereignties is in many ways absurd: a geopolitical Beckett play. The notion of indivisible sovereignty may itself be absurd for similar reasons. But Vattel's linked assertion of formal equality among states is anything but absurd. For Vattel, this formal equality arises from the parallel between plural sovereign entities (polities or states) existing in a 'state of nature', and individual natural persons doing so as in the philosophy of Hobbes or Locke. In either case, natural rights flow and the upshot of these rights is equality in the sense that all are at the same level. According to Lake, Vattelian equality of states can be identified as the direct precursor of 'the concept of national self-determination' that has been so significant since the early twentieth century (Lake 2009: 38). To conceive of states as independent entities may have served as a 'normative ideal in the service of the project of state building' from the seventeenth century onwards (2009: 39).

Against this orthodox background, Lake presents an argument for 'hierarchy' in international relations. He contrasts this with the traditional account centred on 'anarchy' as pertaining between a plurality of sovereign states. Even if one finds Lake's alternative, hierarchy-based model incompletely worked out, his work usefully demonstrates that models other than the orthodoxy are plausible. It assists international law in standing back from the conceptual presuppositions which Lake has identified. If the (so-called) anarchy model is flawed, then there may well be more than one alternative view. Features of the anarchy model, once examined and even problematized, may reveal more possibilities. Thus Lake suggests a close association between the notions of self-help and of the balancing of power, with the anarchy analysis (Lake 2009: 11). Generally speaking the term 'anarchy' is used loosely in international law's own accounts of itself. In some ways a preferable term might be 'competition' which captures the partial independence of the different entities while recognizing that the entities have no choice but to share a globe and a system of regulation. Such terminological suggestions raise the problem of constitutionality, an 'umbrella' term that covers a range of issues in international co-ordination and structure. Neil Walker has noted that constitutionalism in the context of the European Union behaves like a 'cluster concept', 'associated simultaneously with a number of different but themselves interrelated definitive criteria' (Walker 2010: 154).

International constitutionalism; sovereignty; statehood; governmentality: a collectives-centred approach to international law would illuminate these interrelated issues. It may be that international relations theory stands in need of this new initiative just as much as international law. International relations theory, like international law, treats of individuals. They may be cold-hearted 'realists' or warm-hearted 'constructivists' but states remain persons, actors on the world stage. In this context, Prozorov argues that the influence of Carl Schmitt has been almost hegemonic in defining the task of international relations (Prozorov 2009: 223). Transcending Schmitt has turned out, according to Prozorov, to be extraordinarily difficult. Prozorov's proposals for transcending the Schmittian worldview call upon formulations of Agamben and of Badiou, both of whom challenge the role of identity and of identity politics. Moreover, and consistent with the arguments of Waldron discussed earlier, Sergei Prozorov refers to 'the painstaking process of the fragmentary emergence of the world community defined in non-identitarian terms' (Prozorov 2009: 241). This is the challenge of the collective.

According to Eugene Holland, the Schmittian state 'enjoys a monopoly not only on violence but also on citizenship, on people's sense of belonging and the degree and kind of their investment in social groups' (Holland 2011: 62). Non-state collectivities such as communes, and co-operation in general, constitute forms of resistance. Within social and political theory the association of the state with violence, whether symbolic or actual, is so familiar as to be cliché. Thus Holland refers to 'the prelegitimate act of violence necessary for founding the State' (Holland 2011: 159).

Hardt and Negri agree that Schmitt remains a powerful intellectual presence. They observe that Schmitt 'manages to bring together the various medieval and feudal theories of sovereignty of the ancien régime with the modern theories of dictatorship' (Hardt and Negri 2004: 330). For Hardt and Negri, modern sovereignty 'does not require that a single individual … stand alone above society … but it does require that some unitary political subject – such as a party, a people, or a nation – fulfil that role' (2004: 331). Hardt and Negri continue:

> [W]e have passed from national government to imperial governance, from the hierarchy of fixed national powers to the mobile and multilevel relations of global organizations and networks. (Hardt and Negri 2004: 323)

Sociological theory of geopolitics is in agreement that 'sovereignty remains a systemic property but its institutional insertion and its capacity to legitimate and absorb all legitimating power, to be the source of law, have become unstable' (Sassen 2006: 415). Sassen continues: 'The politics of contemporary sovereignties are far more complex than notions of mutually exclusive territorialities can capture'. This approach to sovereignty in the contemporary world suggests that a focus on the state is anachronistic. But for collectives to be thought of as benevolent alternatives to the state, would clearly be inadequate. There is more than a little romanticism in such a formulation, not to mention kitsch (Koskenniemi 2005b). International relations, like international law, needs to come to terms with collectives in their dark sides as well as in their bright sides. As Adorno said, '[m]ere affability is participation in injustice' (Aust 2011: 427).

Chapter 9
Toward a Law of People

Cosmopolitanism and Solidarity

There is a long and honourable tradition of scholars and even the occasional politician raising their eyes above their home turf. Gladstone once remarked that 'each train that passes a frontier weaves the web of the human federation' (Koskenniemi 2001: 223). And there is an undeniably cosmopolitan flavour to the approach being advocated here. It might be thought to be 'cosmopolitanism lite', the kind of easy-going cultural worldliness that disavows national or ethnic identity and which seems to come easily to the Western elite. Just as the English language is happily acknowledged by its native speakers as a grab-bag of other linguistic influences over the centuries, so it is easy from a position of comfort to repudiate identity politics as, in effect, primitive. The possessor of dual passports has a certain 'belt and braces' level of security as well as the complacent sense of representing the future. The step from two to many passports seems much smaller than the step from one to two, which in turn is very much smaller than the step from none to one. Of course, it would all look and feel very different if global power relations were otherwise: following the above analogy, as if the English language, accumulating the cast-offs of the speech of its overlords, were the language of slaves. Having no nation may not be the same as needing no nation.

The argument being made in this book is that international law must take on board these questions and that the first step (but only the first step) is to recast its vocabulary. Reconstituting its grammar is another task. The collectivist paradigm in international law is intended to be a contribution to the cosmopolitanism project more broadly. Cosmopolitanism has been a feature of numerous philosophical and political theory traditions over the centuries, going back at least to the assertion of Diogenes the Cynic that he was 'a citizen of the world' (Appiah 2006). Diogenes' existence was 'dog-like' (the origin of the word 'cynic' in this case) and involved a life of both poverty and openness to the public gaze. Diogenes was famously unimpressed by the visit of Alexander the Great and his cosmopolitanism was of a quietist variety so far as knowledge of, or involvement in the lives of, anyone beyond his place of residence was concerned. To this extent the Cynical version of cosmopolitanism joins hands with the many faith-based movements to withdrawal from society over subsequent centuries. That is to say, the monastic life and the life of the hermit or ascetic involve a rejection of political life and of citizenship which in a negative way is a form of cosmopolitanism, which rejects all polities equally. Of course in some of its faith-based variants, collective commitment takes the form of a proselytizing and sometimes a militant religious imperialism. Faith-based conquest or aspirations to wholesale conversion of the world's population are forms of cosmopolitanism because political boundaries would be dissolved in such a millennial triumph.

Identity is a key problem for cosmopolitanism because it seems to shackle the person to his or her locality. Identity politics, as defined for example by Jeremy Waldron, might be thought of as anathema to the cosmopolitan project. By its nature cosmopolitanism calls into question local loyalties and local identities. The term has indeed been employed as a term of accusation in the rhetoric of oppression, especially in the context of post-war anti-Semitism in the USSR and elsewhere (Rensmann and Schoeps 2011). In that hateful discourse rootlessness is treated as a sign not merely of the seriousness of the projected threat, but of its universality. More generally, theorists differ over the scale and over the consequences of the cosmopolitan dethroning of patriotism and of its fellow-travellers. The universalizing thrust of the cosmopolitan project would seem to eradicate cultural differences along with political boundaries. In so doing the threat of what might turn out to be cultural hegemony cannot be ignored. This is one way of thinking about cosmopolitanism lite: as a product, and '[t]he same product is offered everywhere' (Badiou 2003:121).

In relation to a cosmopolitan 'dethroning of patriotism' it has been suggested by Schwartz, following Habermas and others, that a benevolent 'constitutional' genus of patriotism is in fact needed. Thus 'a vague cosmopolitan commitment to democracy and human rights would seem incapable of engendering the kind of solidarity needed to supplant competing nationalisms' (Schwartz 2011: 505). This claim is contestable, and needs somewhat more support than Schwartz provides, but it makes the point that patriotism is a complex phenomenon and that its connections with nationalism are themselves complex. One significant contemporary contributor to the debate proposes a way in which cosmopolitanism can be synthesized with the 'rootedness' in the local that so strongly characterizes identity politics. Kwame Anthony Appiah's 'rooted cosmopolitanism' thus seeks to 'marry our cultural differences to a common humanity' (Adelman 2012: 187). Appiah's 'partial cosmopolitanism' is an attempt to yoke together the individualism of the liberal subject, shaping her or his own path through a landscape of choices, with the aspirations of the internationalist. Rooted cosmopolitanism is an attempted synthesis of the apologist and the utopian. Other formulations include what has been termed cultural cosmopolitanism (Knop 2008: 320).

Onora O'Neill has argued (Nussbaum 2007: 275) that an adequate political theory of cosmopolitanism would need to be based on duties rather than entitlements. As Martha Nussbaum comments, cosmopolitanism as most widely known prefers the latter focus. O'Neill's approach is consistent with Kant's argument that those who can influence each other, 'must accept some civil constitution', which is to say, in the international context, some form of supranational regulation (Capps 2009: 273). Pat Capps shares the Kantian orientation according to which human dignity is the touchstone for law of all kinds. With particular reference to international law, Capps proposes that 'global civil incorporation' is the appropriate instrument for the delivery of the 'solidarist values' that are the end of law (Capps 2009: 272). In a related mode, Nussbaum has proposed that 'we should give our first allegiance to no mere form of government, no temporal power, but to the moral community made up by the humanity of all human beings' (Adelman 2012: 201). Nussbaum asserts what she sees as a Kantian view of 'the moral importance of the state': 'an expression of human autonomy ... already a prominent feature' of the writings of Grotius (Nussbaum 2007: 256). This approach is for Nussbaum closely connected with the respect for other states signalled by a reluctance to intervene and a preference to negotiate with elected representatives. 'The ability to join with others to give one another laws is a fundamental aspect of human freedom. Being autonomous in this sense is no trivial matter: it is part of having the chance to live a fully human life' (2007: 257).

Such an expression of course relies on an individualistic approach to human autonomy. This deontological and highly aspirational form of the cosmopolitan requires, I think, rigorous scrutiny, not least in the context of a desired convergence with international law. Thus Fleur Johns has discussed the 'recurring attempts to restore to international law an imperative if paradoxical sociality'. Johns refers to the 'peripatetic lineage of "the social" in international law' and has also referred to the work of Hannah Arendt and the 'impulses towards solidary renewal of and through law' (2012: 76). Johns refers enigmatically to a loyalty that 'may be relied upon, but ... will not reassure' (Johns 2012: 84). In the international law context 'solidarity rights' have been discussed by Morgan (2011: 51), a category said to include rights to development, to environmental protection and to the alleviation of poverty, again an aspirational rather than a parsimonious definition. More generally, an approach to justice that emphasizes non-domination rather than egalitarianism as such seems appropriate for a collectivist frame in international law. According to Shapiro, 'non-domination [is] in an important sense the primary political value' (Shapiro 2012: 294). The negative register of 'non-domination' is consistent with a sensitivity to the fluidity of identity and of political arrangements. Identity is not only fluid, it is 'compromised' (Waldron 2010: 398), and this term captures important features of the instability of territorial connectivities between populations and spaces.

To attempt to contribute to the articulation of a global solidarity through international law is to stand on the shoulders of giants (Koskenniemi 2005a: 611). But there are pitfalls in the invocation of the collective and of solidarity. Any reference to 'we' is problematic and, so to speak, potentially violent. Who is this 'we'? Florian Hoffmann (2006: 239) criticizes social theorist Richard Rorty for the inadequacy of his understanding or deployment of the 'we'. According to Hoffmann, Rorty 'seeks to a prori undermine attempts to show that "we" as fractured, asymmetrical and full of cross-cutting social antagonisms'. Hoffman cites Nancy Fraser who has written, also in critique of Rorty, of the 'conflicting solidarities and opposing we's' in social space (2006: 227). The 'we' of professional international lawyers is both cohesive and deeply fragmented: collective subjectivities are constructed, negotiated and transgressed in the workaday world of the Plenary Hall (Tallgren 1999). What we do is our collective responsibility: as my local road transport authority has recently reminded me, 'You're not stuck in traffic. *You are traffic*'. It should also be noted that any discussion of cosmopolitan theory, solidarity and the collective brings us face to face with the challenge of hospitality (Knop 2008: 312). As Kant and Derrida have discussed, and as Lemuel Gulliver found in his *Travels*, that is what it all comes down to.

Individualisms and Collectivisms

It is important to be cautious about 'individualism', a term with 'multiple ambiguities' (Nussbaum 2007: 441 n28). Yet the question of the collective as the other to the individual still requires further consideration. The question is not novel. In the context of international law 'Self and Other', a collective self and related issues are discussed by Nijman (2007: 33, 48). More widely, it is the discipline of psychology that has in most of its manifestations commandeered the individual person as its scientific domain, and has on that basis attempted to explain how people interrelate, communicate and act in groups. Group psychology, crowd psychology and the psychology of dyadic communication – from mothers and babies onwards – have been topics of speculation and of empirical investigation for centuries (Bradley 2005: 81). As a lapsed psychologist it would be easy for the present author to damn these traditions of enquiry with faint praise, or to overlook them entirely, in the context of the work at hand. Some reference should be made to the sophisticated ways in which for example the psychology of affect and of volition are currently being explored. The emotional life can be defined not only in orthodox, subjectivist terms but also in terms of shared discourses and processes for the construction of meaning that are at the same time collaborative and performative (Wetherell 2012). Critique has been offered in the present book of the lingering notion of the 'will' of states. 'Will' in individual persons is scarcely less troublesome as a concept, and continues to be of forensic significance (Motzkau 2009).

Much of psychology over recent centuries, including social psychology, has adopted the experimental methodologies of the natural sciences, and has intersected little with international law. In relation to international law it has been. above all, psychoanalysis that has made an impact. To some extent scholars of international law have shared a fascination with psychoanalysis with political, cultural and sociological scholars over the last century (Parker 2011). Thus it has been observed (Anghie 2007: 133) that conceptualizations of international law between the two World Wars were significantly influenced by psychoanalysis as well as by other movements in the social sciences and humanities. The work of both Hans Kelsen and Carl Schmitt has been shown to reflect that influence (Carty 1995). Sigmund Freud had argued for the significance in the mental life of both individuals and societies of unconscious processes, such as those that are manifested in dreams and in cultural products such as religions (Rose 2007: 62). In English discussions, Brierly's 1936 edition of *The Law of Nations* referred to the 'social consciousness of states' (Anghie 2007: 134). Employing psychological language in this way to describe the characteristics of states of course exemplifies, in a striking manner, the problems associated with thinking of states as kinds of individual. Such tropes may be considered iconic of the forms of discourse in international law that this book has sought to highlight. As we have seen, international relations theory is on occasion guilty of the same practices. According to Sandholtz and Sweet, '[c]itizens, groups, firms, non-governmental organisations, and governmental officials may … be led to alter their own cognitive schema, values, and decision-making' (Reus-Smit 2004c: 271). This style is methodologically as one with the psychologism of Rawls, for whom '[n]o people will be willing to count the losses to itself as outweighed by gains to other peoples' (Rawls 1999a: 60). This *ex cathedra* statement by Rawls might be considered a counter-motto for this book: it seems to me to be misguided and misleading in every possible way. Its only virtue, a technical one, is its consistency with Rawls' previous statements about attachment (Rawls 1999b: 429) which, equally, adhere to traditional values in the guise of philosophical findings.

We know that Freud was dubious about the supposed role played by a postulated 'oceanic feeling' in religious adherence (Koskenniemi 2012), leaning to earthier explanations. As Koskenniemi suggests, questions of motivation and of the complex interplay of the subjective and the objective – questions pressed by Freud over many features of social life – arise just as much in relation to 'projects of world community'. Indeed psychoanalytic language remains of significance in contemporary debate within jurisprudence, including international legal theory (Focarelli 2012: 10). Costas Douzinas suggests, with an oblique reference to psychoanalytic theory, that '[w]hen jurisdiction is itself called into question then the original difference between creating and stating the law returns like the repressed' (Douzinas 2006: 53). It is not entirely clear what Douzinas means by 'original' here, and what weight he wishes to place on this concept. To some extent Douzinas' reference is to a mythological origin of law that might perhaps compete, as a form of explanation of the genealogy of law, with both a social contract and a Rawlsian 'original position'. Any of these three could be a candidate for the Eliadean founding moment referred to by Taylor (2007: 208), as could the origin myth of Oedipus and of the primal horde, as postulated by Freud (Morss 1990: 141). All of these proposed explanations for law's origins make claims about a social milieu in which the mystical knot was first tied. All law, then, may be said to have its birth in the societal, in the community. Unless international law is to be distinguished radically from all other kinds of law, the claim could then be made that the collective dimension of international law has in some sense gone 'underground' insofar as its recognition is concerned. The collective nature of international law might therefore be colourfully said to have 'returned like the repressed' if the arguments made in the present book are accepted.

Sisyphus Needs Allies

I have argued that it is the task of international law to focus on people in their masses, not people as individuals, still less states or their surrogates. From that perspective, international law has followed the time-worn example of the drunk and the lamp-post: looking for his keys not where he may have dropped them but where there is a light, however dim. International law has looked for a systematic understanding of global mass conduct by the light of individuality. Thus it has been a law of Newtonian pebbles, while the ocean has lain neglected before us. This book thus throws down a challenge to the theory of international law: to take collectives seriously. International law has accepted the responsibility for the conceptualization of jural relationships at the global level. This is our diplomatic bag so to speak. As things stand, international law comes in two styles, neither of which successfully recognizes collectives. A third style is needed. No claim is being made as to extensive progress with a new paradigm. But it is hoped that the need for such a new paradigm is demonstrated.

This is all very messianic of course, and should be brought down to size somewhat. International law always has need to restrain a tendency to hyperbole, as Aust emphasizes (Aust 2011: 426). Levelling down all these kinds of institutions, entities and social groups to the single ontological level of 'collectives' is in some respects a bathetic project. It is consistent with a recognition of 'the all-too-human shabbiness of existing law' (Waldron 1992b: 25). But it may still be challenging. If all international law is about collectives, then all legitimate human rights protections are protections of collectives. Even when individual natural persons are directly involved in international law, their involvement arises and is given meaning only by their collective affiliations or shared fate. The role played by lone natural persons, like the role played by individualistic actors such as states and peoples, is to be thought of as legal fiction. Kafka's Joseph K in *The Trial* is, precisely, fictive; as Walter Benjamin urged, the natural or psychological reading of Kafka is mistaken (Benjamin 2009: 212).

International criminal justice, the machinery of which was designed to address the conduct of individual leaders, is trying to respond to the collective and systemic nature of international atrocities. The collective responsibility arising from 'system criminality' calls for conceptual developments in the law of the accessory such as those Douglas Guilfoyle (2011) advocates. Similarly human rights and humanitarian law issues involving private agencies have become increasingly prevalent in recent decades. The activities of multinational private companies often impact on the welfare of communities both positively and negatively. Those companies are themselves collectives. Private security agencies are playing an increasingly significant role in military campaigns and policing operations, and their obligations under humanitarian law (for example) are still being worked out. The argument could equally be made that the defence of the civil rights of an individual against her or his state of nationality, under international human rights instruments and machinery, only has meaning when that 'plaintiff' is thought of as a representative of a class of persons thus protected. In both kinds of context the language of will, consent and choice seem unhelpful. Rather, interests of various collectives are defended (and corresponding benefits realized) as a consequence of procedures and mechanisms that are likewise collective ones. The possibility of conflicting interests, and of conflicting readings of interests, is not only acknowledged but built into the descriptive framework.

If these suggestions are to be entertained then not only are there some interesting challenges, but also new perspectives emerge on the familiar. But the gesture to collectivity is not enough by itself. Toni Erskine has observed that '[c]ollectivities come in a multitude of forms. They include tribes and teams, faculties and families, biker gangs and battalions, corporations and queues at the supermarket, academic bodies and, indeed, states' (Erskine 2003c: 22). And as Maitland remarked, in a not unrelated context, '"[c]ollectively" is the smudgiest word in the English language' (Runciman 2003: 49).

Who Speaks For Whom?

Representation is a key question not only in a democracy, but in any polity. It was of central concern to Hobbes and remains a key problem in political theory (Runciman 1997; 2007). Representation brings into sharp relief the relationships between individual, collective and society (Sajó 2011: 92), and this would include those relationships sometimes labelled as 'managerial' (Koskenniemi 2009). The collective approach to international law radically reframes the role of the individual, yet it has not even 'scotch'd' this snake of representation, let alone dealt it a death blow. We finish then with the agony of representation: with Shakespeare's *Coriolanus*.

Coriolanus has a mixed reputation among the citizenry of Rome, despite his military successes in defending the city. The political elite is able to exploit his disinclination or inability to perform for the population, in the political arena, in order to procure his banishment. (What could possibly go wrong?) As first performed when Hobbes was a teenager, if that can be imagined, Coriolanus is depicted as by nature inarticulate except as war machine. He could have been a contender. Everything Coriolanus does and says is visceral. He is no populist. 'You common cry of curs, whose breath I hate/ As reek o' th' rotten fens ...' But Coriolanus' attitude to the people is much more than aristocratic disdain or the contempt of the soldier for stay-at-homes. These citizens are no mere rabble (and Shakespeare knew how to put a mob on the stage). Coriolanus is angry: and his anger is interconnected with his representational role in the society:

> For your voices I have fought/ Watched for your voices; for your voices bear/
> Of wounds two dozen old; battles thrice six/ I have seen and heard of; for your
> voices have/ Done many things, some less, some more. Your voices! (II iii 133)

We are the voices.

References

Aalberts, T. 2012. *Constructing Sovereignty Between Politics and Law*. London: Routledge.

Adelman, H. 2012. The doctrine of the right to protect: a failed expression of cosmopolitanism, in *Rooted Cosmopolitanism: Canada and the World*, edited by W. Kymlicka and W. Walker. Vancouver: University of British Columbia Press, 178–205.

Anghie, A. 1996. Francisco de Vitoria and the colonial origins of international law. *Social & Legal Studies*, 5, 321–36.

Anghie, A. 2007. *Imperialism, Sovereignty, and the Making of International Law*. Cambridge: Cambridge University Press.

Appiah, K.A. 2006. *Cosmopolitanism: Ethics in a World of Strangers*. New York: Norton.

Arbour, L. 2008. The responsibility to protect as a duty of care in international law and practice. *Review of International Studies*, 34, 445–58.

Aust, H. 2011. *Complicity and the Law of State Responsibility*. Cambridge: Cambridge University Press.

Aust, H. 2012. The Kosovo opinion and issues of international responsibility, in *Kosovo and International Law: The ICJ Advisory Opinion of 22 July 2010*, edited by P. Hilpold. Leiden: Brill, 209–32.

Badiou, A. 2003. *Infinite Thought*. London: Continuum.

Baker, R. 2010. Customary international law in the 21st century: old challenges and new debates. *European Journal of International Law*, 21, 173–204.

Bass, G.J. 2008. *Freedom's Battle: The Origins of Humanitarian Intervention*. New York: Vintage.

Beard, J. 2011. The international law in force: anachronistic ethics and divine violence, in *Events: The Force of International Law*, edited by F. Johns, R. Joyce and S. Pahuja. London: Routledge, 18–28.

Beard, J. and Noll, G. 2009. *Parrhesia* and credibility: the sovereign of refugee status determination. *Social & Legal Studies*, 18, 455–77.

Benjamin, W. 2009. *One-Way Street and Other Writings*. London: Penguin.

Berman, P.S. 2012. *Global Legal Pluralism: A Jurisprudence of Law Beyond Borders*. Cambridge: Cambridge University Press.

von Bernstorff, J. 2010. *The Public International Law Theory of Hans Kelsen: Believing in Universal Law*. Cambridge: Cambridge University Press.

Besson, S. 2010. Theorizing the sources of international law, in *The Philosophy of International Law*, edited by S. Besson and J. Tasioulas. Oxford: Oxford University Press, 163–85.

Booth, K., Dunne, T. and Cox, M. 2001. Introduction, in *How Might We Live? Global Ethics in the New Century*, edited by K. Booth, T. Dunne and M. Cox. Cambridge: Cambridge University Press, 1–28.

Bowden, S. 2011. *The Priority of Events: Deleuze's Logic of Sense*. Edinburgh: Edinburgh University Press.

Bradley, B. 2005. *Psychology and Experience*. Cambridge: Cambridge University Press.

Buchanan, A. 2004. *Justice, Legitimacy, and Self-Determination: Moral Foundations for International Law*. Oxford: Oxford University Press.

Buchanan, A. 2010. The legitimacy of international law, in *The Philosophy of International Law*, edited by S. Besson and J. Tasioulas. Oxford: Oxford University Press, 79–96.

Burke, E. 1997. *Reflections on the Revolution in France*, extracted in *Classics of Modern Political Theory: Machiavelli to Mill*, edited by S. Cahn. Oxford: Oxford University Press, 667–81.

Burman, E. 2008. *Deconstructing Developmental Psychology*. 2nd Edition. London: Routledge.

Byrd, B.S. and Hruschka, J. 2010. *Kant's Doctrine of Right: A Commentary*. Cambridge: Cambridge University Press.

Cahn, S. (ed.) 1997. *Classics of Modern Political Theory: Machiavelli to Mill*. Oxford: Oxford University Press.

Campbell, T. 2001. *Justice*. 2nd Edition. Houndmills: Macmillan.

Campbell, T. 2004. Collective rights and individual actors, in *Law, Legal Culture and Politics in the Twenty-First Century*, edited by G. Doeker-Mach and K. Ziegert. Stuttgart: Steiner, 127–47.

Capps, P. 2004. Positivism in law and international law, in *Law, Morality, and Legal Positivism*, edited by K. Himma. Stuttgart: Steiner, 9–18.

Capps, P. 2009. *Human Dignity and the Foundations of International Law*. Oxford: Hart.

Carty, A. 1995. Law and the postmodern mind: interwar German theories of international law: the psychoanalytical and phenomenological perspectives of Hans Kelsen and Carl Schmitt. *Cardozo Law Review*, 16, 1235–92.

Carty, A. 1996. *Was Ireland Conquered? International Law and the Irish Question*. London: Pluto Press.

Carty, A. 2005. Review essay: international legal personality and the end of the subject: natural law and phenomenological responses to new approaches to international law. *Melbourne Journal of International Law*, 6, 534–52.

Cassese, A. 1995. *Self-Determination of Peoples*. Oxford: Oxford University Press.

Charlesworth, C. and Chinkin, C. 2000. *The Boundaries of International law: A Feminist Analysis*. Manchester: Manchester University Press.

Covell, C. 2004. *Hobbes, Realism and the Tradition of International Law*. Houndmills: Palgrave Macmillan.

Crawford, J. (ed.) 2002. *The International Law Commission's Articles on State Responsibility: Introduction, Text and Commentaries*. Cambridge: Cambridge University Press.

Crawford, J. 2006. *The Creation of States in International Law*. 2nd Edition. Oxford: Oxford University Press.

Crawford, J. 2007. Multilateral rights and obligations in international law. *Recueil des Cours*, 319, 325–482.

Criddle, E. and Fox-Decent, E. 2009. A fiduciary theory of *jus cogens*. *Yale Journal of International Law*, 34, 331–87.

Damrosch, L. 2007. *Jean-Jacques Rousseau: Restless Genius*. Boston: Houghton Mifflin.

Dare, T. 2002. Group rights and constitutional rights, in *Litigating Rights: Perspectives from Domestic and International Law*, edited by G. Huscroft and P. Rishworth. Oxford: Hart.

Davies, N. 2011. *Vanished Kingdoms: The History of Half-Forgotten Europe*. London: Allen Lane.

Delmas-Marty, M. 2009. *Ordering Pluralism: A Conceptual Framework for Understanding the Transnational Legal World*. Oxford: Hart.

Domingo, R. 2011. Gaius, Vattel, and the new global law paradigm. *European Journal of International Law*, 22, 627–47.

Douzinas, C. 2006. Speaking law: on bare theological and cosmopolitan sovereignty, in *International Law and its Others*, edited by A. Orford. Cambridge: Cambridge University Press, 35–56.

Engle, K. 2010. *The Elusive Promise of Indigenous Development: Rights, Culture, Strategy*. Durham NC: Duke University Press.

Erskine, T. (ed.) 2003a. *Can Institutions Have Responsibilities? Collective Moral Agency and International Relations*. Houndmills: Palgrave Macmillan.

Erskine, T. 2003b. Introduction: making sense of 'responsibility' in international relations: key questions and concepts, in *Can Institutions Have Responsibilities? Collective Moral Agency and International Relations*, edited by T. Erskine. Houndmills: Palgrave Macmillan, 1–16.

Erskine, T. 2003c. Assigning responsibilities to institutional moral agents: the case of states and quasi-states, in *Can Institutions Have Responsibilities? Collective Moral Agency and International Relations*, edited by T. Erskine. Houndmills: Palgrave Macmillan, 19–40.

Erskine, T. 2010. Kicking bodies and damning souls: the danger of harming 'innocent' individuals while punishing 'delinquent' states. *Ethics and International Affairs*, 24, 261–85.

Everdell, W. 1997. *The First Moderns: Profiles in the Origins of Twentieth-Century Thought*. Chicago: University of Chicago Press.

Finnemore, M. 2005. *National Interests in International Society*, extracted in *Foundations of International Law and Politics*, edited by O. Hathaway and H.H. Koh. New York: Foundation Press, 112–20.

Focarelli, C. 2012. *International Law as Social Construct: The Struggle for Global Justice*. Oxford: Oxford University Press.

Fox, H. 2007. Time, history and sources of law peremptory norms: is there a need for new sources of international law? In *Time, History and International Law*, edited by M. Craven, M. Fitzmaurice and M. Vogiatzi. Leiden: Martinus Nijhoff, 119–40.

Fox-Decent, E. 2011. *Sovereignty's Promise: The State as Fiduciary*. Oxford: Oxford University Press.

Freud, S. 1964. *Moses and Monotheism. The Standard Edition of the Complete Psychological Works of Sigmund Freud*, Vol. XXIII. London: The Hogarth Press.

Fulbrook, M. 2004. *A Concise History of Germany*. 2nd Edition. Cambridge: Cambridge University Press.

Gaeta, P. 2010. Introduction, symposium: the human dimension of international law. *European Journal of International Law*, 21, 7–9.

Gilbert, M. 2006. *A Theory of Political Obligation*. Oxford: Oxford University Press.

Golder, B. and Fitzpatrick, P. 2009. *Foucault's Law*. London: Routledge.

Gould, C. 2004. *Globalizing Democracy and Human Rights*. Cambridge: Cambridge University Press.

Gover, K. 2010. *Tribal Constitutionalism: States, Tribes, and the Governance of Membership*. Oxford: Oxford University Press.

Grbich, J. 2006. Secrets of the fetish in international law's messianism, in *International Law and its Others*, edited by A. Orford. Cambridge: Cambridge University Press, 197–220.

Gross, L. 1948. The Peace of Westphalia, 1648–1948. *American Journal of International Law*, 42, 20–41.

Guilfoyle, D. 2011. Responsibility for collective atrocities: fair labelling and approaches to commission in international criminal law. *Current Legal Problems*, 64, 255–86.

Hardt, M. and Negri, A. 2004. *Multitude*. Harmondsworth: Penguin.

Hathaway, O. and Koh, H.H. 2005. *Foundations of International Law and Politics*. New York: Foundation Press.

Hitchens, C. 2002. *The Trial of Henry Kissinger*. London: Verso.

Hoeffe, O. 2002. *Categorical Principles of Law: A Counterpoint to Modernity*. University Park PA: Penn State University Press.

Hoeffe, O. 2006. *Kant's Cosmopolitan Theory of Law and Peace*. Cambridge: Cambridge University Press.

Hoffmann, F. 2006. Human rights, the self and the other: reflections on a pragmatic theory of human rights, in *International Law and its Others*, edited by A. Orford. Cambridge: Cambridge University Press, 221–44.

Holland, E. 2011. *Nomad Citizenship: Free-Market Communism and the Slow-Motion General Strike*. Minneapolis: University of Minnesota Press.

Horne, A. 2002. *Seven Ages of Paris: Portrait of a City*. London: Pan.

Hughes, M. 1992. *Early Modern Germany, 1477–1806*. London: Macmillan.

Johns, F. 2012. Living in international law, in *Reading Modern Law: Critical Methodologies and Sovereign Formations*, edited by R. Buchanan, S. Motha and S. Pahuja. London: Routledge, 74–86.

Johns, F., Joyce, R. and Pahuja, S. (eds) 2011. Introduction, in *Events: The Force of International Law*, edited by F. Johns, R. Joyce and S. Pahuja. London: Routledge, 1–17.

Jones, P. 2001. Individuals, communities and human rights, in *How Might We Live? Global Ethics in the New Century*, edited by K. Booth, T. Dunne and M. Cox. Cambridge: Cambridge University Press, 199–215.

Jütersonke, O. 2010. *Morgenthau, Law and Realism*. Cambridge: Cambridge University Press.

Kant, I. 1997. *Perpetual Peace*, extracted in *Classics of Modern Political Theory: Machiavelli to Mill*, edited by S. Cahn. Oxford: Oxford University Press, 571–600.

Kellogg, C. 2010. *Law's Trace: From Hegel to Derrida*. London: Routledge.

Kelsen, H. 1967. *Pure Theory of Law*. Berkeley CA: University of California Press.

Kennedy, D. 2004. *The Dark Sides of Virtue: Reassessing International Humanitarianism*. Princeton: Princeton University Press.

Kingsbury, B. 1999. The applicability of the international legal concept of 'indigenous peoples' in Asia, in *The East Asian Challenge for Human Rights*, edited by J. Bauer and D. Bell. Cambridge: Cambridge University Press, 336–77.

Kingsbury, B. 2000. Reconstructing self-determination: a relational approach, in *Operationalizing the Right of Indigenous Peoples to Self-Determination*, edited by P. Aikio and M. Scheinin. Turku: Abo Akademi, 19–37.

Kissinger, H. 1994. *Diplomacy*. New York: Simon & Schuster.

Klabbers, J. 2002. *An Introduction to International Institutional Law*. Cambridge: Cambridge University Press.

Klabbers, J. 2012. International institutions, in *The Cambridge Companion to International Law*, edited by J. Crawford and M. Koskenniemi. Cambridge: Cambridge University Press, 228–44.

Knop, K. 2008. Citizenship, public and private. *Law and Contemporary Problems*, 71, 309–41.

Koh, H.H. 2005. Why do nations obey international law? extracted in *Foundations of International Law and Politics*, edited by O. Hathaway and H.H. Koh. New York: Foundation Press, 12–19.

Koskenniemi, M. 2001. *Gentle Civilizer of Nations: The Rise and Fall of International Law 1870–1960*. Cambridge: Cambridge University Press.

Koskenniemi, M. 2005a. *From Apology to Utopia: The Structure of International Legal Argument*. Cambridge: Cambridge University Press.

Koskenniemi, M. 2005b. International law in Europe: between tradition and renewal. *European Journal of International Law*, 16, 113–24.

Koskenniemi, M. 2009. The politics of international law – 20 years later. *European Journal of International Law*, 20, 7–19.

Koskenniemi, M. 2011. The political theology of trade law: the scholastic contribution, in *From Bilateralism to Community Interest: Essays in Honour of Judge Bruno Simma*, edited by U. Fastenrath et al. Oxford: Oxford University Press, 90–112.

Koskenniemi, M. 2012. Projects of world community, in *Realizing Utopia: The Future of International Law*, edited by A. Cassese. Oxford: Oxford University Press, 3–13.

Kramer, M. 1991. *Legal Theory, Political Theory, and Deconstruction: Against Rhadamanthus*. Bloomington IN: Indiana University Press.

Kramer, M. 1998. Rights without trimmings, in M. Kramer, N. Simmonds and H. Steiner, *A Debate Over Rights*. Oxford: Oxford University Press, 7–111.

Kramer, M. 1999. *In Defense of Legal Positivism: Law Without Trimmings*. Oxford: Oxford University Press.

Kramer, M., Simmonds, N. and Steiner, H. 1998. *A Debate Over Rights*. Oxford: Oxford University Press.

Kritsiotis, D. 2004. When states use armed force, in *The Politics of International Law*, edited by C. Reus-Smit. Cambridge: Cambridge University Press, 45–79.

Kroslak, D. 2003. The responsibility of collective external bystanders in cases of genocide: the French in Rwanda, in *Can Institutions Have Responsibilities? Collective Moral Agency and International Relations*, edited by T. Erskine. Houndmills: Palgrave Macmillan, 159–82.

Kutz, C. 2000. *Complicity: Ethics and Law for a Collective Age*. Cambridge: Cambridge University Press.

Kymlicka, W. 2011. Beyond the indigenous/minority dichotomy? in *Reflections on the UN Declaration on the Rights of Indigenous Peoples*, edited by S. Allen and A. Xanthakis. Oxford: Hart, 182–208.

Lake, D. 2009. *Hierarchy in International Relations*. Ithaca: Cornell University Press.

Lalonde, S. 2002. *Determining Boundaries in a Conflicted World: The Role of Uti Possidetis*. Montreal: McGill-Queen's University Press.

Lauterpacht, E. 2010. *The Life of Sir Hersch Lauterpacht, QC, FBA, LLD*. Cambridge: Cambridge University Press.

Lefkowitz, D. 2010. The sources of international law: some philosophical reflections, in *The Philosophy of International Law*, edited by S. Besson and J. Tasioulas. Oxford: Oxford University Press, 187–203.

Lepard, B. 2010. *Customary International Law*. Cambridge: Cambridge University Press.

List, C. and Pettit, P. 2011. *Group Agency: The Possibility, Design, and Status of Corporate Agents*. Oxford: Oxford University Press.

Lister, M. 2012. Who are refugees? *Law and Philosophy*. [Online]. Available at: <http://link.springer.com/article/10.1007/s10982-012-9169-7> [accessed: 15 January 2013].

Locke, J. 1997. *Second Treatise of Government*, extracted in *Classics of Modern Political Theory: Machiavelli to Mill*, edited by S. Cahn. Oxford: Oxford University Press, 217–92.

Malcolm, N. 1998. *Kosovo*. New York: New York University Press.

Marks, S. (ed.) 2008. *International Law on the Left*. Cambridge: Cambridge University Press.

Martin, R. and Reidy, D. (eds) 2006. *Rawls's Law of Peoples: A Realistic Utopia?* Oxford: Blackwell.

Mégret, F. 2006. From 'savages' to 'unlawful combatants': a postcolonial look at international humanitarian law's 'other', in *International Law and its Others*, edited by A. Orford. Cambridge: Cambridge University Press, 265–317.

Merquior, J.G. 1980. *Rousseau and Weber: Two Studies in the Theory of Legitimacy*. London: Routledge and Kegan Paul.

Meyerson, D. 2010. Persons and their rights in law and morality. *Australian Journal of Legal Philosophy*, 35, 122–33.

Mill, J.S. 1974. *On Liberty*. London: Penguin.

Miller, D. 2006. Collective responsibility and international inequality, in *The Law of Peoples*, in *Rawls's Law of Peoples: A Realistic Utopia?* edited by R. Martin and D. Reidy. Oxford: Blackwell, 191–205.

Moltchanova, A. 2009. *National Self-Determination and Justice in Multinational States*. Dordrecht: Springer.

Morgan, R. 2011. *Transforming Law and Institution: Indigenous Peoples, the United Nations and Human Rights*. Farnham: Ashgate.

Morgenthau, H. 2005. *Politics Among Nations*, extracted in *Foundations of International Law and Politics*, edited by O. Hathaway and H.H. Koh. New York: Foundation Press, 31–42.

Morss, J.R. 1990. *The Biologising of Childhood: Developmental Psychology and the Darwinian Myth*. Hillsdale NJ: Erlbaum.

Morss, J.R. 1996. *Growing Critical: Alternatives to Developmental Psychology*. London: Routledge.

Morss, J.R. 2004. Heteronomy as the challenge to nation: a critique of collective and of individual rights. *Law, Text, Culture*, 8, 167–90.

Morss, J.R. 2005. Sources of doubt, sources of duty: HLA Hart on international law. *Deakin Law Review*, 10, 41–50.

Morss, J.R. 2008. Can custom be incorporated in law? On the place of the empirical in the identification of norms. *American Journal of Jurisprudence*, 53, 85–99.

Morss, J.R. 2009. The legal relations of collectives: belated insights from Hohfeld. *Leiden Journal of International Law*, 22, 289–305.

Morss, J.R. 2010. On having your legalism and eating it too. *Australian Journal of Legal Philosophy*, 35, 116–21.

Morss J.R. 2011. Book Review, S. Besson and J. Tasioulas (eds), *The Philosophy of International Law, International and Comparative Law Quarterly*, 60, 286–8.

Morss, J.R. 2012. Pluralism and international law. Panel Presentation, American Society for International Law Annual Meeting, Washington DC, March 2011. *American Society for International Law Proceedings*, 105, 459–62.

Morss, J.R. forthcoming. Riddle of the sands: time, power and legitimacy in international law, to appear in *Critical International Law: Post-Realism, Post-Colonialism and Transnationalism*, edited by P. Singh and B. Mayer. New Delhi: Oxford University Press, 2014.

Motzkau, J. 2009. Exploring the transdisciplinary trajectory of suggestibility. *Subjectivity*, 27, 172–94.

Neff, S. 2005. *War and the Law of Nations*. Cambridge: Cambridge University Press.

Newman, D. 2011. *Community and Collective Rights: A Theoretical Framework for Rights Held by Groups*. Oxford: Hart.

Nijman, J. 2007. Paul Ricoeur and international law: beyond 'the end of the subject'. Towards a reconceptualization of international legal personality. *Leiden Journal of International Law*, 20, 25–64.

Nine, C. 2012. *Global Justice and Territory*. Oxford: Oxford University Press.

Nollkaemper, A. and Nijman, J. (eds) 2007. *New Perspectives on the Divide between International and National Law*. Oxford: Oxford University Press.

Nolte, G. and Aust, H. 2009. Equivocal helpers – complicit states, mixed messages, and international law. *International and Comparative Law Quarterly*, 58, 1–30.

Nolte, G. and Aust, H. 2013. European exceptionalism? *Global Constitutionalism*, 2, in press.

Nussbaum, M. 2007. *Frontiers of Justice: Disability, Nationality, Species Membership*. Cambridge MA: Harvard University Press.

Obregón, L. 2006. Completing civilization: Creole consciousness and international law in nineteenth-century Latin America, in *International Law and its Others*, edited by A. Orford. Cambridge: Cambridge University Press, 247–64.

Oeter, S. 2012. Secession, territorial integrity and the Security Council, in *Kosovo and International Law: The ICJ Advisory Opinion of 22 July 2010*, edited by P. Hilpold. Leiden: Brill, 109–38.

Oklopcic, Z. 2009. *Populus interruptus*: Self-determination, the independence of Kosovo, and the vocabulary of peoplehood. *Leiden Journal of International Law*, 22, 677–702.

Orakhelashvili, A. 2006. *Peremptory Norms in International Law*. Oxford: Oxford University Press.

Pahuja, S. 2011. *Decolonising International Law*. Cambridge: Cambridge University Press.

Panayi, P. 1999. *Outsiders: A History of European Minorities*. London: Hambledon.

Parker, I. 2011. *Lacanian Psychoanalysis: Revolutions in Subjectivity*. London: Routledge.

Parsons, T. 2010. *The Rule of Empires: Those Who Built Them, Those Who Endured Them, and Why They Always Fall*. Oxford: Oxford University Press.

Patton, P. 2010. *Deleuzian Concepts: Philosophy, Colonization, Politics*. Stanford CA: Stanford University Press.

Paulus, A. 2010. International adjudication, in *The Philosophy of International Law*, edited by S. Besson and J. Tasioulas. Oxford: Oxford University Press, 207–24.

Paulus, A. 2011. Reciprocity revisited, in *From Bilateralism to Community Interest: Essays in Honour of Judge Bruno Simma*, edited by U. Fastenrath et al. Oxford: Oxford University Press, 113–37.

Pentassuglia, G. 2009. *Minority Groups and Judicial Discourse in International Law*. Leiden: Martinus Nijhoff.

Perreau-Saussine, A. 2010. Immanuel Kant on international law, in *The Philosophy of International Law*, edited by S. Besson and J. Tasioulas. Oxford: Oxford University Press, 53–75.

Peters, A. 2012. Are we moving towards constitutionalization of the world community? in *Realizing Utopia: The Future of International Law*, edited by A. Cassese. Oxford: Oxford University Press, 118–35.

Pettit, P. 2006. Rawls's peoples, in *Rawls's Law of Peoples: A Realistic Utopia?* edited by R. Martin and D. Reidy. Oxford: Blackwell, 38–55.

Pettit, P. 2010. Legitimate international institutions: a neo-republican perspective, in *The Philosophy of International Law*, edited by S. Besson and J. Tasioulas. Oxford: Oxford University Press, 139–60.

Pincus, S. 2009. *1688: The First Modern Revolution*. New Haven: Yale University Press.

Pogge, T. 2006. Do Rawls's two theories of justice fit together? in *Rawls's Law of Peoples: A Realistic Utopia?* edited by R. Martin and D. Reidy. Oxford: Blackwell, 206–25.

Pogge, T. 2010. The role of international law in reproducing massive poverty, in *The Philosophy of International Law*, edited by S. Besson and J. Tasioulas. Oxford: Oxford University Press, 417–35.

Prozorov, S. 2009. Generic universalism in world politics: beyond international anarchy and the world state. *International Theory*, 1, 215–47.

Quirico, O. 2012. Disentangling climate change governance: a legal perspective. *Review of European Community & International Environmental Law*, 21, 92–101.

Rajagopal, B. 2003. *International Law from Below*. Cambridge: Cambridge University Press.

Rawls, J. 1999a. *The Law of Peoples with 'The Idea of Public Reason Revisited'*. Cambridge MA: Harvard University Press.

Rawls, J. 1999b. *A Theory of Justice*. Revised edition. Cambridge MA: Harvard University Press.

Raz, J. 2003. Comments and responses, in *Rights, Culture and the Law: Themes from the Legal and Political Philosophy of Joseph Raz*, edited by L. Meyer, S. Paulson and T. Pogge. Oxford: Oxford University Press, 253–74.

Rensmann, L. and Schoeps, J. (eds) 2011. *Antisemitism and Counter-Cosmopolitanism in the European Union*. Leiden: Martinus Nijhoff.

Reus-Smit, C. 2004a. Introduction, in *The Politics of International Law*, edited by C. Reus-Smit. Cambridge: Cambridge University Press, 1–13.

Reus-Smit, C. 2004b. The politics of international law, in *The Politics of International Law*, edited by C. Reus-Smit. Cambridge: Cambridge University Press, 14–44.

Reus-Smit, C. 2004c. Society, power and ethics, in *The Politics of International Law*, edited by C. Reus-Smit. Cambridge: Cambridge University Press, 272–90.

Rose, J. 2007. *The Last Resistance*. London: Verso.

Rousseau, J.J. 1997. *The Social Contract*, extracted in *Classics of Modern Political Theory: Machiavelli to Mill*, edited by S. Cahn. Oxford: Oxford University Press, 420–485.

Ruggie, J. 2005. What makes the world hang together? Neo-utilitarianism and the social constructivist challenge, extracted in *Foundations of International Law and Politics*, edited by O. Hathaway and H.H. Koh. New York: Foundation Press, 120–127.

Runciman, D. 1997. *Pluralism and the Personality of the State*. Cambridge: Cambridge University Press.

Runciman, D. 2003. The problem of representing the state, in *Can Institutions Have Responsibilities? Collective Moral Agency and International Relations*, edited by T. Erskine. Houndmills: Palgrave Macmillan, 41–50.

Runciman, D. 2007. The paradox of political representation. *Journal of Political Philosophy*, 15, 93–114.

Russell, B. 1961. *History of Western Philosophy*. London: Routledge.

Said, E. 2000. *The End of the Peace Process: Oslo and After*. London: Granta Books.

Sajó, A. 2011. *Constitutional Sentiments*. New Haven: Yale University Press.

Sanchez Brigido, R. 2009. Collective intentional activities and the law. *Oxford Journal of Legal Studies*, 29, 305–24.

Sassen, S. 2006. *Territory, Authority, Rights: From Medieval to Global Assemblages*. Princeton: Princeton University Press.

Schwartz, A. 2011. Patriotism or integrity? Constitutional community in divided societies. *Oxford Journal of Legal Studies*, 31, 503–26.

Schwöbel, C. 2010. Organic global constitutionalism. *Leiden Journal of International Law*, 23, 529–53.

Sellers, M. 1998. *The Sacred Fire of Liberty: Republicanism, Liberalism, and the Law*. Houndmills: Macmillan.

Sellers, M. 2006. *Republican Principles in International Law: The Fundamental Requirements of a Just World Order*. Houndmills: Palgrave Macmillan.

Sen, A. 2012. Thirteenth annual Grotius lecture series: the global status of human rights. *American University International Law Review*, 27, 1–15.

Shapiro, I. 2012. On non-domination. *University of Toronto Law Journal*, LXII, 293–335.

Simma, B. 1994. From bilateralism to community interest in international law. *Recueil des Cours*, 250. Leiden: Martinus Nijhoff.

Simpson, G. 2011. Paris 1793 and 1871: *Levée en masse* as event, in *Events: The Force of International Law*, edited by F. Johns, R. Joyce and S. Pahuja. London: Routledge, 81–90.

Skouteris, T. 2010. *The Notion of Progress in International Law Discourse*. The Hague: TMC Asser Press.

Smith, R. 2003. *Stories of Peoplehood: The Politics and Morals of Political Membership*. Cambridge: Cambridge University Press.

Steiner, H. 1998. Working rights, in M. Kramer, N. Simmonds, and H. Steiner, *A Debate Over Rights*, Oxford: Oxford University Press, 233–301.

Stilz, A. 2009. Why do states have territorial rights? *International Theory*, 1, 185–213.

Stilz, A. 2011. Nations, states and territory. *Ethics*, 121, 572–601.

Tallgren, I. 1999. We did it? The vertigo of law and everyday life at the diplomatic conference on the establishment of an International Criminal Court. *Leiden Journal of International Law*, 12, 683–707.

Tamir, Y. 2003. Against collective rights, in *Rights, Culture and the Law: Themes from the Legal and Political Philosophy of Joseph Raz*, edited by L. Meyer, S. Paulson and T. Pogge. Oxford: Oxford University Press, 183–204.

Tasioulas, J. 2010. The legitimacy of international law, in *The Philosophy of International Law*, edited by S. Besson and J. Tasioulas. Oxford: Oxford University Press, 97–116.

Taylor, C. 2007. *A Secular Age*. Cambridge MA: Harvard University Press.

Teubner, G. 2012. *Constitutional Fragments: Societal Constitutionalism and Globalization*. Oxford: Oxford University Press.

Tuck, R. 1979. *Natural Rights Theories*. Cambridge: Cambridge University Press.

Van Hartesveldt, F. 2000. *The Boer War*. Stroud: Sutton.

Vattel, E. de 2008. *The Law of Nations*. Indianapolis: Liberty Fund.

Waldron, J. 1992a. Minority cultures and the cosmopolitan alternative. *University of Michigan Journal of Law Reform*, 25, 751–93.

Waldron, J. 1992b. Enemies of nomos. Book review of D. Kelley, *The Human Measure. The Times Literary Supplement*, 21 February, 25–6.

Waldron, J. 1998. Is Coleman Hobbes or Hume (or perhaps Locke)? in *Analyzing Law: New Essays in Legal Theory*, edited by B. Bix. Oxford: Oxford University Press, 117–39.

Waldron, J. 1999a. All we like sheep. *Canadian Journal of Law and Jurisprudence*, 12, 169–86.

Waldron, J. 1999b. *The Dignity of Legislation*. Cambridge: Cambridge University Press.

Waldron, J. 2000. What is cosmopolitan? *Journal of Political Philosophy*, 8, 227–43.

Waldron, J. 2002. Taking group rights carefully, in *Litigating Rights: Perspectives from Domestic and International Law*, edited by G. Huscroft and P. Rishworth. Oxford: Hart, 203–20.

Waldron, J. 2005. Torture and positive law: jurisprudence for the White House. *Columbia Law Review*, 105, 1681–750.

Waldron, J. 2006. The rule of international law. *Harvard Journal of Law & Public Policy*, 30, 15–30.

Waldron, J. 2008. The dignity of groups, public law and legal theory. Research Paper Series, Working Paper No 08–53, NYU School of Law. [Online]. Available at: <http://ssrn.com/abstract=1287174> [accessed: 15 January 2013].

Waldron, J. 2010. Two conceptions of self-determination, in *The Philosophy of International Law*, edited by S. Besson and J. Tasioulas. Oxford: Oxford University Press, 397–413.

Walker, N. 2010. Multilevel constitutionalism: looking beyond the German debate, in *The Many Constitutions of Europe*, edited by K. Tuori and S. Sankari. Farnham: Ashgate, 143–67.

Waltz, K. 2005. *Theory of International Politics,* extracted in *Foundations of International Law and Politics*, edited by O. Hathaway and H.H. Koh. New York: Foundation Press, 42–7.

Wenar, L. 2006. Why Rawls is not a cosmopolitan egalitarian, in *Rawls's Law of Peoples: A Realistic Utopia?* edited by R. Martin and D. Reidy. Oxford: Blackwell, 95–113.

Wendt, A. 2005. Anarchy is what states make of it: the social construction of power politics, extracted in *Foundations of International Law and Politics*, edited by O. Hathaway and H.H. Koh. New York: Foundation Press, 127–32.

Wetherell, M. 2012. *Affect and Emotion: A New Social Science Understanding*. London: Sage.

Widder, N. 2012. *Political Theory After Deleuze*. London: Continuum.

Wilde, R. 2008. *International Territorial Administration: How Trusteeship and the Civilizing Mission Never Went Away*. Oxford: Oxford University Press.

Wright, J. 2006. *The Ambassadors: From Ancient Greece to the Nation State*. London: Harper Collins.

Young, I.M. 2007. *Global Challenges: War, Self-Determination and Responsibility for Justice*. Cambridge: Polity Press.

Zamoyski, A. 2007. *Rites of Peace: The Fall of Napoleon and the Congress of Vienna*. London: Harper Collins.

Žižek, S. 2008. *Violence*. New York: Picador.

Cases

Accordance with International Law of the Unilateral Declaration of Independence in Respect of Kosovo, Advisory Opinion, *ICJ Reports*, 2010, 403.

Legal Consequences of the Construction of a Wall in the Occupied Palestinian Territory, Advisory Opinion, *ICJ Reports*, 2004, 136.

Western Sahara, Advisory Opinion, *ICJ Reports*, 1975, 12.

Index